Blind Narrations and Artistic Subjectivities

Blind Narrations and Artistic Subjectivities: Corporeal Refractions makes an important contribution to the field of blindness studies by highlighting the centrality of blindness in literary compositions. It presents a critical interpretation of selected prose writings by three blind authors: Argentine poet, short story writer, and essayist Jorge Luis Borges; Australian religious educator and diarist John M. Hull; and the American memoirist and poet Stephen Kuusisto. The volume discusses themes like

- theorising the corporeality of writing
- aesthetic turn to the experience of blindness
- altered sensation and self-understanding
- lived experience of growing blind
- self-knowledge through interaction with the world
- artistic subjectivity, narrative choices, and the 'implied' author

This book will be useful for scholars and researchers of blindness studies, disability studies, arts and aesthetics, literature, cultural studies, and philosophy.

Aravinda Bhat is an Assistant Professor at the Department of Languages, Manipal Academy of Higher Education, Manipal, India. He holds a PhD in English Literature from The English and Foreign Languages University in Hyderabad, India. He teaches European literatures in translation, the intellectual history of Europe, research practices, critical thinking, creative writing, and German. His research interests include literature by blind and visually impaired authors, Disability Studies, philosophy, and the novel. Through his work, he indulges his love of books.

Blind Narrations and Artistic Subjectivities
Corporeal Refractions

Aravinda Bhat

Routledge
Taylor & Francis Group

LONDON AND NEW YORK

First published 2024
by Routledge
4 Park Square, Milton Park, Abingdon, Oxon OX14 4RN

and by Routledge
605 Third Avenue, New York, NY 10158

Routledge is an imprint of the Taylor & Francis Group, an informa business

© 2024 Aravinda Bhat

British Library Cataloguing-in-Publication Data
A catalogue record for this book is available from the British Library

ISBN: 978-1-032-04761-4 (hbk)
ISBN: 978-1-032-50789-7 (pbk)
ISBN: 978-1-003-39966-7 (ebk)

DOI: 10.4324/9781003399667

Typeset in Sabon
by SPi Technologies India Pvt Ltd (Straive)

To Appa and Amma

... a recourse to the most primitive ground: the body as the site of first and last resort.

— Meena Alexander, "In Whitman's Country"

Contents

Acknowledgements

I developed this book from my doctoral thesis, which I submitted in August 2016 to the Department of English Literature, The English and Foreign Languages University (EFL-U), located in Hyderabad, India. So, I wish to offer heartfelt thanks to my PhD supervisor, Dr Jibu Mathew George, who was (at the time) Assistant Professor at the School of Indian and World Literatures, EFL-U. He more than fulfilled his remit as a PhD advisor by expertly guiding me over the uncertain terrain of doctoral research from July 2011 to August 2016. The regular discussions we had about literature and philosophy not only contributed immensely to my intellectual growth, but also directly informed this work. I have been touched by his kindness over the last fifteen years.

I count it as my good fortune to have got the opportunity to pursue my MA in English Literature at the Central Institute of English and Foreign Languages (CIEFL, later EFL-U), an institution which promoted higher learning in the humanities like no other place in the country. Significantly, I was introduced to Western philosophy by the late and much missed Prof. Javeed Alam in a course which ran from August to November 2005. I read Modernist poetry (again in August–November 2005) and James Joyce's one hundred-year-old novel, *Ulysses* (January–April 2007), with the poet and teacher par excellence, Dr Rajiv C. Krishnan. These sterling scholars introduced me to the two closely allied practices of meticulous textual study and careful reasoning. Further, it was Dr Krishnan who first suggested, over fifteen years ago, that I pursue research on writings by blind authors. Therefore, I want to acknowledge the crucial role that these two mentors played in the maturing of my intellectual life.

I am grateful beyond words to Prof. Geetha Durairajan, formerly of EFL-U, for being a friend and advisor through thick and thin over a period of seventeen years. Without her support and editing skills, the doctoral thesis on which the present book is based would have remained incomplete. The educator, writer, and peace worker Chintan Girish Modi has enriched the chapters contained in this work with his careful proofreading. I thank him for this, and for his friendship spanning over sixteen years. Without the long-standing friendship and invaluable help of the enormously talented

multilingual poet, translator, script-writer, and cinema critic BA Samvartha
(Sahil), and through him, the good offices of Dr Shashi Kumar, Department
of English and Film Studies, University of Alberta, Canada, this monograph
could never have been published.

Sincere thanks go to Dr Upamanyu Sengupta, who is Assistant Professor
at Maharashtra National Law University Mumbai, for standing by me
through the duration of the PhD programme and beyond. Our stimulating
discussions centring on literature, philosophy, and politics carry great value.
I am deeply indebted to Dr Max Ubelaker Andrade, Associate Teaching
Professor in Latin American Studies at the University of Massachusetts
Lowell, for his unstinting friendship. He has helped me think carefully about
Borges while writing, initially two conference papers on the Argentine's
works, and later four chapters for this book. I am especially grateful to him
for writing a generous foreword to this monograph.

The Librarian in Charge during my PhD tenure, Dr N. Satish, and the staff
of Ramesh Mohan Library, EFL-U, gave me timely help in procuring books
and articles for the research. The Cell for the Disabled, especially Ms.
Lavanya and Mr Sampath Kumar who worked in that department, provided
invaluable support to students with disabilities. In this way, the cell enabled
such students to pursue their studies at the university. Senior professors such
as Mahasweta Sengupta, Lakshmi Chandra, A. V. Ashok, Alok Bhalla, and
Syed A. Sayeed encouraged me over the years with their exemplary teaching
and varied styles of thinking. The following people contributed greatly in
making my life on campus comfortable: the ward boys of Basheer Men's
Hostel, workers at both the men's and ladies' messes, and the two Sagar
brothers who run the campus store. I wish to thank all these persons, and the
Department of English Literature, EFL-U, for supporting my graduate
studies.

I presented two papers on Borges's short fiction at a couple of interna-
tional conferences where I was fortunate to receive useful feedback. These
scholarly gatherings helped me develop my arguments. In this regard, I wish
to express warm thanks to Prof. Elizabeth Abele, the Executive Director of
Northeast Modern Language Association during their 45th Annual
Convention held in April 2014 at Harrisburg, PA; and to Prof. Hannah
Thompson and Prof. Vanessa Warne, co-organisers of "Blind Creations: An
International Conference on Blindness and the Arts" held in June 2015 at
Royal Holloway, University of London, UK.

A big thank you to Prof. David Lelyveld, husband of the late poet and
essayist Prof. Meena Alexander and copyright holder of her literary works.
He generously granted me permission to use a few words from Prof.
Alexander's essay entitled "In Whitman's Country" as the epigraph to the
present work. I stumbled upon the essay in the anthology entitled *Book of
Indian Essays* (2020), edited by the poet and scholar, Arvind Krishna
Mehrotra. The moment I read the said words, I was struck by their aptness
to my book and decided to somehow contact Prof. Lelyveld.

I wish to give profuse thanks to Mr Rahul Putty, Head of the Department of Languages (DoL), Manipal Academy of Higher Education (MAHE), Manipal, India, where I have been working as Assistant Professor since May 2019. Mr Putty has been a steadfast friend and colleague since August 2016, and has given me unfailing support while I laboured to turn my thesis into this book. Work on it has continued in a staggered fashion for more than six years as I taught first at Manipal Centre for European Studies (MCES), MAHE, till May 2019, and then at DoL. So, I wish to thank Prof. Neeta Inamdar, Head of MCES, for her encouragement at the start of my teaching career.

Portions of Chapter 4 and Chapter 5 of this monograph have appeared in considerably modified forms in two book chapters, namely "Being on the Brink of a Blind Abyss: Stepping Back from a Religion Defined by the Opposing Archetypes of Light and Darkness" (259–94) published in the third volume of *De Natura Fidei: Rethinking Religion across Disciplinary Boundaries* (2021), edited by Jibu Mathew George; and "Faith Healing and Blindness Across Cultures: Disability, Religion, and the Scientific Milieu" (83–92) appearing in *Finding Blindness: International Constructions and Deconstructions*, edited by David Bolt, 2023. Material dealt with in Chapter 6 and Chapter 7 appears in altered and concise form in the article entitled "Narrative Lacunae and Variable Articulation in Stephen Kuusisto's Memoirs: Uncovering an Aesthetic Dialectic" (1–11) in *EFL Journal*, volume 13, issue 2, 2022. I wish to express my gratitude to the editors of these publications for enabling me to contribute my writings.

Warm thanks go out to Dr Shashank Shekhar Sinha, Ms. Antara Ray Chaudhury, and Ms. Brinda Sen at Routledge India for welcoming my book proposal and nurturing the project. I am grateful to the three anonymous reviewers for providing useful comments on my book proposal and manuscript. They helped me sharpen the arguments presented in the sequel. Ms. Saritha Srinivasan, Project Manager at Straive, is a thorough professional; I truly appreciate her patience during the book production process. I want to thank Mr Nick Brock for expertly, and generously, copy-editing each part of the manuscript.

Finally, I inscribe my loving gratitude to my family for their constant support, without which my work would be impossible: my mother Lakshmi M. Bhat, father Prof. Dr K. Mahalinga Bhat, sister Gayatri, brother-in-law Vinay Kumar V., nephew Advaith, and niece Kavya. Folks, this is an academic work! hopefully I'll write a book someday that will be of greater interest to you.

Aravinda Bhat, April 2023, Manipal

Foreword

Aravinda Bhat writes that at times it is possible to discern a tension between the immediacy of a sensorial reality (which is different for every human being) and a more internal, imagined reality that idiosyncratically gathers and transforms a shifting assortment of cultural, social, and psychological constructs. He argues that it is important to not underestimate our senses, the unique configuration of senses that you or someone else might possess, for they condition the nature of our experience, our sense of self, and our relationships with others. Bhat directs these arguments to the reader with the knowledge that for many people who are not disabled, the senses can be forgotten for considerable stretches of time; they can slip out of mind with the ease of distraction or inattention. This, of course, is because the world is quite often built for and by people without disabilities; they do not run into the same impediments, restrictions, disregard, and disrespect that disabled people encounter, negotiate, and work to change. They are not required to pay the same degree of attention. Emphasizing the nature of the various overlapping cultural, psychological, social constructs at the expense of the specific, sensing body (in other words) comes at a cost: it diminishes one's ability to perceive the diversity and complexity of our intersubjective reality and it makes it more challenging to understand the roles our own bodies and senses play as we navigate the world, establish relationships with others, and interpret or attempt all forms of creative work.

The tension between these dimensions of experience (the sensory and the cultural) is, for Bhat, generative. It might be borrowed here to suggest that he, as a blind person and a disabled person, draws from his sensory experiences to interpret, rearrange, and question works of literature, philosophy, and memoir paying special attention to blindness and disability. The result is an urgent academic engagement with the work of Jorge Luis Borges, Stephen Kuusisto, and John M. Hull that explores how different experiences of blindness shaped the creation of unique intellectual and artistic contributions. Bhat takes his readers on a journey through his approach to reading, bringing them close to his own experience of interpretation so that they might perceive his form of encountering the interrelated ideas that link sight, blindness, imagination, temporality, self-actualization, and creativity in diverse texts and contexts.

I first met Aravinda Bhat in 2014. He travelled from Hyderabad, India to Harrisburg, Pennsylvania, in the United States, to participate in the annual convention of the Northeast Modern Language Association and deliver a talk in a panel discussion that I chaired titled "Jorge Luis Borges and the Five Senses." I remember how he connected with the audience during his lecture; he had prepared a carefully written text for the event that he drew from as he spoke. Where many of the other invited scholars read directly from print-ed-out papers, he spoke in the moment while listening to the audience's reactions. As he offered his observations on how Borges's strategies of literary representation connected with Bergson's approach to temporality and self-hood, he cited memorised passages and offered present-moment analysis of their significance, tying them in to the ideas of the other speakers. In the context of this introduction, and the themes of Bhat's book, it is worth mentioning how his sensory experiences, his blindness, combined with a tremendous amount of work and preparation to create the conditions for a different mode of engaging with the audience and panelists that was particularly impactful.

Afterwards, we met for dinner and began a series of conversations that have continued up until the present day. Often these conversations involved discussions of Borges's stories, but they also found their way into countless other topics and subjects. On two occasions—the 2015 "Blind Creations International Conference on Blindness and the Arts" at Royal Holloway, University of London and the 2022 virtual conference "Critical Blindness Studies: Current Debates and Future Directions"—we were able to present our individual work and bring our dialog into public settings.

Aravinda Bhat's *Blind Narrations and Artistic Subjectivities* guides the reader through a sensitive, attentive, academic engagement with three writers whose creativity, insights, and brilliance have special resonance within Critical Blindness Studies. Bhat is interested in the direct, idiosyncratic experiences of blindness of the three selected writers, as well as the tropes of blindness, the metaphors and discourses that are used, challenged, reworked, or rejected. His work points to the creation of blind cultures that develop new stories and traditions around visuality, sight, and blindness or, in turn, work to simply clear open space for other blind people to articulate their own experiences, on their own terms. It is (to borrow his language) both a window and a mirror that will give readers opportunities to perceive the author's mode of thought and interpretation and also to consider their own sensory and cognitive approaches to reading, perception, and selfhood.

Max Ubelaker Andrade
University of Massachusetts Lowell

1 Introduction

Theorising the Corporeality of Writing

1.1 Introduction

On a pleasant afternoon in November 2015 (it was Tuesday the 24th), a classmate and I were sitting in the university canteen. Both of us were doctoral students at The English and Foreign Languages University in Hyderabad, India. We had just returned from the Rajiv Gandhi International Airport outside the city and were having a late lunch. We had gone to the airport to receive the prominent Indian novelist, late Kiran Nagarkar. He was at the university to deliver the keynote address at an international conference entitled "Words Words Words: The Future of Literary Writing," which took place on 25–27 November 2015.

While my peer and I were waiting for our food to be served, it struck me that the cook was beating out a catchy rhythm with his cooking spoon as he prepared food – very likely noodles – in his frying pan. I asked my companion if she had noticed the foot-tapping beat, and her puzzled question "Noticed what?" amazed me. Was the loud, rhythmic sound not even apparent to her? At that moment – late in the ninth semester of my PhD programme – the philosophical validity of my doctoral research became crystal clear to me: my experience, as a visually impaired person, of listening to events transpiring around me was not as mundane as I had taken it to be: sighted people, it dawned on me as I heard the girl's question, were more or less oblivious to stimuli other than the visual (cf. *On Sight* 225). So, my literary-philosophical inquiry into the influence of blindness on the process of literary composition, it occurred to me, did possess some scholarly value. The project attempted to clarify how their variable experiences of blindness inform the work of three blind and visually impaired authors: the Argentine poet, essayist, and short story writer Jorge Luis Borges; the Australian-British religious educator and diarist John M. Hull; and the American poet and memoirist Stephen Kuusisto.

To state the problem baldly, if you learn that the author of a book you are reading is blind, would you conclude that their particular experience might have a bearing on the content and/or the stylistic quality of the writing? Or would you argue that understanding the book's content need not actually depend upon the experience of disability? I set out in what follows to find an

DOI: 10.4324/9781003399667-1

answer to the question of why it is important to consider blindness in conjunction with literature. It is possible that the reader will ask what, if any, impact an author's blindness may have on their writing. Such a question implies that blindness is a medical condition trivial to literature. This book demonstrates that the experiential dilemma of blindness and selfhood exercises a profound influence on the writings of Borges, Hull, and Kuusisto. Further, examining the ways in which blindness comes into their writings will reveal their divergent subjectivities as blind artists. It will become evident through their literary works, or worlds, that "the body is [not] a sheet of plain glass through which the soul looks straight and clear" (Woolf 4), but, on the contrary, that blindness structures the subject's every perception and creates a uniquely different world. This book will attempt to flesh out, in eight chapters, the aesthetic dynamics that defines the said three authors' respective oeuvres.

1.2   Narrative Choices, Bodily Condition, and Artistic Subjectivity

Two questions drive this inquiry forward: How does the visually impaired writer's particular bodily condition bear on narrative choices? Is it possible to extrapolate from this on authorial subjectivity? By 'subjectivity,' I mean how the self may be conceived of with reference to time, space, and the author's artistic works. The questions enunciated above guide my inquiry as I interpret the following texts with a view to tracking the shaping influence of blindness: selected short fiction and non-fiction by Borges; two diaries, *Touching the Rock: An Experience of Blindness* (1990) and *On Sight and Insight: A Journey into the World of Blindness* (1997);[1] I will also draw upon two exegetical works on the Bible, namely *In the Beginning There was Darkness: A Blind Person's Conversations with the Bible* (2001) *and The Tactile Heart: Blindness and Faith* (2013) by Hull; and *Planet of the Blind: A Memoir* (1998), *Eavesdropping: A Life by Ear* (2006), and *Have Dog, Will Travel* (2018) by Kuusisto. It must be noted, obvious though the point might seem, that the titles of the works themselves suggest the power of blindness to give birth to a distinct world.

In his earliest poetry written in the 1920s, Jorge Luis Borges "experimented with a jagged avant-garde style he would soon leave behind" (Kristal x), and dwelt on symbols that he would return to in various genres throughout his writing career: "the night, the dark, and the crepuscular

---

1 These volumes are two versions of the same diary, the latter being an expansion of the former. Hull enlarged *Touching the Rock* by adding "a number of passages which had not been included in the original book, and ... two new chapters which had been written after August 1986" (*On Sight* xi). For this reason, when I supply parenthetical references for quotations drawn from the material common to both diaries, I will cite page numbers from the second volume. Conversely, when I quote words that are not present in both diaries, I will provide citation for each volume as is appropriate. However, I offer bibliographical information for both diaries in the 'Works Cited' page at the end of the book.

world of visions and dreams, themes that speak to the blindness that would overtake him slowly, over a long period of time" (Kristal ix). Efran Kristal points out that Borges's poetry of the 1920s "combined the geography (and even the history) of the Rio de la Plata region of his birth with a metaphysical aura that would surround most of his subsequent literary works" (x). Thus, Borges's oeuvre is defined by thematic continuities. His 'fictions' and non-fictions are notable for their erudition (*Selected Non-Fictions* xi; xv). Eliot Weinberger's observation on Borges's fictional and non-fictional writings reveals something of their character: "'Fiction' and 'non-fiction' are notoriously blurred boundaries in Borges' fiction, but not in his non-fiction" (xiv). It is recognised that Borges's later poetry, which may be dated to 1960 during a crucial phase in his writing career, deals with the multifarious meanings of the blind condition ("Blind Spot in the Mirror"; Yudin 11–13). But it is less widely noted that blindness and other disabilities receive comprehensive attention in his prose writings.

John Hull was Professor Emeritus of religious education at the University of Birmingham, England. In *Touching the Rock* and *On Sight and Insight*, he presents two books developed from a cassette diary in which he recorded his "daily experiences" (*Touching the Rock* ix) over a number of years. In the process of reflecting on his blindness and talking to the cassette, he examines "the blind condition" (*On Sight* xiii) in all its complexity. *In the Beginning There was Darkness* and *The Tactile Heart* are interpretative works which offer a blind person's critical perspective on the Bible and Christian theology.

While *Planet of the Blind* is a long narrative memoir that reflects with profound artistry on Stephen Kuusisto's life 'with blindness,' *Eavesdropping* is a collection of short personal essays which the memoirist calls "auditory postcards or tone poems" (xii). While the writer develops an aesthetic of listening in this volume of essays, *Have Dog, Will Travel* tells in fine detail the story of how being partnered with guide dog Corky transforms his life.

I interpret these texts with critical focus on corporeality. More specifically, the readings that follow take cognisance of the ways in which differences in embodiment, or deviations from the 'normal' body, are inscribed in aesthetic expression. The first reason for selecting literary compositions by these particular authors who come from diverse countries is that I wish to understand how these persons, with widely differing socio-political backgrounds, treat blindness. The second reason arises out of a desire to study the above authors' responses to blindness in the personal realm. When people become blind halfway through life, or when they realise that they are different from other people due to blindness (or any other disability for that matter), the first reaction is self-reflexive in nature; that is to say, they tend to look at their own embodiment. The blind person comes to a political conception of the self, meaning knowledge of one's interconnectedness with others, much later. A further point of significance is that the texts under study represent different genres of literature. This fact necessitates a narrative analysis which is sensitive to the aesthetic differences particular to authors and genres.

Differing formulations of the questions to which I seek answers in this book compete with one another. The particular phrasing of the problem is of paramount importance because it shapes the inquiry. It should be noted at the outset that a strong logic connects the three articulations of the problematic. I initially phrased it in the form of two related questions: How does visual impairment inflect the authorial voice (in selected literary texts composed by Borges, Hull, and Kuusisto)? How can one reflect on the use of language and trace the contours of the author's subjectivity? These questions entail reflection on the modalities of language used by the blind authors. Tracing the (visually) disabled author's subjectivity in their writings necessarily involves the problematisation of the very category of disability. The interdisciplinary field of disability studies, which incorporates significant reflections on literary texts, provides helpful means of developing a critical appreciation of the problem at hand. We may conclude that the above questions would involve a study of subjectivity through the examination of literary texts composed by blind and visually impaired writers, the authorial voice, and the use of language and interpretation.

The second question above must be refined further in order to prevent the blind author's subjectivity from being reduced to just one aspect of their identity, viz. blindness. The problem of how artistic subjectivity may be traced in the literary use of language requires careful scrutiny. While, on the one hand, this formulation runs the risk of implying that authorial subjectivity can be deciphered within the linguistic fabric of the text, on the other, it can hardly be said that the text as a whole represents that creative entity (see Borges's text "Borges and I" [*Collected Fictions* 324]). The point of this objection is not that subjectivity is here reduced to "mere" language.[2] It is possible only to study language because our interest is limited to literary texts. The critic must probe which elements (textual features and parameters) in the author's work constitute the "contours" of artistic subjectivity. Therefore, certain crucial changes have to be made in the way the research problem is articulated.

This task may be accomplished by positing three new questions. The first conceptualises subjectivity as a composite whole: How does disability interact with other posited elements of subjectivity such as memory, culture, and so on? Questions two and three are bound up by the common concern of language: What is the relation between the text and its referents,[3] namely the characters, their actions, events, and the world? What is the relation between the text and subjectivity? These questions not only point to the referentiality of language in narratives (a matter that will be examined in the course of the book), but also suggest the theoretical approaches to be adopted.

I believe that in literary analysis the texts – novels, short stories, essays, poetry, and so on – must be treated as the primary material to be examined, and the various theories used only as aids to reading the former. Instead of giving prime importance to reading philosophical and narratological theories

2 The social-constructionist theorists argue that subjectivity is indeed determined by discourse.
3 I shall discuss the conflict between meaning and reference in literature in Chapter 2.

and automatically – or 'uncritically' – applying concepts found therein to the texts under study, a more fruitful exercise from the critical point of view would be to read the primary texts, and then elucidate issues dealt with therein on the basis of a sound philosophical grounding. We may recall here Wayne C. Booth's words which express a similar concern: "... for in a time when too much criticism, pursuing 'autonomy,' floats off into the Great Inane, with never a reference to anything but its own concept spinning, there is surely room for a criticism that is openly embedded in and respectful of the stuff that it criticizes" (xii). Contemporary theories, with their emphasis on rhetoric, afford considerable freedom to the critic in defending arguments, but considering literary texts as being of prime importance will allow us to provide evidence for the claims made in this book.

The problem as I formulate it here provides access to the authors' self-exploration. The authors negotiate with who they are, or what the self is, after reflecting on "a matrix of other, web-interrelated possible selves" (Hagberg 147). These negotiations take place reflexively with the self, dialogically with society and literary conventions. The problem at hand, then, necessitates a narratological-philosophical analysis of the primary texts. The focus must, therefore, shift from inflections of the authorial voice to the wider domain of narrative choices. Generally speaking, inflections of the authorial voice acquire importance in longer narratives such as Kuusisto's first and third memoirs, *Planet of the Blind* and *Have Dog, Will Travel*. A long work of fiction or non-fiction presents greater opportunities to move between different voices and idioms, whereas a work of short fiction possesses more or less a stable voice. Another reason why narrative choices assume importance is that, as mentioned above, the works I am reading include not only short stories, but also lectures, essays, diaries, and memoirs, the last two being episodic in character.

1.3 Contribution to Scholarly Conversation

The recent book entitled *Borges Beyond the Visible* (2019) by Max Ubelaker Andrade examines the Argentine author's literary theology[4] by paying particular attention to his visual aesthetics. In his critical commentary on Borges's key short stories, Ubelaker Andrade illuminates how the author exposes through ingenious fictional devices the very nature of the act of reading literature. While Ubelaker Andrade approaches the question of Borges's blindness indirectly by analysing the nature of fictional textuality, the present book interprets the ways in which the author's bodily being bears on his writings.

The article "Borges in the Mind's Eye" (37–51) by Christopher Krentz analyses two prominent short stories – one of which I write about in my book[5] – by Borges to show "how his oncoming blindness shaped and enriched

---

4 See chapter 1, "Borges's Literary Theology: Fiction and the Visible" (9–60).
5 The story in English translation is titled "Funes, the Memorious," which is not the version I interpret in Chapter 3 (9–14) and Chapter 8 (8).

such memorable works" (37) which were published in the 1940s and 1950s. Krentz draws extensively on Borges's autobiographical writings, biographies of the author, insights on his blindness offered by sighted critics, and disability studies to make his case. Perhaps due to an absence of a blindness-centric approach in this body of more or less critical literature, except in the last-mentioned discipline, Krentz's conclusions fail to convince the reader.

Two studies of Borges's poetry consider the literary-philosophical importance of blindness to the poet. The first one is the article "The Blind Spot in the Mirror: Self-Recognition and Personal Identity in Borges's Late Poetry" (307–25) by David Laraway. This critic presents his argument against the backdrop of very little scholarly attention to the question of blindness in Borges's poetry:

> Given the significance of blindness as a trope throughout the western literary tradition ... and the role it played in the heady days of deconstruction of the 1970s and early 1980s, surprisingly few attempts have been made to explore its significance as a structuring principle of Borges's poetry.
>
> (Laraway, "The Blind Spot in the Mirror" 308)

So, he analyses some of Borges's later poems and discusses themes such as "the poet's sight" (Laraway, "The Blind Spot in the Mirror" 308), identity, memory, and knowledge, "the figure of the face as a site where identity is at once consolidated and undermined" (Laraway, "The Blind Spot in the Mirror" 309), "the relationship between blindness and the problem of anagnorisis, or self-recognition," and "the motif of the mirror" (Laraway, "The Blind Spot in the Mirror" 311) in Borges's aesthetics. Through his analysis, Laraway illustrates not only that blindness is a theme in the Argentine's poetry, but that it also structures his texts because the mirror that they constitute can reflect the self of the author ("the identity of 'Borges'") only when they are read. It is in this way that this mirror contains a blind spot that prevents Borges from recognising who he is unless his readers complete his literary texts in the process of interpreting them (Laraway, "The Blind Spot in the Mirror" 322). Chapter 2 and Chapter 3 of this book treat these themes in some detail while examining Borges's short fiction.

The second critical work to consider the significance of blindness in Borges's poetry is the slim volume *Nightglow: Borges' Poetics of Blindness* (1997) by Florence L. Yudin. While this study explicates a "stunning dialectical arc, from radiance to Tenebrae" (Yudin 15) in Borges's poetry, the present book examines a complementary dialectic of withdrawal from the world and the artistic turn to the experience of blindness in Borges's fictional and non-fictional writings.

In his article "'A River that No One Can See': Body, Text, and Environment in the Poetry of Stephen Kuusisto" (183–94), Michael L. Melancon inquires into the strong influence exercised by blindness and sensory variation on literary writing. His argument is based on Kuusisto's poems from the collection *Only Bread, Only Light* (2000), and relies upon the first two memoirs written by the poet, namely *Planet of the Blind* and *Eavesdropping*. In the *Poetics* (XVII), Aristotle exhorts the poet to maintain "objectivity in art" (Melancon 183), that is, to preserve "artistic distance" from "the object of creation" in order to achieve excellence. This view, which incidentally is unequivocally visual in tone, has decisively guided thinking on literary composition and theory in the West. However, when the artist's body "becomes more visible as another, due to illness or disability," that is to say, when the experience of disability makes the artist more keenly aware of his bodily make-up, he draws upon the embodied state in creating his art. Concepts from disability studies and scholarship on "the sites of language production and reception" help Melancon make his case against the dominant discourse on art and language which keeps the disabled body separate from the process and products of creativity.

Melancon examines "the way that Kuusisto's poetry interrogates and challenges traditional concepts of language and the body, shaping a new discourse that begins within the body and travels outward to the world" (184–85). Through an analysis of select poems, the critic shows how the disabled artist "is able to explore more fully the subjectivity of artistic creation" (Melancon 183). He, thus, throws light on the role of the embodied self in creativity. He describes Kuusisto's poetic technique in this way: "In his poetry he explores the bodily senses in a myriad of ways, investigating how sight, hearing, and touch can serve to facilitate expression and communication by both receiving information and transmitting information" (Melancon 184). By discussing the poetic figuration of Braille, recorded books for the blind, the experience of nature, and music, Melancon demonstrates how the poet probes the relation between language, self, the blind body, and experience. At the beginning of the essay, the author states, "The art of disabled people, however, is often overlooked in a society in which" (Melancon 183), and continues with words he quotes from Sharon L. Snyder: frequently, "corporeal otherness is viewed as an impediment to art" (qtd in Melancon). While this statement points to the alienation of disabled artists, it becomes evident by the concluding section of the article that artistic excellence demands a degree of separateness from the world. Extending the insight he draws from the speaker's experience in the poem "Awake All Night," Melancon offers, "This sense of ghostliness, of being in, but not entirely as one with the world might well describe the ethos of disabled artists as they observe, record, create, and shape their experiential world while struggling with a language system that has" (193), as Jay Dolmage formulates the problem, "inscribed and controlled the experience of disability for disabled and non-disabled alike" (qtd. in Melancon). To unpack these words, in the case of disabled artists, a difficult-to-close gulf prevents the satisfactory expression of personal experience in language. In their practice of the art of writing poetry, fiction, and non-fiction, such artists have to struggle to fashion a language which is adequate for their needs. In spite of this difficulty, we see how it is possible for an artist to succeed, as Snyder states, not despite but "as a result of disability experiences" (qtd. in Melancon 183). Kuusisto, thus, brings the body into poetics by writing poems that explore his blindness and the aesthetic power of the other senses.

In the essay "Disabilities, Bodies, Voices" (283–95), Jim Swan articulates ideas that are crucial for the argument of this book. Explaining the significance of disability studies, Swan asks, "... what's new about the new field of disability studies ... How does it stand apart from other instances of historically silenced groups making themselves heard?" (283–84). His answer to the two questions contains the seeds for a fresh examination of disabled writers' selfhood:

> The answer, I think, is the particular viewpoint that disability studies brings to an understanding of the body—an understanding that writing is not only *about* the body but *of* and *from* the body too. As Nancy Mairs puts it—in words that should be stitched permanently into the memory of every writer, disabled or not: 'No body, no voice; no voice, no body'.
>
> (Swan 284)

Thus, disability scholarship gives importance to the body and voice, both in relation to writing. Corporeality is, then, a significant factor in narrativising subjectivity. It is noteworthy that Swan is concerned not just about our understanding of the body, but more to the point, about the body itself in writing. He states,

> The embodied perspective of disabled persons ... is the necessary ground for realizing the agency of the disabled subject, and it must be a fundamental part of any curriculum in disability studies. Otherwise, the pervasive cultural studies model, with its strong Foucauldian commitment, its tendency to view the body as no more than the site of contested cultural discourses, renders the question of the disabled subject unapproachable.
>
> (Swan 284–85)

This quotation captures the thrust of Swan's argument. He wishes to broaden the scope of disability studies by including disabled persons' writings, and aims to protect disability writing (in its task of making the voices of disabled subjects heard) from the dangers of the cultural studies model. He considers it important to examine issues such as the self, subjectivity, body, "cognitive difference" (Swan 286), disability experience, language, and writing. Important in this regard is his perceptive analysis of Hull's diary, *Touching the Rock* (290–92).

While the resources reviewed here make valuable contributions to the critical literature on Borges, Hull, and Kuusisto, there exists a gap in the scholarship on their literary works: the study of blindness as it relates to their respective aesthetics is restricted mainly to poetry of two among the three artists. This book fills the scholarly lacuna by presenting a study of prose narratives by them. It concentrates on, as stated above, the question of narrativising subjectivity in relation to blindness.

1.4 Theoretical Approaches and Concepts

In this section, I write about the philosophical arguments and conceptual nets that have shaped my literary research. The idea of everyday experience occupies an important place in thinking about corporeality, which may be understood as including various kinds of bodies, viz. disabled and non-disabled ones. This in turn bears on the question of (differential) perception and epistemology. We are present in the world as incarnate subjects. As Maurice Merleau-Ponty asserts, sense experience "always involves a reference to the body" (61). The kind of body the subject possesses conditions how they experience the world, live in it, know it, and know the self (Savarese 205). Thus, any kind of disability exercises an all-pervasive influence on the experience of the subject. S. Kay Toombs asserts that phenomenology provides "a window into lived experience" (10). Coming to the study of narrative, Monika Fludernik introduces the novel concept of "experientiality" in developing a "'natural' narratology." This narratological system differs from the older, formal models. Fludernik explains, "Unlike the traditional models of narratology, narrativity ... is here constituted by what I call experientiality, namely by the quasi-mimetic evocation of 'real-life experience'" (9). Thus, for Fludernik, the representation of human experience constitutes "narrativity." She develops a "cognitive" (Fludernik 5) and constructivist theory of narrative. Her definition of mimesis reveals this aspect in elucidating the notion of "experientiality":

> ... mimesis must NOT be identified as imitation but needs to be treated as the artificial and illusionary projection of a semiotic structure which the reader recuperates in terms of a fictional reality. This recuperation, since it is based on cognitive parameters gleaned from real-world experience, inevitably results in an implicit though incomplete homologization of the fictional and the real worlds.
>
> (Fludernik 26)

Clearly, the reader of the literary text interprets the thoughts and actions of characters in the fictional world on the basis of "cognitive parameters gleaned from real-world experience." This means that they understand the experience represented in the literary world by consulting – and depending upon – their experience in the environment shared with humans and other living beings. Thus, Fludernik says with reference to oral narrative, which she takes as the model for analysis: "Narrative mimesis evokes a world, whether that world is identical to the interlocutors' shared environment, to a historical reality or to an invented fictional fantasy" (27). When the literary text deals with the experience of disability, the reader interprets it in such a way that the shape of that experience becomes evident through its relationship to the real world.

This model may be applied to both fictional and non-fictional texts. Fludernik clarifies that the two concepts of narrativity and fictionality are closely related through the notion of human experientiality (28). She defines the former "as mediated human experientiality (which can be plotted on the level of action or on the level of fictional consciousness)" (Fludernik 26). So "narrativity" in this model may be found in a wide range of texts cutting across the traditional divide between fiction and non-fiction. It is not limited by "the criteria of mere sequentiality and logical connectedness" (Fludernik 19), which play a "central role … in most discussions of narrative." She defines "fictionality" as a literary concept, describing it in relation to "narrativity" as "the subjective experience of imaginary human beings in an imaginary human space, that correlates with narrativity since the emphasis on human experientiality can be manifested most perfectly in the ideal realm" (Fludernik 29). We see that literary worlds are conceived here as "the ideal realm" which enables the uncovering of human experientiality. I shall, therefore, draw upon Merleau-Ponty's phenomenology, and narratological concepts based on Fludernik's notion of experientiality to bolster my argument about disability experience, narrative choices, and blind literary subjectivities.

The question of sensation gains significance as the principle ordering this literary inquiry. So a brief sketch of a few significant problems that modern philosophy is engaged with will help prepare the ground. German idealist thought, taking off from Immanuel Kant's work, responds to Enlightenment philosophy. In "The Enlightenment and Idealism" (18–36), Frederick Beiser traces the relationship between the two philosophical movements: "the fundamental principles" (18) of the former, namely "rational criticism and scientific naturalism," lead to the following "disastrous consequences" for knowledge: scepticism and materialism. The two principles and their results have serious implications for conceptions of the self and the external world: "If skepticism undermines our common-sense beliefs in the reality of the external world, other minds, and even our own selves, materialism threatens the beliefs in freedom, immortality, and the sui generis status of the mind." Starting with René Descartes, European philosophers had been finding it hard to account for "the reality of the external world and other minds" (Beiser 20) because of conflicting concepts of reason, namely "criticism and naturalism" (Beiser 23). Enlightenment thought seems to lead to the subject being irrevocably separated from the world and other subjects due to the uncertainty inherent in knowledge. In dealing with reason, then, the idealist philosophers grappled with epistemological questions, thus thinking about how to establish verifiable contact between our knowledge of the world (and, therefore, the knowing subject), and the world in which we live and of which we are a part. Another important question that they thought about was intersubjectivity: how to establish contact between different subjects in the world? Thus it is that "intuition" assumes importance starting with Kant's philosophy.

Kant's explication of truth has significant implications, from the point of view of the present argument, for an account of experience. Beiser summarises the position taken in the critical philosophy as follows: "... Kant proposes that we see truth as the conformity of objects with our concepts, as the agreement of our perceptions with certain universal and necessary concepts that determine the form or structure of experience" (23). Under the heading "Transition to the transcendental deduction of the categories" (224–26) of the *Critique of Pure Reason* (1998), Kant writes,

> Now, however, all experience contains in addition to the intuition of the senses, through which something is given, a **concept** of an object that is given in intuition, or appears; hence concepts of objects in general lie at the ground of all experiential cognition as *a priori* conditions; consequently the objective validity of the categories, as *a priori* concepts, rests on the fact that through them alone is experience possible (as far as the form of thinking is concerned). For they then are related necessarily and *a priori* to objects of experience, since only by means of them can any object of experience be thought at all.
>
> (emphasis as in the source, 224)

Kant's conception of truth offers a solution, then, to the unacceptable consequences of Enlightenment philosophy, viz. skepticism and materialism. Beiser explains the implications of the transcendental deduction for truth thus:

> ... it is no longer necessary to get outside our own representations to see if they conform to objects in themselves. Rather, the standard of truth will be found within the realm of consciousness itself by seeing whether a representation conforms to the universal and necessary forms of consciousness itself.
>
> (23–4)

The operative words here are "the universal and necessary forms of consciousness" which make it clear that the experience of all conscious beings is structured by "certain universal and necessary concepts," that is, by the ways in which subjects perceive and know. Patricia Kitcher explains how Kant's transcendental idealism provides the means for philosophy to prove the validity of knowledge and the connection between subjects. Kant's central epistemological problem is, she writes, "that the standards by which we distinguish truth from illusion originate, in part, from our own subjective$_{SF}$ constitution, but that they are nonetheless objective, because they are indispensable for any cognition at all" (Kitcher 416). Here, the term 'subjective$_{SF}$' indicates that which originates "'in the subject's faculties'." This thesis provides the basis for articulating a dynamic notion of subjectivity, where the self's faculties of thought and imagination play a creative role in cognition. This conception of truth, by its reliance on "the universal and necessary forms of consciousness itself," links the subject to other subjects/minds in the world.

Beiser highlights Kant's belief that "knowledge requires the most intimate interchange between understanding and sensibility" (28). While "understanding and theoretical reason" (Guyer 39) deal with concepts, the body, with its sensory faculties, plays a significant role in "sensibility," and helps in the generation of intuitions. Intuition is the immediate experience of objects in the world by the subject. The paramount importance of intuition in talking about experience emerges from Kant's understanding that an intuition is a singular representation that is in immediate relation to its object, while a concept is a general representation that can be related to many objects but is not in immediate relation to any, and for that reason can be related to an object only through an intuition (Guyer 40). Intuition occupies an important place in describing experience (and thus "all cognition") because it enables the subject to have an immediate relation to objects which concepts alone cannot do (see Kant 110; 224). Commenting on Kant's arguments leading to "the distinction between intuition and concept" (41), Paul Guyer explains that, in the 1760s, the former developed an argument in favour of "the contrast between logical and real relationships" (42), and "the argument that we can recognise features of the spatial structure and orientation of objects that cannot be contained in the concepts of those objects" (43). Both arguments show that "sense perception" puts the subject in immediate touch with the world. Further, they demonstrate that concepts in the mind do not directly relate to the world as an intuition does. The immediacy of intuition arises, as suggested above, through "the medium" (Guyer 42) of sensations (sensing with the faculties of perception) or, in other words, by means of the subject's bodily experience of objects. Kirk Dallas Wilson states, "Intuitive representations 'show forth' ['anschauen'] their object by representing its mereological structure [the 'part-whole relation' characterising 'individuals' 254] and, in the case of empirical intuitions, its empirical properties" (258). As a result, sensual contact between the body and objects in the world assumes importance. Taking into account the fact that "the immediacy-mediacy distinction is critical" (264) in distinguishing between concepts and intuitions, Wilson gleans "a definition of immediacy" with the help of the doctrine of transcendental idealism, that belongs to "the Aesthetic," and states that "appearances, the objects of empirical intuitions, are just representations in the mind":

Now one cannot distinguish within consciousness of an object its appearance from its intuition. I cannot distinguish within my perception (intuition) of my desk a separate item which is my desk. The implication of transcendental idealism is that we must identify the appearance qua object of intuition with the intuition itself. Thus, we can define immediacy as isomorphic identity between an intuition and its object.

(264–65)

This line of thinking, where the subject's contact with the world moves centre stage, enables us to give a fuller account of everyday experience. The metaphysical thought of the French philosopher, Henri-Louis Bergson, particularly his insights on duration or subjective time, intuition, and selfhood form the bases for the argument in Chapter 3 of this book.

The 19th-century Danish philosopher, Soren Aabye Kierkegaard (1813–55), whose work investigates philosophical questions in distinctly literary ways, may help illuminate Borges's use of alter egos. Kierkegaard was deeply concerned with questions regarding the self, subjectivity, and representation, questions to which he offered sophisticated answers. Alastair Hannay and Gordon D. Marino offer the following observation concerning the question of selfhood which Kierkegaard made on Socrates and himself (see *Soren Kierkegaards Papirer* [Pap. X1 A 266 p. 177]):

Writing of himself Kierkegaard was reminded of what he had once written pseudonymously about Socrates ... that "his whole life was a personal preoccupation with himself, and then guidance comes along and adds something world-historical to it." This was Kierkegaard's own perspective on his life in retrospect. He came to believe that he had had a religious mission from the start.

(3)

This passage leaves the reader in little doubt about Kierkegaard's concern with self-inquiry. While the postmodernist literary critic Roger Poole explains that the Danish thinker's "irony and his many-voiced-ness, his *heteroglossia*, distance him from any position that could be asserted to be finally 'his' position" (48), Katalin Nun and Jon Stewart caution against Poole's extreme stance on philological grounds (xiii–xiv). Such a position is represented in the following quotation: "Kierkegaard has made any final 'closure' on the matter of 'his' meaning impossible" (Poole 48). With such an interpretation, Poole aims to foreground Kierkegaard's affinity to poststructuralist thought, which considers "meaning" as finally undecidable. By contrast, Nun and Stewart advocate acknowledging "the importance of the pseudonyms" if being "attentive to them" (xv) makes sense in the case of the topic being researched. However, they go on to counsel that "there is no reason to insist on this absolutely or to push this to extremes" if the question of the pseudonyms does not bear on a particular "issue in Kierkegaard" (Nun and Stewart xvi). Instead, they advance a measured view, namely that "by taking seriously each of ... [Kierkegaard's pseudonyms] as individuals, we will be able to gain new insights into the texts which they are ostensibly responsible for" (Nun and

Stewart xv). In this regard, Kierkegaard's suggestive words appearing in "A First and Last Explanation" may be highlighted:

> Therefore, if it should occur to anyone to want to quote a particular passage from the books, it is my wish, my prayer, that he will do me the kindness of citing the respective pseudonymous author's name, not mine—that is, of separating us in such a way that the passage femininely belongs to the pseudonymous author, the responsibility civilly to me.
>
> (Kierkegaard 627; Poole 62)

The concluding words of this quotation make it clear that while Kierkegaard regards the pseudonymous authors as individuals who are intellectually independent, he still bears legal "responsibility" for works 'authored' by his pseudonyms. This intricately literary reflection on the question of subjectivity in Kierkegaard's writings will play a role in interpreting Borges's narrative technique in short stories where characters bearing his name make an appearance.

The philosopher Shelley Tremain claims that "the ways in which concepts, classifications, and descriptions are imbricated in institutional practices, social policy, intersubjective relations, and medical discourses structure the field of possible action for humans" ("On the Government of Disability" 187). If we accept the position that "the field of possible action for humans" is structured by discursive practices, the question that arises is: Where in all this is the place for the human will to perform independent action?[6] Tremain goes on to clarify that there is no such room because, as she puts it, "that intentional action always takes place under a description" is a truism. She elaborates, "... the approach assumes that the materiality of 'the body' cannot be dissociated from the historically contingent practices that bring it into being, that is, bring it into being as that sort of thing." If our corporeal existence and activity are at root structured by language or descriptions, the person is reduced to a non-entity that can be conceived as being, from root to tip, a mechanical part of a complicated machine. This conclusion stands despite what Tremain says next:

> Disciplinary practices enable subjects to act in order to constrain them. For juridical power *is* power (as opposed to mere physical force or violence) only when it addresses individuals who are free to act in one way or another ... the production of seeming acts of choice (*limits* of possible conduct) on the everyday level of the subject makes possible hegemonic power structures.
>
> (Tremain, "On the Government of Disability" 187–188)

---

6 This perspicacious question, on which my argument in this chapter is based, was asked in early 2012 by my second philosophy teacher, Prof. Syed A. Sayeed. When he posed it to a student during a discussion in which she was unreflectively using Foucault's concepts to counter his argument, it stopped her short and clearly made her think, as Prof. Sayeed remarked.

Although this "juridical power" is said to act upon "individuals who are free to act in one way or another," that is to say, its forces "enable subjects to act" as free agents, I want to suggest that only they cannot do so. Significant phrases such as "in order to constrain them," "the production of seeming acts of choice" (with emphasis on the word 'seeming'), "*limits* of possible conduct," and "hegemonic power structures" make it clear that this philosophical system does not recognize, or allow for, the functioning of free will. In fact, Tremain indicates this very idea in her adaptation of Michel Foucault's theory in disability studies:

> Foucault introduced the term "dividing practices" to refer to modes of manipulation that combine a scientific discourse with practices of segregation and social exclusion in order to categorize, classify, distribute and manipulate subjects who are initially drawn from a rather undifferentiated mass of people. Through these practices, subjects become *objectivized* as (for instance) mad or sane, sick or healthy, criminal or good. Through these practices of division, classification, and ordering, furthermore, subjects become tied to an identity and come to understand themselves scientifically. In short, this "subject" must not be confused with modern philosophy's *cogito*, autonomous self, or rational moral agent.
>
> ("On the Government of Disability" 186; *Foucault and the Government of Disability* 10; Foucault 777–78)

This passage summarises Foucault's genealogical explanation of how subjects come to be governed by bio-power. Bio-power classifies, segregates, and objectivises them as "mad or sane, sick or healthy, criminal or good" in order to separate disabled and other unwanted people, and exclude them from society. Thus, Tremain's nominalist analysis relies on the archaeology of medical and social practices to enable resistance against such government ("On the Government of Disability" 188). In the institution of these practices, it is said, subjects "are initially drawn from a rather undifferentiated mass of people." Is this to say, then, that no criteria are used to achieve these classifications? This explanation rests on a vague notion of how, in the first place, subjects are classified before they are distributed and manipulated. Then, Tremain turns to Foucault's suggestion "that analyses of power should take as their starting point a new kind of counter-politics (what he called 'strategic reversibility') that these knowledges have inadvertently spawned" (*Foucault and the Government of Disability* 7). Admirable, but the Foucauldian philosopher cannot have it both ways. The concept of "strategic reversibility" seems to conveniently make it possible for people subjugated by bio-power to formulate "needs and imperatives of … 'life' as the basis for political counterdemands." A theory which conceives of subjects as being completely determined by disciplinary practices fails to recognize the power of the human body-mind to tell their story, or, in other words, to narrate their experience – in their own voice. If "subject" is not to be understood as "modern philosophy's *cogito*, autonomous self, or rational moral agent," there can be no free will to resist subjugation.

I argue, in opposition to Tremain's Foucauldian analysis, that our corporeal existence must not be thought of as being constituted by discursive practices because this denies value to the person's experiential autonomy. Such a position sidesteps the question of experience by merely casting it as a construct. I hold that a blind person, for example, knows what it is like to be blind or experience his or her disability in a way that a sighted person cannot know it. If we consider the impairment, blindness, as something constituted by socially shared language or by "historically contingent practices," the private nature of that experience becomes lost – insignificant at best, unthinkable at worst – due to its being conceived of as a construct. This is to say that the experience of blindness and other disabilities is not merely produced by language and discursive practices. To clarify further, it is certainly not to say that the blind person has "privileged access" to their experience because of the misconceived notion that "autobiographical language ... provides a representation after and apart from the inward facts of the first-person case" (Hagberg 149). Although such a person uses shared language in describing their experience, their self-descriptions allow for the self-creative expression of experience in a way that the productive discursive practices of bio-power clearly do not. Garry L. Hagberg explains the power of self-descriptive language as follows: "Such language is in truth more self-defining than self-describing. Or (cautiously): more self-creative than self-reflective" (149). It should be noticed that this conception of self-creative language gives the self autonomy to oppose subjection by describing their experience on their own terms.

According to the social model understanding of disability, while people do bear physical, sensory, and/or intellectual impairments, society must be held responsible for the "economic and social" discrimination faced by them, and not those individuals themselves (Oliver and Barnes 548). Tremain criticises the concept of impairment as understood by the social model. Instead, she argues that the "allegedly 'real' impairments must ... be identified as constructs of disciplinary knowledge/power" (Tremain, "On the Government of Disability" 192; *Foucault and the Government of Disability* 10) because the realist conception of impairments helps "**sustain**, and even augment, current social arrangements" (emphasis as in the source). The said constructs are 'uncritically' incorporated by "some subjects" into their "self-understandings." Further, the disabled subject's "testimonials, acts, and enactments" are significant only as performative actions that constitute "the allegedly 'natural' impairment." Impaired body-minds are, as per Tremain's account, to be conceived as illusions. As Swan points out, this "tendency to view the body as no more than the site of contested cultural discourses renders the question of the disabled subject unapproachable" (284–85), and also "runs the risk of excluding ... the writing of the embodied subject." Tobin Siebers describes the approach adopted by Tremain, which relies on Foucault's exposition of the constitutive role played by bio-power, as strong social constructionism (174–75). In an endnote to his essay, Siebers points out the social-constructionist conception of the body to be "merely a ghostly fantasy produced by the power of language" (182). So he cautions, "If it is true that bodies matter to people with disabilities, it may be worth thinking at greater length about the limits of social construction" (Siebers 174). In this way, Siebers brings our attention back to the body, which is the vehicle of experience. Tremain's deterministic approach does not, as is clear from this discussion, consider the experience of the self to be of philosophical significance, as it is concerned overwhelmingly with "the historically contingent practices [that] bring [the material body] into being," as if the will of the individual did not matter.

This book presents a resolute argument against the strong social-constructionist stance represented by Tremain. Let us allow Merleau-Ponty to speak on the matter of the self:

> I am not the outcome or the meeting-point of numerous causal agencies which determine my bodily or psychological make-up. I cannot conceive myself as nothing but a bit of the world, a mere object of biological, psychological or sociological investigation. I cannot shut myself up within the realm of science. All my knowledge of the world, even my scientific knowledge, is gained from my own particular point of view, or from some experience of the world without which the symbols of science would be meaningless.
>
> (ix)

Here, the phenomenologist clarifies that the person is "the absolute source" (Merleau-Ponty ix) of "the symbols of science" and of knowledge, because it is the former's experience that sustains them. To say that a bodily and/or mental impairment is constituted by "discursive and institutional practices" (Tremain, "On the Government of Disability" 190) is to deny the radically corporeal nature of disability experience. While I hold the belief that body-minds with impairments are different kinds of subjects, and not 'abnormal' creatures living in "a harmed condition" (Harris 96) as various societies regard them in accordance with the medical model of disability,[7] I am aware of Siebers's recognition that many people with disabilities very often live with pain and suffering on a daily basis. Therefore, they do not regard their

---

7 Scholars working in disability studies distinguish between different models or frames of understanding disability, viz. the medical model, the social model, and the cultural model. Siebers describes the first one as follows: "The medical model situates disability exclusively in individual bodies and strives to cure them by particular treatment, isolating the patient as diseased or defective" (173). The social and cultural models of disability theorise that medical doctors and rehabilitation professionals overwhelmingly consider the body of the disabled individual as defective. As a result of this, these professionals ignore the role played by powerful social and cultural forces such as negative attitudes and barriers in the built environment in disabling that individual. Thus, although illness and bodily make-up condition the individual's functioning in the world, the barriers imposed upon them by society place obstacles in their path.

disabilities as opportunities to resist various repressive "ideological constructions" (Siebers 177–178). This state of affairs makes it imperative that disability theory deals with corporeal experience. I do think that scholars working in this field should not consider the impaired body merely as an effect which is "always already signified and formed by discursive and institutional practices" (Tremain, "On the Government of Disability" 190), but should retain impairment as an experiential category in philosophical vocabulary. The reason is as follows: having an impairment does not mean that the person experiences only pain and/or inconveniences, or that they are perceived as different and inferior to the non-disabled. It has an ontological value, and therefore has wide-ranging implications for epistemology. Being blind, for instance, means (1) that the person inhabits the world of the blind, which is different from, but connected to, the world of the sighted (*On Sight* xiii); and (2) that they create, or can do so, a different world (poetry, art) based on how they know, and interact with, the world.

Virginia Woolf states with wisdom in her essay "On Being Ill" (193–203) that:

> ... literature does its best to maintain that its concern is with the mind; that the body is a sheet of plain glass through which the soul looks straight and clear, and, save for one or two passions such as desire and greed, is null, and negligible and non-existent. On the contrary, the very opposite is true. All day, all night the body intervenes; blunts or sharpens, colours or discolours, turns to wax in the warmth of June, hardens to tallow in the murk of February. The creature within can only gaze through the pane—smudged or rosy; it cannot separate off from the body like the sheath of a knife or the pod of a pea for a single instant ...
>
> (4)

Due to the important role played by the (ill) body in life, Woolf argues for the treatment in literature of illness and, by extension, of corporeality. Nearly half a century later, Hélène Cixous opens her iconoclastic essay "The Laugh of the Medusa" (875–93) giving a passionate call to women to write:

> Woman must write her self: must write about women and bring women to writing, from which they have been driven away as violently as from their bodies—for the same reasons, by the same law, with the same fatal goal. Woman must put herself into the text—as into the world and into history—by her own movement.
>
> (875)

This decisive statement may be applied with equal truth to the position of the disabled in writing, in the world, and in history. The words are decisive because they recognize the importance of acting by one's will, of breaking free of imposed constraints, in the phrase "by her own movement." Ecriture feminine emphasises a strong bodily component. Cixous not only forcefully urges women to write their selves, but also gives men the space to write: "I write woman: woman must write woman. And man, man" (877). If we proceed along this line of reasoning, it becomes clear that the disabled woman and man must write "her self" and his self, respectively. To write one's self as a blind person, for example, or to put one's self "into the text," indicates the significance of artistic subjectivity. Cixous's words are similar to what Swan says concerning the subject matter of disability studies: "... it is people with disabilities making themselves heard politically, socially, culturally" (283). This declaration reveals the bodily nature of writing subjectivity.

The following words clarify that writing and the body go together: "And why don't you write? Write! Writing is for you, you are for you; your body is yours, take it" (Cixous 876). It is sexual desire that unites the two: "... or because you wrote, irresistibly" (Cixous 877), she explains, "as when we would masturbate in secret, not to go further, but to attenuate the tension a bit, just enough to take the edge off." This writing in secret is similar to masturbating, as the quotation indicates, not to explore the sexual potential of one's being but always in fear. Due to this fear and secrecy, says Cixous to women, their writing was not good (876–77). She celebrates the sexual power of women's writing when she avers that the male-dominated market for books does not "like the true texts of women—female-sexed texts" (Cixous 877). She argues for the female body in desire to come to the text, thus advocating that writing be understood as emanating from the desiring body. Later in the text, she stresses the importance, to put it in Swan's words, of the "voiced body" (284) to characterise the embodied logic of the woman who speaks "at a public gathering" (Cixous 881): "... all of her passes into her voice, and it's with her body that she vitally supports the 'logic' of her speech. ... she physically materializes what she's thinking; she signifies it with her body." This thought represents a fresh interpretation of the role that the body plays in writing. Importantly, her stance actually goes against the views that see writing as an impersonal exercise in language. So she repudiates the commonly recognized division "between the logic of oral speech and the logic of the text" in order to stress the importance of the body in women's speech and writing. Thus, Cixous offers a personal view that takes into account the ground of living and writing, viz. the body.

It would be fruitful to begin the study of narrative by asking a straightforward narratological question: How do narratives develop? The narrative art is, first and foremost, an art in – and with – language. Working in – and with – language and its resources, such as tropes, and using certain narrative techniques, the artist tells the story. Examining the role of language in the art of storytelling, and the techniques that are used to develop the discourse of narratives is important for this monograph. The issues that merit consideration fall under the broad umbrella of narrative choices, and involve narratological questions of voice and perspective; narrators and characters in the stories; narrated actions, events, situations including epiphanies, and setting; temporality and causal connections in narrative; and the crucial question of everyday experience in narrative. All these themes may be explored by examining "narrative discourse" (Genette 26), which in literature is the "narrative text."

I conceive disability as difference. As Henri-Jacques Stiker states in the introductory chapter to his book, *A History of Disability* (1999), "the real ... generates difference and singularity" (12). We may understand from these words that the disabled body is marked as different from the 'normal' body. Lennard J. Davis argues that the "concept of the normal" (100) arose in Europe during the nineteenth century. This idea developed in association with "the concept of the bell curve" (Davis 101) in statistics. "In this paradigm," writes Davis, "the majority of bodies fall under the main umbrella of the curve. Those that do not are at the extremes and therefore are abnormal." So people came to be forced "to conform" to the requirements of the norm. It is important to note that this "imperative" of normalcy lies heavy equally on those bodies considered to fall within the bell curve, as well as on those that lie outside it. However, adopting the approach of theorising disability experience as difference requires caution, because, in Western thought, difference is always already charged with moral values which grade those that are different from one another as superior and inferior, pure and impure. As David Mitchell states in his foreword to Stiker's book, the existence of disability in a body shows that the body is not a perfect whole – corporeal integrity being a conception that our cultures subscribe to, but that it is susceptible to illness and disability: "As a beginning principle, Stiker posits that an encounter with disability inaugurates a break in the observer's perceptual field—'a tear in our being that reveals [the body's] open-endedness, its incompleteness, its precariousness.' The visceral nature of this 'tear' reveals the extent of our investment in the fantasy of the normal" (viii). This investment in the fantasy of 'normal' existence is something that disabled persons have to deal with, both in themselves and in others, on a daily basis because it determines attitudes towards disability. Both a non-disabled person and one who is blind, for instance, can be taken aback when they encounter a disability in another person; the blind person may even loathe themselves because of their disability, or can have a negative attitude such as fear, pity, disgust, horror, dislike, or even hatred towards somebody with a different disability. This means that the blind person, like the non-disabled person, regards themselves as being 'normal.' Thus, the "tear in our being that reveals [the body's] open-endedness, its incompleteness, its precariousness" plays a major role in self-understanding. With the help of this basic conception of disability, we will consider how the experientiality of blindness has a bearing on narrative choices in the texts under study.

Hannah Arendt's thoughts about the limit of philosophical discourse and the potential of literature to define the self form "an important starting point" (Kottman viii) for the philosophy of storytelling developed by the feminist philosopher, Adriana Cavarero.[8] The question of selfhood receives

8 I thank Dr Upamanyu Sengupta for bringing to my notice Cavarero's work on storytelling.

two distinct kinds of treatment in philosophy and literature: the vocabulary of the former can manage only a definition of 'what' someone is (Kottman vii). This limitation exposes philosophy's aim of achieving universal knowledge. The language of the latter becomes necessary to know 'who' someone is, that is, their uniqueness (Kottman viii). Paul A. Kottman writes,

> 'Who' someone is ... remains inexpressible within the language of philosophy; but does not, as a result, remain utterly ineffable. Rather, 'who' someone is can be 'known' (although this is not epistemological knowledge) through the narration of the life-story of which that person is the protagonist.
>
> (viii)

This divergence in the goals achievable by the discourses of literature and philosophy has a crucial bearing on the work presented in this book. This fact is suggested by the phrase "who they are, or what the self is"(5) in the present chapter. It indicates the split between the vocabularies of literature and philosophy with regard to personhood. While I adopt an amalgam of philosophical/narratological approaches in discussing blind artistic subjectivities, the varied literary works written by Borges, Hull, and Kuusisto reveal their respective individual uniqueness. This singularity informs my discussions of their varying aesthetic approaches to blindness and selfhood. The distinct literary imagination of each of the authors and my philosophical approach interact to produce a study that examines plural literary forms.

1.5 The Research Claim and Chapter Summaries

The claim which I seek to defend in this monograph develops out of the questions which start off this chapter. Certain concerns that the narratives foreground are indicators of the fact that, for Borges, Hull, and Kuusisto, blindness and visual impairment were a major factor in making narrative choices. (By 'blindness' I mean complete lack of sight, and 'visual impairment' indicates low vision which does not really allow the person to use the sight they have to do their work.) Examining the narrative choices will enable us to talk about authorial subjectivity. The process of positing the two research questions and making the claim requiring substantiation in the rest of the book allows the author to set before his reader the problem which motivated him to compose the chapters that follow. These chapters will show the unique, divergent ways in which the three authors' artistic subjectivities emerge. I find crucial points of convergence in their selfhoods, but the various phases of the understanding of blindness and subjectivity evident in their works bring out the richness of interaction between blindness and literature. It is this critical analysis which lends credibility to the research presented here.

Having laid down the conceptual framework structuring the monograph, and discussed the theoretical approach informing this work, I will now proceed to a brief sketch of the chapters that follow. Chapter 2, "Blindness in Borges's Fictions," examines the various phases of Borges's aesthetic of blindness by critically reading a number of short stories which he wrote over nearly half a century, from 1934 to 1983. At the centre of this aesthetic may be perceived a dialectical movement in the responses to blindness captured by his short fiction from the 1940s and 1950s. His fictional practice during this period bodies forth a dialectical movement between self-sufficient esoteric systems and the experiential world (Chapter 2, p. 27). The move into the archives of recondite knowledge reflects withdrawal from the external world, while the artistic turn to the experience of blindness symbolises creativity. I contend that Borges shows through this dialectic the importance of engaging with corporeality and selfhood while grappling with life as a blind person.

Chapter 3, "Altered Sensation and Self-Understanding in Borges's Fictions," interprets six short stories which cover most of Borges's literary career to show that he was keenly aware of various kinds of disability experience. I will focus on instances of direct emphasis on disability experiences such as paralysis and blindness in these selected 'fictions,' and will illustrate the point that being reflective about disability indicates a deepened awareness of, and interest in, the fragility of corporeal existence. It becomes clear in the course of the chapter that deformities are, in the lives of those who are disabled, one among the many aspects of experience which define their subjectivities. The underlying premise and structuring principle of the argument is that bodily deformities affect self-conception in diverse, observable ways. In the short stories taken up for this study,[9] one can observe that when characters lose, in part or whole, the faculty of the senses, they come to acquire a different understanding of time; time slows down for many of them. I argue that the reasons for this novel sense of time are as follows. The character with the deformity is restricted in movement, and spends his time in physically non-active but intensely contemplative ways. He has a heightened awareness of reality, and an expansive sense of time. He also begins to notice unmistakable similarities in experiences, perceptions, and memories from day to day. The disabled character's experiential homogeneity, thus, calls up the theme of repetition and the idea of circular time. My contention is that Borges pertinently foregrounds the consequence of bodily deformities in a differential matrix of sensations, which in these short stories appears as a creative temporal consciousness.

Chapter 4, called "The Everyday Experience of Growing Blind: Narrative Subjectivity in Hull," and Chapter 5, entitled "Self-Knowledge through Interaction with the World," treat a movement in the selfhood of John M.

---

9 The titles of the narratives are as follows: "Hakim, the Masked Dyer of Merv" (1934), "Funes, His Memory" (1942), "The End" (1953), "The Maker" (1960), "The Other" (1972), and "August 25, 1983" (1983).

Hull as represented in his two diaries, *Touching the Rock: An Experience of Blindness*, and *On Sight and Insight: A Journey into the World of Blindness*. He has developed these books from the recordings that he made on cassette over approximately four years and spanning the experience of eight years, starting in June 1983, as he grappled with his blindness. Hull reflects on his daily experiences 'in blindness' in narrative sections composed on a regular basis, which demonstrates the dynamic connection between maintaining the cassette diary and realising his condition of being blind. The fragmentary form of the diaries with their cumulative effect is well-suited to describe and examine this process of leaving one kind of consciousness (the sighted self) and experiencing the birth of a new consciousness (the blind self). The first of the chapters on Hull explores the relationship between his dreams and conscious life to discover how he gains a fuller understanding of the blind self that was once sighted. He regularly makes entries interpreting his dreams. There he connects the experiences he has in the stories that the dreams present with his most immediate concerns centring on interactions with his wife, children, friends, and colleagues, and other details in conscious experience. The chapter shows how Hull, through reflection on the mind's activity in dreams, comes to integrate his past sighted life and his present blind life. The second chapter on the diarist's works examines his reflections on two key concerns, viz. knowledge and social relationships as they impact his selfhood. He considers both factors as having a formative influence on him as a person. The diaries show why knowledge is fundamental to the day-to-day living of life, and how this fact necessitates reflection on one's experiences, thereby producing self-knowledge. What impact does blindness have on Hull's knowledge? How does his ability to gain knowledge in the blind condition affect his being-in-the-world? It is clear from his reflections that the ways in which he knows the world exercise a formative influence on his existence in, and passage through, it. The chapter also traces a dialectical movement from Hull's initial conception of the self as it is visually based on the body image to one that is not determined by visual considerations, but is related to being-in-the-world.

Chapter 6, "The Poetical Subjectivity of Kuusisto," interprets the first of three memoirs by Kuusisto, *Planet of the Blind: A Memoir*, which follows a movement in his selfhood from a long-term rejection of blindness to an eventual, full acceptance of the blind self. Chapter 7, "The Narrative Dialectic of Silences and Articulations in the Memoirs of Kuusisto," describes the aesthetic of listening that the memoirist develops in the twenty-nine essays that form *Eavesdropping: A Life by Ear*. Further, it explains an aesthetic dialectic enacted in the narrative fabric of the two memoirs mentioned above. This dialectic may be recognised once Kuusisto's aesthetic of listening is understood. The former is constituted by variations in the narration of a series of memories from childhood and youth to be found in Kuusisto's first two works. Thus, we see that his writings embody a self-conscious art of blindness in two ways that are not separate but contiguous: the art of living as a blind person, and the art produced in and through blindness.

Chapter 8, "Artistic Subjectivity, Narrative Choices, and the Author: Their Relation as a Function of Bodily Being," presents concluding reflections on the narrative modes used by Borges, Hull, and Kuusisto to tell their various stories. Doing so will help tie the arguments of the chapters together in such a way that the authors' individual artistic subjectivities become evident. Drawing upon Merleau-Ponty's discussion of abstract movement as the defining principle of consciousness (139), and upon Kierkegaard's explanation of pseudonymity in his works (627), the chapter advances the argument that Borges engages in self-examination and self-representation through his short stories which narrate multiple disability experiences. Also discussed are the implications of the gaps between the writing, or reflecting, self and the experiencing self, or selves, in Hull's and Kuusisto's autobiographical works. The titles and summaries of the eight chapters forming this book make it clear, then, that strong connections exist between blindness in literature, corporeality, and subjectivity. This study enables us to engage in a sustained reflection on, and discovery of, selfhood through the medium of the literary imagination as it explores the experience of blindness.

2   Blindness in Borges's Fictions

Jorge Luis Borges (1899–1986) lost his sight gradually over three decades, eventually becoming blind after he turned fifty-eight (Manguel 15–16). In Borges's 1969 poem "In Praise of Darkness" (*Selected Poems* 298–301), the speaker states as a matter of fact, "In my life there were always too many things./Democritus of Abdera plucked out his eyes in order to think:/Time has been my Democritus" (lines 14–16). The force of these lines becomes evident in the Argentine's 1977 lecture entitled "Blindness" (*Selected Non-Fictions* 473–83), where he describes his blindness using the metaphor "slow nightfall" (*Selected Non-Fictions* 474), which speaks to his experience of gradually becoming blind. He understands his sight loss to have started in 1899 and to have "lasted more than three quarters of a century" (*Selected Non-Fictions* 474–75). In his long life as a blind person, he displayed conflicting attitudes towards his disability, and adopted differing ways of dealing with its consequences. Here I will examine Borges's narratives to track the various phases through which his aesthetic of blindness developed. The various stages in the aesthetic mirror the evolution of his self-conception as a blind man. I substantiate this claim by citing Laraway's explanation of why Borges appropriates the mirror as a symbol of art ("The Blind Spot in the Mirror" 311). At the centre of the aesthetic may be perceived a dialectical movement in the responses to blindness captured by Borges's short fiction from the 1940s and 1950s.

Borges's literary career was long, spanning more than six decades. Kristal writes in his introduction to the volume entitled *Poems of the Night* (2010) that the Argentinian author "began writing poetry during World War I as a teenager living with his family in Geneva" (x), and continued writing up until 1985, a short while before his death. I divide his career into three periods: the early period, that begins with the publication of his first collection of poetry *Fervor de Buenos Aires* (1923), and runs up to 1940; the middle period, that includes two decades from the publication of the short story "Tlön, Uqbar, Orbis Tertius" in 1940 to the publication of the collection *El Hacedor* (*The Maker*) in 1960; and the late period, from 1960 to his death in Geneva in June 1986. The two publications defining the middle period, which is crucial due to the advancement of blindness in Borges's life, form milestones in the

DOI: 10.4324/9781003399667-2

progress of the aesthetic under consideration. I base this division on the author's engagement with blindness in selected prose writings.

Alberto Manguel[1] writes in his memoir, *With Borges* (2006), that Borges's

> was a blindness expected since his birth, because he always knew that he had inherited feeble eyesight from his English great-grandfather and his grandmother, both of whom died blind; also from his father, who had gone blind at about the same age as Borges.
>
> (16)

This fact is important for Borges's writings because the theme of blindness winds through them, colouring all with its presence. Since Borges had weak eyesight as a boy, and knew that he might lose his sight over time, the world of the blind was never far from his thoughts. A plethora of references to blindness – both direct and veiled – may be found throughout his oeuvre, but the present chapter will focus on his narrative fiction.[2] Ubelaker Andrade suggests that one way to approach Borges's relationship with blindness is to consider it in terms of anticipation and direct experience.[3] This idea may be aligned with the broad themes of metaphoric and experiential engagement with blindness as evident in Borges's short stories. As Naomi Schor writes, "both real and metaphoric" manifestations of blindness "are bound up with each other" (83). I combine the themes of "anticipation" of blindness by Borges, and his "direct experience" of it – the way that blindness is a fact in his life, with its metaphoric and experiential forms in the narratives, respectively (cf. Krentz 39). This conceptual amalgam enables me to make the point that when Borges deploys blindness as a metaphor in many of his short stories, it informs the narratives with an anticipated sense of presence. As I endeavour to demonstrate in this chapter, his turn to blindness as experience in his literary composition reflects the achievement of creative excellence.

During the middle period of his career, due to advancing blindness, Borges experienced an evolving relationship with the world, as attested by his immersion in memorised texts. The fact that he assimilated a vast body of writing during the time he had enough sight to read is well-documented. Paul S. Piper states that Borges, who worked as a librarian from 1937 to 1946, read widely at the library where he worked, translated, and wrote a number of his short stories (56). In his "Introduction" (5–8) to *Seven Nights* (1984), referring to Borges's "remembered library" (5), Alastair Reid writes that,

---

1 The blurb of Manguel's memoir states that he "is an award-winning writer and translator." Manguel says that in 1964, Borges engaged him to read aloud to him. According to him, Borges is "one of the world's great readers" (Manguel 13). He writes that he had the good fortune to read to Borges from 1964 to 1968 (Manguel 12).

2 All references in Chapters 2 and 3 to the short stories of Borges are from the volume *Collected Fictions* (1998).

3 Dr Ubelaker Andrade and I had a conversation (among several immensely important ones) on 13 September 2014 about Borges's short stories via Skype.

after being dismissed from the Municipal Library of Buenos Aires in 1946, the Argentine man of letters found it necessary to give lectures to make a living. However, by then, he could not "read a written text" due to the encroaching blindness. He had to prepare his lectures with the help of his mother, and then "memorize his material." In this way, he created "a considerable private library of reference and quotation" in his capacious memory.

Borges's self-conscious withdrawal into the erudite textual world signifies increasing perceptual limitations. I argue that his fictional practice during the middle period embodies a dialectical movement between self-sufficient esoteric systems and the experiential world. When the author, responding to his growing blindness, withdraws from the external world into a hermetic 'thought-world,' his fictions display a penchant for the archaeology of knowledge, interest in scholarly archives, old traditions, and knowledge restricted to a small circle of scholars and concealed from the wider world. On examining the aesthetics of Borges's narratives, we find that they are not merely short stories characterised by features typical to the genre; they also deal with deeply intellectual themes, and tend to be extremely reflective, as I argue in this chapter. As a result of their subject matter, such short stories may be described as esoteric fiction. The move into the archives of knowledge reflects withdrawal from the external world, while the turn to the experience of blindness symbolises creativity. Here, I offer a reading of a few short stories that dramatise this dialectic, namely "Tlön, Uqbar, Orbis Tertius" (1940), "The Library of Babel" (1941), "The Aleph" (1945), "The Immortal" (1947), "The Zahir," "The Writing of the God" (1949), and "The Maker" (1960). In the first two narratives, yielding to the impulse to disengage from the world, Borges offers an encyclopaedic detailing of the contingencies entailed by an ideal realm. While blindness precipitates the author's withdrawal, the desire for systems of knowledge which impose order in a chaotic world drives those who are enamoured of various forms of idealism along this course. Both of them do so in order to evade the complexities of human embodiment. The next four short stories exemplify narratives dealing with an inward turn, away from visual plenitude, and towards self-discovery. "The Maker" narrates the poet's engagement with the experience of the world by imagining Homer's experience as he progressively becomes blind. My contention is that Borges shows, through this dialectic of withdrawal from the world and the artistic turn to experience, the importance of engaging with corporeality and selfhood while grappling with life as a blind person.

In "Blindness," Borges refers to "the pathetic moment" (*Selected Non-Fictions* 475) in 1955, when, to express it in his memorable words, "I knew I had lost my sight, my reader's and writer's sight." At the end of that year, he was appointed the director of the National Library of Argentina. He says that he gradually "came to realize the strange irony of events" whereby he became almost completely blind at the same time as being given charge of "nine hundred thousand books in various languages." Piper adds that, on being named the director of the National Library, Borges referred in his "acceptance speech" to "'God's splendid irony in granting me at one time 800,000 books and darkness'" (57). Further, both Borges (*Selected Non-Fictions* 475) and Piper (57) refer to the "Poem of the Gifts." The former composed this poem soon after coming to recognise the inexplicable and ironic twist in his life (*Selected Non-Fictions* 475). It deals with that "splendid irony" in a poignant and masterful manner. I would pair with this poem the short story "The Maker" for its rich aesthetic engagement with the experience of blindness and the resulting creativity. Edwin Williamson suggests in his biography of the author, *Borges: a life* (2004), that he wrote "The Maker" in 1957 (338) at a time when he was in despair. These approximate dates for the poem and the short story, as well as the fact that both compositions appeared in 1960 in the collection entitled *The Maker*, support my argument in the chapter. I propose that the aesthetic shift suggested by Ubelaker Andrade – which forms part of the dialectical movement identified in Borges's writings – occurred during the five years between 1955 when the author recognised that he had become blind, and 1960 when *The Maker* was published.

2.1 The Metaphorical Articulation of Blindness

Variations on the theme of blindness are present in many short stories by Borges, starting with the earliest anthology entitled *A Universal History of Iniquity* (1935) up to and including the last collection that was published nearly half a century later, *Shakespeare's Memory* (1983). The references and allusions to blindness constitute a narrative exploration of sensory difference, and of the world of the blind. Consider, for instance, the brief appearance of "blind Danny Lyons, a towheaded kid with huge dead eyes" (26) in "Monk Eastman, Purveyor of Iniquities" (25–30) from the first collection. The words describing the blind man are befittingly graphic for a New York gangster-pimp. In the underworld of that city, Danny Lyons's blindness is not a liability for the daily performance of his chosen activities. His end, which is brutal and which comes at the hands of one of his peers, testifies to the dangerous life he led. That world was also home to the gangster Dandy Johnny Dolan, who "wore [a 'delicate copper pick'] on his thumb to gouge out his enemies' eyes" (26). This statement, with its brutal energy, gives us to understand that blinding was thought of as an act of cruel punishment, as revenge, and finally as a ritual of victory. Although the act is considered by the narrator and the fictional characters he portrays as a punishment that will devastate the victim, the presentation of the life of the blind gangster Danny Lyons shows that the criminal world could be shaped by its blind members as well.

Analogous to the power of the blind to mould the world is the power of tactile and auditory images – which allude to the world of the blind – to shape the narrative. The impersonal narrator lays stress on sound and touch in telling the story. This approach becomes evident in the description of Monk Eastman's physical presence: "He had a short, bull neck, an unassailable chest, the long arms of a boxer, a broken nose; his face, though legended with scars, was less imposing than his body" (27). Drawn from Herbert Asbury's description of the gangster (255),[4] this linguistic sketch is significant for its tactile imagery, although visual appreciation is undoubtedly possible. What is striking about the highlighted features of Monk Eastman's physique – a broken nose and a body that is more imposing than the face – and his activities such as the fatal blows he administered with knives and bludgeons (27–28) is that all these features are overwhelmingly physical in the sense of being tactile even though they appeal, by default, to the visual faculty. The above quotation and examples such as fading mug shots of gangsters and men "reeking of cigar smoke and alcohol" (28) are typical of the narratorial statements to be found in the short stories that point to a world without sight. Among the statements that relate temporal events, we find descriptive phrases denoting sound or its lack. This feature strengthens the view expressed above: "the dance without music" and "telling the story" (25) concerning a knife fight in Argentina; "the senseless, deafening noise of a hundred revolvers" (28) characterising a savage gun battle between two criminal gangs of New York City; "The Crackle of Gunfire" (29) used as the title of a narrative section; and the narratorial indication "he [Monk Eastman] was heard to say" (30) used to report the gangster's derisive opinion of the Great War, all stress the importance of hearing.

This mode of narration offers details in a way that suggests the relegated importance of sight. The aesthetic principle of blindness shapes other narratives as well. The events in "Man on Pink Corner" (45–52) – a short story about separate encounters between three knife fighters in the city of Buenos Aires – take place in the course of a night. Although vision and colours are mentioned in the narrative, they belong to the night. They are dark and sombre. The words 'Night' and 'darkness' in Borges's art suggest, according to Kristal, "themes that speak to [his blindness]" (*Poems of the Night* ix). There are quite a few scenes involving music, dance, the body, sound, and listening in the story. Talking about the physical appearance of Francisco Real, also known as the Yardmaster, the narrator-character says, "The man resembled the voice a good deal" (46). Here the voice has precedence both in time and importance because the man's voice is heard before he is seen. The narrator tells the reader how he pays attention to the body of his dance partner, describing her as "a girl that could follow like she could read my mind." Narrative details, such as the tango which creates an atmosphere of "drunken dizziness" (49), "[t]he melonga [that] ran like a grass fire from one end of the room to the other," and the Yardmaster's soundless death (51), demonstrate the significance of corporeal presence both in erotic play and in mortality. They also highlight the significance of elements involving sightlessness in this

4 We should note here that Borges himself lists Asbury's work as the source for "Monk Eastman, Purveyor of Iniquities" in the index (*Collected Fictions* 64) appended to his first collection, *A Universal History of Iniquity* (1935).

narrative. The presence of a blind violinist in the dance hall (where a major portion of the action takes place) strengthens such an understanding. Also noteworthy in this regard are narrative statements that exploit blindness as a metaphor – a man "steps forward and stands there like he's dazzled by all the women and all the light" (48), and "He [the Yardmaster] stood there tall, and unseeing" (50). We can discern blindness in its metaphorical form in this narrative in the contrasting behaviour of the various characters. The knife fighter, Rosendo Juárez, refuses to fight the man from the north, the yardmaster, who insolently challenges him to a duel, and instead throws his knife out of the window. The way he does this indicates the insight he has gained: "Then all of a sudden he reared back and flung that knife straight through the window, out into the Maldonado" (48). This bold action is not that of a man without courage, but of one who is disgusted with the meaningless violence indulged in by the macho men of the streets. Metaphorically expressed, then, he sees the violent character of the life he has been leading thus far for what it is, whereas the Yardmaster, La Lujanera, the narrator, and the other tough people present in the dance hall do not see, or in other words are blind to, the utter meaninglessness of such an existence. In fact, in "The Story from Rosendo Juárez" from the collection *Brodie's Report* (1970), Juárez himself, narrating the story from his point of view, says that this was what happened to him that evening.

In "Hakim, the Masked Dyer of Merv" (40–4), the protagonist Hakim uses the two blind men who accompany him when he appears as the masked Prophet (41), the leopard which is blinded (42), and later his "harem of 114 blind wives" (43) as signs which proclaim his power. This power, he declares, was granted him by the Almighty (42). By putting out the eyes of the above-mentioned humans and animal, he intends to reduce them from living beings to mere signs that serve to glorify him. Thus, blindness becomes a potent symbol – in the eyes of the people of Hakim's land, one of sacred power; to the reader, that of brutality, because the man does violence without compunction. Further, he uses his mask (and subsequently a rich veil that hides his face [42]), and his "extraordinarily sweet" (41) voice as means of keeping the world ignorant about his body. This is because it has been deformed by leprosy. In this way, he 'blinds' everybody. If he were to be honest and not deceive the world, he would be killed or banished from society into oblivion. (I shall discuss this point in detail in the next chapter [71–3].) Thus, for five years, from 158 to 163 Hegira, he succeeds in preventing the rulers of the land and the population from realising that he is an impostor and outcast masquerading as a prophet. Ironically, however, his downfall is brought about by the revelation made by one of his blind wives as she was being strangled to death for adultery: "… she … screamed that the third finger was missing from the Prophet's right hand, and that his other fingers had no nails" (44). This defiant act, performed as she was on the verge of death, restores to the blind woman her agency, while at the same time leading to Hakim's assassination by two of his followers. Thus, blind men, women, and even a blind animal make significant appearances in Borges's fictions written before 1940, the year when "Tlön, Uqbar, Orbis Tertius" was published. These narrative occurrences reflect Borges's preoccupation with blindness even during the 1930s.

"Hakim, the Masked Dyer of Merv" also features the metaphorical use of blindness with reference to Hakim's psychology, and knowledge of the state of affairs during the time of the veiled Prophet in Turkistan. At the end of the section entitled "The Scarlet Dye" (40–1), the narrator reports that among Hakim's things found broken after his disappearance from "his native city" (41) of Merv is a brass mirror. We can safely conclude that when he discovers that he is infected with leprosy, Hakim breaks the mirror so that he does not have to see the image of his afflicted face and body reflected in it. The view expressed in his cosmogony that "mirrors ... are abominable" (43) is significant from this point of view. Similarly, he uses "a fourfold veil of white silk" (42) to hide his deformed face as much from himself as from the world. Thus, the breaking of the mirror and the donning of the veil enforce a kind of blindness in its wearer.[5] At the same time, the broken mirror and the magnificent gemmed veil serve as symbols of deception that hide from the world – thereby blinding everybody to – his devious plan to win power and glory. Hakim's reference to the divine gift of "words of such antiquity that speaking them burned one's mouth" (42), an allusion to the veiled Prophet's "sweet" voice (41), Hakim's practice of "tenor chanting of prayers" in battle, the "words" of "confidential friends of God," the voice of fire in the hell of Hakim's cosmogony which tortures those who deny the Prophet's Word, and other similar instances demonstrate the stress the narrator lays on the voice and hearing to call attention to the preclusion of sight, both real and metaphorical.

In certain short stories found in the section named "Et Cetera" (53–63) of *A Universal History of Iniquity*, there is a more or less veiled, metaphorical use of blindness to indicate various defects in human character. In "A Theologian in Death" (53–4), the focalising character Melancthon[6] is a theologian who writes "nothing whatever concerning charity" (53) in the hereafter, which is "not heaven." The house where he resides after his death is "like that in which he had lived in the world," and all the things in the room in which he awakens after departing from the world resemble his earthly possessions. Thus, they constitute a kind of mirror that confuses Melancthon and keeps him ignorant of his current reality. He is, as it is, too arrogant in his scriptural knowledge to perceive it. He shows disdain towards charity, a virtue favoured by the angels. The first sign that he will soon learn of his folly is the initial obscurement and eventual disappearance of "the things which he used in his room." This description mirrors the gradual advance of blindness, an experience to which Borges could easily relate. Later, when Melancthon

---

5 Gandhari, the Kaurava queen of Hastinapur, voluntarily assumes this kind of blindness in the *Mahabharata*.

6 This name alludes to the sixteenth-century reformer, Philip Melancthon.

cannot see what he has written about charity the day after he has committed it to paper as an expedient to protect himself from divine wrath (54), we are reminded again of blindness. I will cite certain words from the short story titled "August 25, 1983" (489–93), published nearly five decades later, to suggest that, for the author, the phenomenon of letters disappearing from the pages on which they are written symbolises blindness. In that narrative, the eighty-four-year-old double of Borges uses the expression "'touch the books that have no letters'" (491) to allude to his blindness. Thus, Borges uses sightlessness in "A Theologian in Death" as a metaphor for the arrogance of the theologian.

"The Wizard that was Made to Wait" (57–60) is another short story that foregrounds the blindness of ecclesiastic arrogance. When a dean of the cathedral of Santiago de Compostela arrives at the house of the wizard Illán in the city of Toledo "to learn the art of magic" (57), the latter informs "him that he had divined that his visitor was a dean, a man of good position and promising future" (58). Illán is a man with supernatural sight who can see into the future. His taking the dean by his hand and leading him metaphori-cally suggests his knowledge that the dean lacks sight, and thus is ignorant of the weakness of his character. Sight here is linked with self-knowledge, and acts as a metaphor for wisdom – an important thematic feature in much of Borges's writings ("The Blind Spot in the Mirror" 308). The influence of this aesthetic principle becomes clear in the course of the present narrative when a dream acts as a mirror. As the wizard subtly guides the dean through a dream forecasting his future rise in the church, and his simultaneous neglect of his teacher of "the occult science" (59) Illán, the dean finally recognises his arrogant, ungrateful self.

"The Chamber of Statues" (54–6) is adapted by Borges from Sir Richard Burton's *Book of the Thousand Nights and a Night* (*Collected Fictions* 531), and is a tale about forbidden sight and the consequences for the ruler of "the kingdom of the Andalusians" who violates this law. He must not open the gates of "a strong tower" (54) in the capital city of the kingdom and see the things that are hidden within. The meaning is clear: their sight and knowl-edge are prohibited. However, the wilfulness of the "evil man, who was not of the old royal house" (55), makes him 'blind' to the danger that threatens him and the realm when he enters the tower and views its treasures. As a means of alluding to the different kinds of blindness to be found in the story, the narrator paradoxically foregrounds corporeality and touch as a sensory modality suited to a blind person's perception. Referring to the king's act of opening the gates of the tower, he says that the man "pulled off the locks with his right hand (which will now burn through all eternity)"; the "figures of Arabs on their horses and camels [inside the tower] were round, as in life," such that "a blind man could identify them by touch, and the front hooves of their horses did not touch the ground yet they did not fall, as though the mounts were rearing." Both the "marvellous mirror … which had been made for Suleyman, son of David," and the "terrible inscription" (56) that the king views in the inner chambers of the tower indicate that he understands the folly of his action just before being vanquished and slain by the Arab conqueror, Tarik ibn Zayid.

Thus, we see that Borges makes variegated use of blindness to connote situations and traits of character. Schor observes that blindness appears in literary texts as a metaphor with unfailing regularity because it belongs to a "category of figures ... to which language offers no alternative" (77). However, as already explained, this metaphorical figuring of blindness forms part of the dialectical movement between the ideal and the experiential, which is the topic of this chapter.

The unnamed narrator who opens "The Mirror of Ink" (60–2) describes Yāqub[7] as "the crudest of the governors of the Sudan" (60) since he does not care for the welfare of his subjects. The former calls the governor "Yāqub the Afflicted." The epithet, which makes an unflattering allusion to the man's physical appearance, indicates that he has an ailment or disability. Yāqub is one of the two focalising characters of the narrative. Although both the first narrator and the sorcerer Abderramen-al-Masmud call Yāqub "the Afflicted" one, the reader is never told what the tyrant's affliction is. Abderramen-al-Masmud is the other main character of the narrative, and the one who narrates the manner in which Yāqub meets his doom. By his repeated use of the above epithet, the sorcerer seems to hint throughout his narrative that Yāqub's afflicted body represents his cruel personality. But Borges does not allow the completion of such a move in the reader's mind, because, as mentioned above, we do not learn what Yāqub's affliction is.

Abderramen-al-Masmud possesses the skill to show Yāqub marvellous "forms and appearances" (60) in a magical mirror of ink. Ubelaker Andrade elucidates the connection that this "circular pool" (*Borges Beyond the Visible* 56) bears with a pigment which blots out the sight of a man in Sir Richard Francis Burton's work (*Borges Beyond the Visible* 57). By means of the sorcerer's craft, Yāqub encounters himself in the mirror drawn in his "right palm" (60). The striking phrase 'mirror of ink,' besides signifying the magical mirror of the story, may also be interpreted as connoting a paradoxically veiled mirror which conceals even as it reflects or reveals appearances. Further, the words may allude to writing, which is created by putting ink on paper. (The pages that follow contain an examination of literature as a special kind of mirror.) The tyrant discovers in the mirror that he is a "condemned man" (62) who is about to be executed. Although he sees his face and other appearances clearly in the mirror, he lacks the ability to see past his worldly power and self-importance, and comprehend his own cruel nature. Thus, the veil worn by "the Masked One" (61), who appears in the mirror of ink, reflects Yāqub's inability to see. We may say, then, that the Quranic words concerning the unveiling of sight do not possess the power to enable Yāqub to see and know himself. For although he commands the sorcerer to show him the vision of "a just and irrevocable punishment" (62), he hides his eyes "[i]n fear and madness" when he sees that the guilty man who is to be put to death is himself. However, the sorcerer forces him "to look upon the ceremony of his death." Thus, when the veil of the condemned man is "stripped from him" in the mirror, Yāqub recognises himself by means of his face. As Laraway indicates, "Only when his death is imminent does the revelation occur" ("The Blind Spot in the Mirror" 320). The critic explains, "The connections between death, the face, and a moment of self-revelation are to be found throughout Borges's works." However, the sight of his visage does not enable Yāqub to achieve any insight into his character because he is overwhelmed by the prospect of imminent death. In this recognition, as Laraway observes, "the figure of the face [acts] as a site where identity is at once consolidated and undermined" ("The Blind Spot in the Mirror" 309, 313).[8] The narrative importance of "the motif of the mirror" (Laraway, "The Blind Spot in the Mirror" 311) lies, then, not in enabling the tyrant to understand the self, but in metaphorically showing his blindness with regard to himself. Thus, the prominent theme of the short story is the exploration of sight and its obscurement.

2.2 The Dialectic of the Ideal and the Experiential

The first move in the dialectical arc under examination is the withdrawal by the blind subject into the ideal realm. The word "ideal" and its various forms appear in the present chapter in three main senses: firstly, as that which relates to thoughts or mental phenomena which are non-material in character; secondly, in the related sense of linguistic phenomena such as words and literary expressions; and thirdly, in the sense of utopian conceptions of human society. The narrator of "Tlön, Uqbar, Orbis Tertius" (hereafter "Tlön" [68–81]) is an alter ego of Borges. He opens the narrative by stating that he came to discover the "fiction[al]" "country" (69) of Uqbar with the help of "a mirror and an encyclopedia" (68).[9] The combination of the two images is not a coincidence: they are deployed to serve the common purpose of reflection. The "mirror" and "*The Anglo-American Cyclopaedia* (1917)" are meant to reflect the self and the world, respectively. Hence they act as twin symbols in the narrative, with a common role to play. We have seen that the mirror has been used as a symbol in a number of Borges's short stories examined above, notably in "The Mirror of Ink" in a sustained manner. Laraway explains the reason for the author's appropriation of "the well-worn trope that art is a kind of mirror" ("The Blind Spot in the Mirror" 311):

---

8 On the importance of the face for self-recognition in Borges's writings, see Laraway, "Dissemblances" (52–4) and Laraway, "The Blind Spot in the Mirror" (309–14).

9 In the version of "Tlön" that I read, Borges's translator uses three spellings of the word "encyclopedia," viz. "encyclopedia," "encyclopaedia," and "encyclopœdia."

It is not the capacity of art to reflect the world that makes the mirror such a powerful symbol; it is rather the mirror's unique ability to reveal to the viewer a perspective of him or herself that would otherwise be unavailable.

("The Blind Spot in the Mirror" 311)

(I will take up the question of fictional epistemology/ontology later in this chapter [43–5].) For Borges, then, the mirror acts as the reflective surface par excellence that enables "one [to] see one's own face as others see it" ("The Blind Spot in the Mirror" 312). It serves as a motif pointing to self-recognition from "a strictly visual standpoint" ("The Blind Spot in the Mirror" 311). So, we can say that the joint appearance of the mirror and the encyclopaedia[10] symbolises the epistemological role of art.

Although the two devices are designed to help in the acquisition of specific kinds of knowledge, they fail to perform the functions they are meant to in a reliable manner. In the case of the encyclopaedia, the presence of an article in one of its copies about a country that does not exist on earth generates a doubt in the minds of the narrator and his friend, Bioy Casares. This doubt pertains not only to this particular encyclopedia, but it also calls into question the efficacy of the encyclopaedia as a class of books, and ultimately of language itself, to represent the world. The narrator's passing remark about the misleading nature of the title of *The Anglo-American Cyclopaedia*, which is actually a "literal ... laggardly reprint of the 1902 *Encyclopœdia Britannica*" (68), hints at the misleading character of its contents. Borges's distrust of the mirror as a device which would reflect his face and reveal the self is evident in his literary practice. In an interview conducted by Seamus Heaney and Richard Kearney "in Dublin on 16th June, 1982, Bloomsday" (71) on the occasion of James Joyce's centenary celebration, Borges says,

I am ... obsessed by a dream in which I see myself in a looking glass with several masks or faces each superimposed on the other; I peel them off successively and address the face before me in the glass; but it doesn't answer, it cannot hear me or doesn't listen, impossible to know.

(77)

Thus, as the narrator of "Tlön" says, the mirror can only "shadow us" (68). Moreover, the mirror is "inaccessible" ("The Blind Spot in the Mirror" 312) to Borges as "a key to ... identity" "in his blindness." The author's deployment of the mirror and the encyclopaedia as mediums that reinforce uncertainties about the self and the power of language to represent the world suggests his anxiety about blindness and its consequences. It also demonstrates his desire to withdraw from the world.

---

10 Which, like Borges's narrative, is a work of literary art.

The narrator further declares that the copy of *The Anglo-American Cyclopaedia* which he and his friend Bioy Casares had found in the rented house in Ramos Mejia contained no mention of Uqbar. The same was the case with the copy consulted by Carlos Mastronardi in a Buenos Aires bookshop. An exhaustive hunt for any sign of the country "through atlases, catalogs, the yearly indices published by geographical societies, the memoirs of travelers and historians" (70) proved to be fruitless as they yielded nothing. This bewildering absence is suggestive of the imaginary character of the land of Uqbar. This view is further strengthened by the vagueness of the article on it present in the "copy of the encyclopedia" discovered by Bioy Casares. The suspicion is confirmed when the narrator recalls in Part II of the narrative "a brief description of a false country" (71) in the encyclopedia. To be sure, reference books such as encyclopaedias are subject to revision. This requirement alludes to the provisional character of knowledge. But the cumulative effect of not finding any mention of the country of Uqbar in the pages of a wide range of books deepens the mystery, and casts a doubt on the efficacy of the encyclopaedia and other reference material to represent the world. This inability to locate the country in the maps of the world, and in the pages of various books about the world parallels and implies the blind person's inability to access *"the visible universe"* (italics as in the source, 69), and the optical image of the self in the mirror.

This state of affairs encourages the blind person to dwell in the 'thought-world' rather than in the physical, spatial world as the latter is inaccessible to him, and he is not able to sense objects and other details that are located far from his body. The result is that he loses a sense of control over his own life in the interactive human world, which is shaped by sighted people. Thus, that person is motivated to withdraw from the experiential world into the mental – ideal – realm. Such a move allows him, in the words of Hull, to retain "some kind of inner control" (*On Sight* 46), at least in the sphere of the mind or "the introspective consciousness," which gives him "a sense of being in an ordered environment." The diarist explains further that the blind person's desire to withdraw from the sighted world is a psychological reaction to their inability to absorb the pressure of living in an environment which fails to accommodate such persons' needs. We may comprehend this motivation in the following quotation from Hull: "I did not feel as if I wanted to withdraw from the world of sighted people and lose myself in the less demanding and more comfortable world of blind people who would understand me" (*On Sight* 104). But later, discussing the "poignant sense of loss" (*On Sight* 135) that assails him regularly, he writes, "It is rather as if an intention has taken the place of a feeling. The intention is to withdraw." The situation he describes here concerns his difficulties in playing with his children due to a severe lack of knowledge about certain games. This sense of lack is brought about by his difficulty in adjusting to the demands of blindness, the self-same problem that Borges repeatedly returns to in his literary vocation. Continuing the analysis of "Tlön," the reference in Part I of the narrative to Uqbar's literature of the ideal, and the introduction to the world of Tlön indicate the narrator's (and, by implication, Borges's) withdrawal into the archives of knowledge. The article in the encyclopedia mentioned above says "that its [Uqbar's] epics and legends never referred to reality but rather to the two imaginary realms of Mle'khnas and Tlön" (70).

Significantly, Part II of "Tlön" begins with yet another reference to the capacity of the mirror to reflect, which is quickly followed by the discovery of another encyclopedia by the narrator. Although its effectiveness in revealing the self to one who gazes into it is uncertain, the mirror still holds out a limited possibility of such recognition. This tenuous hope explains the narrator's "attachment to" ("The Blind Spot in the Mirror" 311–12) "reflective surface[s]" in the story. According to Laraway, Borges displays a sustained fascination for "the problem of scepticism regarding the self" which appears as a theme in many of his works. In his view, Borges regarded mirrors with an abiding fear due to "the suspicion that they might somehow conceal a clue to his identity" (Laraway, "The Blind Spot in the Mirror" 312). Apropos of this possibility, we should note the narrator's statement "that there is something monstrous about mirrors" (68). Thus, the short story contains the narratorial suggestion that "the illusory depths of the mirror" and the eleventh volume of "*A First Encyclopaedia of Tlön*" might actually constitute "key[s]" ("The Blind Spot in the Mirror" 312) of different kinds: the former by providing "a clue to [the personal] identity" of the railway engineer, Herbert Ash, and the latter by throwing light on "the universe" (72). The narrator's emphatic words concerning the encyclopaedia reinforce this hope: "I now held in my hands a vast and systematic fragment of the entire history of an unknown planet" (71).

In the literary history of the Occident, we find the tradition of the encyclopaedic novel, where miscellaneous data across disciplines is brought in. Some examples include a number of late mediaeval texts, *The Life of Gargantua and of Pantagruel* (1532–64) by François Rabelais during the Renaissance, the novel *Bouvard et Pécuchet* (1881) by Gustave Flaubert, and the works of James Joyce in modern times. These writers endorse a certain holistic approach to life. So they combine realms of experience which are wildly diverse (eschatology and scatology, the religious and the sexual, violence and the holy) in their works. Borges's 'fictions' belong to this novelistic tradition. Therefore, his semi-biographical engagement with the senses has immense epistemological implications involving perception, memory, and imagination. Given the erudite framework of his oeuvre, this engagement also links up with the perennial Western motif hyphenating 'blindness and insight.'

Due to the reference made in Part I of "Tlön" to "a brief description of a false country" (71) present in *The Anglo-American Cyclopaedia*, a doubt was raised earlier in the chapter about the effectiveness of the encyclopaedia to represent the world. We learn from the narrator's summary of Tlön's "conception of the universe" (72), as dealt with in the eleventh volume of *A First Encyclopaedia of Tlön*, that the realm is one composed of ideas. Thus, although the narrative mentions the southern and northern hemispheres of Tlön, there are no references to its countries, oceans, and other physical features. Instead, we have what amounts to a description of the combined intellectual achievements of many generations of thinkers. Thus, it can be seen that the encyclopaedia provides, to echo Borges's words in the foreword to *The Garden of Forking Paths* (1941), a diagram of the human mind, thereby drawing the reader's attention away from the external world and focussing it on idealist matters.

The narrator is clearly thrilled to discover the encyclopaedia dealing with Tlön, but does not want to reveal his "emotions" and, by extension, the story of his personal existence. His reference to "the irrecoverable colors of the sky" (71) is curious. Considering that he is an alter ego of Borges, it could be an allusion to his growing blindness, which prevents him from perceiving those colours. Therefore, he offers the following reason for his unwillingness to go into personal matters: "... this is the story not of my emotions but of Uqbar and Tlön and Orbis Tertius." It is thus important to note how, on finding the encyclopedia in the bar of "the hotel at Adrogué" (70), he quickly becomes absorbed in its pages, subsequently drawing other scholars into a debate on the existence of "later and earlier volumes" of the encyclopaedia (72).

Tlön is known "today" (72) to be "a cosmos" whose "innermost laws ... have been formulated, however provisionally so." On reading further, we learn that it is a realm of Berkelean ideas. The narrator's observation about Hume's assessment of "Berkeley's arguments" as thoroughly unconvincing is significant. That criticism is, he says, "entirely true with respect to the earth, entirely false with respect to Tlön." The statement carries his conviction that idealist theories cannot explain fully the earth and earthly life, but they can elucidate Tlön totally due to its origins in human intelligence. This conviction, however, proves to be mistaken. It is belied, to a great extent, by developments between 1940 and 1947 which are narrated in the "Postscript" to the short story. Hume's criticism of Berkeley's philosophy is of a general nature.[11] Richard H. Popkin points out that till the year 1964, when Hume's three letters to his "close friend Michael Ramsay" (774) were discovered and published in Poland, it was not known for certain if Hume had actually read Berkeley. This point assumes significance because the former is considered "as Berkeley's successor" (Popkin 773). In Hume's "earliest letter" to Ramsay, dated August 26–31, 1737 (Popkin 774), Hume recommends that the latter read Berkeley among other philosophers so that it will be possible for him to

> enter into them [his intellectual 'Performances'] more easily... . These Books will make you easily comprehend the metaphysical Parts of my Reasoning and as to the rest, they have so litlle Dependence on all former systems of Philosophy, that your natural Good Sense will afford you Light enough to judge of their Force & Solidity.
>
> (Qtd. in Popkin 775)

---

11 I am grateful to Ubelaker Andrade for clarifying the question of Hume's criticism of Berkeley's ideas.

Here, Hume's words hint at the difference of "the metaphysical Parts of [his] Reasoning" from "all former systems of Philosophy," including Berkeley's system. This point is confirmed by Popkin when he states that, although Hume was aware of Berkeley's philosophy, there is

> little trace of Berkeley in Hume's writings... . Berkeley is mentioned only three times in Hume's total published works. No doctrine of Berkeley's is used by Hume to establish any of his own views, and where Hume and Berkeley come closest to discussing the same subject or holding the same view, Hume neither uses Berkeley's terms nor refers to him.
>
> (778)

However, Popkin quotes a statement in his article from a letter written by one Lord Monboddo to one James Harris, dated June 18, 1769, which refers to Hume's opinion of Bishop Berkeley's ideas: "he [Lord Monboddo] says he read Berkeley after having heard 'David Hume say that his [Berkeley's] arguments are absolutely unanswerable'" (775–76). We may conclude from this observation that, although on the surface of it the words seem to suggest the "Force and Solidity" of Berkeley's philosophical arguments, Hume did not think highly of them.

The narrative implications of Hume's opinion are as follows. Everything basic to life in Tlön depends fundamentally upon two premises: first, the language of the "nations of that planet" (72) is the source of "religion, literature, metaphysics;" and second, "their language" and "those things derived from [it] presuppose idealism." Three closely related conclusions about Tlön – which structure my reading of the narrative – may be drawn from the above metaphysical premises. First, all "objects" in "the world" are, in A. C. Grayling's words "mind-dependent" ideas ("Berkeley's Argument" 178), that is to say, they are "'made of mind-stuff'" ("Berkeley's Argument" 175). Second, language can be used in parallel ways to conceive objects and compose literary works due to the ideal nature of both types of entities. And third, idealism leads to totalising narratives that drain all meaning from the existence of individual subjects, and from the plurality of "systems of thought"(74) despite their "countless numbers" in the "paradoxical" intellectual climate of the realm. Thus, as we learn in the closing paragraph of the "Postscript" to the short story, the "[temporally and spatially] scattered dynasty of recluses" (81) who fashioned this idealistic planet has influenced reality (read our world), and the narrator predicts that the latter will "be Tlön." Therefore, these inventors of that realm, which intrudes into our world as the narrative progresses, play the role that Berkeley assigns to the "causally efficacious" (Grayling, "Berkeley's Argument" 176), "single infinite mind — in short, God" (Grayling, "Berkeley's Argument" 166). This view is strengthened by references in the narrative to the "one and eternal" (76–7) "subject of knowledge," "the idea of the single subject," and "a single author who is timeless and anonymous." Thus, Bishop Berkeley's metaphysical theory of existence, offered as an elucidation of our world, is realised in Tlön.

Turning first to the second conclusion above concerning the creative power of language, "the world" (73) according to the inhabitants of Tlön may be said to exist in time, not in space. It is, the narrator reports, "not an amalgam of *objects* in space; it is a heterogeneous series of independent *acts*" *(italics as in the source)* occurring in "successive" order. The "real object[s]" that exist in Tlön are thus equivalent to the "'poetic object[s]'" created by poets there because both classes of objects are conceived by employing the diverse resources of language in an intricate manner. The absence of "nouns in the Ursprache[n]" of both the southern and northern hemispheres of the planet indicates the absence of spatial objects. Even when "nouns are formed by stringing together adjectives" in the latter hemisphere, says the narrator, "no one believes in the reality expressed by these nouns ... ." This state of affairs eloquently testifies to the mental character of what exists in Tlön. The following narratorial statement illustrates this point: "... the people of that planet conceive the universe as a series of mental processes that occur not in space but rather successively, in time." This conception of the universe is purely intellectual because a series of thoughts occurring in time constitutes it.

Concerning the nature of this idealistic realm, let us turn next to the narrator's speculation about "who, singular or plural, invented Tlön" (72). There the "'brave new world'" is identified with the volumes of *A First Encyclopaedia of Tlön*, whose number was unknown in 1940 (78). The references to "a secret society" of philosophers and artists of diverse pursuits, and a vast plan involving writing (72) are significant in this regard. The fact that the world of Tlön has been invented, and that it exists only in the form of writing in an encyclopaedia – a written text – is evidence enough for its ideal character. The narrator's conjecture is proved to be correct in "March of 1941" (79) when "a handwritten letter from Gunnar Erfjord was discovered in a book by Hinton that had belonged to Herbert Ashe." The reader learns that "the mystery of Tlön was fully elucidated by the letter." The reference, made in the "POSTSCRIPT" (as the one above) to "a systematic encyclopedia of the illusory planet," provides conclusive evidence about the character of Tlön. This encyclopaedia is produced by the members of a secret society (78),[12] and the work would ultimately include forty volumes (79–80).

Earlier, I referred to the Tlönian conception of "the universe as a series of mental processes" (73), in short, ideas. What can be said about the objects existing in that universe? This point is critical for two related reasons – one metaphysical, the other political. Since the inhabitants of Tlön are idealists, they regard all objects as not having a "corporeal basis" (Grayling, "Berkeley's

---

12 Erfjord's letter reveals that Berkeley was a member of this secret society.

Argument" 167) with "spatial extension" (73), but as "mental state[s]" (74) or mind-dependent ideas. This position may be described as constituting immaterialism, which philosophical stance may be described in Berkeley's words as follows:

> Some truths there are so near and obvious to the mind that a man need only open his eyes to see them. Such I take this important one to be, viz., that ... all those bodies which compose the mighty frame of the world ... have not any subsistence without a mind, that their being is to be perceived or known; that consequently so long as they are not actually perceived by me, or do not exist in my mind or that of any other created spirit, they must either have no existence at all, or else subsist in the mind of some Eternal Spirit ...
>
> (Sec. 6)

This passage clarifies (1) that nothing can exist independently of a perceiving mind; and (2) consequently that all the bodies which make up the world have their existence only in being perceived by a worldly creature, or by "the mind of some Eternal Spirit." (We may note in passing that Berkeley uses the metaphor of sight – to open one's eyes and see – to talk about knowledge.) Thus, the perceiving mind or self gains supreme importance in this philosophy. This non-materialistic conception of objects is best described by the statement in "Tlön" that "all nouns ... have only metaphoric value" (75). It is for this reason that "space is not conceived as having duration in time" (73–4). Notably "the sophism of the nine copper coins" (75), which propounds the doctrine of materialism, is either not understood at all or philosophically rejected as a fallacious argument. Individual, independent (in the sense of being a series of unconnected) ideas are all that exist, as suggested above in the paragraph on language. As these entities cannot be explained, judged, named, or classified, being "irreducible" (74), they can only be, per Berkeley, perceived by the mind. This is because "there are no necessary connections between ideas" (Grayling, "Berkeley's Argument" 177), and they have "'no power or agency'" to affect or illuminate one another when they are linked together by the subject.

However, the above argument for immaterialism does not deny the sensory aspects of perceived objects. According to idealism, various sensible qualities are "observed" to coalesce together to form objects (Grayling, "Berkeley's Argument" 168), which are perceived by the mind and exist as ideas therein (Grayling, "Berkeley's Argument" 169). With this understanding, let us now turn our attention to the objects referred to in the narrative. The nine copper coins; the "*hrönir*" (77) or "secondary objects" that are duplicated by minds, such as pencils, "a rusty wheel," "a gold mask, an archaic sword, two or three clay amphorae, and the verdigris'd and mutilated torso of a king"; and "the *ur*—the thing produced by suggestion, the object brought forth by hope" (78) are striking for their physicality. These secondary objects result from the Tlönians' expectations. Thus, they symbol-ise the inevitable influence of idealism on reality. The main example of "ur" offered by the narrator is "[t]he magnificent gold mask" mentioned above. To this, we may add the "compass" (79) that appears in Laprida, "a very small yet extremely heavy" (80) "gleaming metal cone" discovered at an inn "in the Cuchilla Negra," and several others in various countries all over the real world. The appearance of "the ur" in the real world symbolises the encroaching influence of "the fantastic world of Tlön" on it.

The significance of the Tlönian problem, as sketched by the narrator, lies in the insidious influence of idealism on the inhabitants of the real world. Since psychology occupies the position of the single most important disci-pline in Tlön's "classical culture" (73), it is safe to infer the paramount importance given to the mind and its works in that culture. This bias results first in a diminished, or even absent, engagement with the experience of indi-vidual subjects, and secondly in the rise of totalising narratives. When the objects produced in that realm make their appearance in our world, they impact people adversely. This influence is indicated by the example of the heavy metal cone, which, as the narrator hints, may be responsible for the insanity and death of the "young man" who possessed it. It inspires "fear and revulsion" (80) in the narrator himself. The terror of *hrönir* becomes evident from the statement that they have been used "not only to interrogate but even to modify the past" (77). The reader learns towards the end of the nar-rative not only that history has been obliterated, but also that several disci-plines of human knowledge are being reformed. The narrator makes it clear that all this results from the spell cast on humanity by Tlön. Given Borges's growing blindness, the detail about the awaited reformation of "biology" (81) may be a veiled reference to eugenics and the purification of the human species by a combination of measures such as involuntary or forced sterilisa-tion and killing off "undesirable" members of society, including disabled persons. These revelations act as further proof of the malefic power that objects and ideas emerging from Tlön possess. The discovery "in 1944 [of] the forty volumes of *The First Encyclopaedia of Tlön*" (79), and their dissem-ination throughout the world herald the collapse of reality and the falling of "the world ... under the sway of Tlön" (81) due to the promise of order it offers. Thus, "the horrifying or banal truth" (68) referred to at the beginning of the narrative in connection with "a first-person novel" with an unreliable narrator is that people are enamoured of simplistic systems of knowledge, that is, various species of idealism, such as "dialectical materialism, anti-Sem-itism, Nazism" (81). Such people hope that these comprehensive systems of knowledge will yield solutions to human problems, and restore order in a chaotic world. Thus, in "Tlön," Borges probes the ethical problems posed by idealistic theories as he traces their trajectory, and exposes the consequences arising from their application in the world.

Clearly, then, "Tlön" is a narrative whose form and content correspond well in an exploration of an ideal realm and its implications. "The Library of

Babel" (112–18)[13] may also be so described on account of its artistic fusion of form and content in an examination of a different kind of ideal realm – one created on the basis of "twenty-five orthographic symbols" (113), that is to say, scriptorial language. The unnamed narrator of the story, a blind librarian who may be considered to be an alter ego of Borges, is portrayed as living in "the Library" (112). This library is "the universe," an eternal realm constituted by an "infinite number of hexagonal galleries." All the inhabitants of this labyrinthine universe are librarians, as evident from the narrator's description of man as "the imperfect librarian" (113). These words bring out the supremely relevant point of the narrative, notwithstanding the narrator's claim that his account is "pointless" (117). Throughout the narrative, there appear references to a number of metaphysical arguments offered by idealists and philosophers of various other hues about the library, its structure, the books, and the writing, suggesting the unabating restlessness of the realm's librarians.

The "epistle" (118) – for that is how the narrator refers to his composition – discusses the problem of meaning in the labyrinthine writing found in "its enigmatic books" (113) housed in the Library. In the first articulation of the problem, the reader is presented with the mysterious case of the writing on "the front cover of each book" which neither indicates nor prefigures "what the pages inside will say." This problem is part of a larger riddle, namely "the formless and chaotic nature of virtually all books." The solution to the riddle is provided by the "fundamental law of the Library" (114), viz. "all books, however different from one another they might be," are constituted by combining "the twenty-two letters of the alphabet" and three punctuation marks. It is worth noting that these characters are the basic building blocks necessary for expression in every language employed in the Library. Towards the end of the short story, the narrator offers his own solution to the problem: that any and all "combination[s] of characters" (117) conceived in the Library carry some significance "in one or more of its secret tongues" without fail, which may be deciphered by means of "cryptographic or allegorical 'reading[s]'."

"The Library of Babel," conceived by the narrator as a personal letter, hints at a mode of self-examination which most librarians in the universe do not practise. I approach this point via Borges's concern with literature and its interpretation. Arthur C. Danto explicates the philosophical significance of literature through the concept of "universality of literary reference" (64). Building upon Hegel's idea that "the work exists for the spectator and not on its own account" so that its "apprehension" by "the individual apprehending it … completes the work and gives it final substance" (63), Danto postulates,

> [A literary] work is about the "I" that reads the text, identifying himself not with the implied reader for whom the implied narrator writes but with the actual subject of the text in such a way that each work becomes

13 Borges developed this narrative out of an essay titled "The Total Library" (Piper 57).

a metaphor for each reader: perhaps the same metaphor for each.... . It is literature when, for each reader I, I is the subject of the story ... literature [is] a kind of mirror, not simply in the sense of rendering an external reality, [nor] in passively returning an image [but] in transforming the self-consciousness of the reader who in virtue of identifying with the image recognizes what he is.

(64)

As discussed earlier in this chapter (33–5), Borges views the literary work as a kind of mirror, while recognising that its power to reveal the nature of the self is seriously limited. His oeuvre makes his position on the self clear, namely that "the search for unity leads ineluctably to a certain scepticism" (Laraway, "The Blind Spot in the Mirror" 317; cf. *Selected Non-Fictions* 3–9; *Collected Fictions* 508–15). Borges declares in an early essay, "After Images" (1923), that authors must write the kind of literature which reflects "an individual [persisting] in his illusory country ... being only a simulacrum" (*Selected Non-Fictions* 11). This fictitious individual appearing in the fictional text may be interpreted as both its author and reader (Laraway, "The Blind Spot in the Mirror" 322). As Ubelaker Andrade explains,

In "After Images" Borges writes of a kind of fiction which would be like a mirror into which the reader would enter, becoming transformed into a being whose world would be destroyed by darkness and lack sounds. In short, one of its purposes is to multiply the self, or to open up new ways of being, possibilities that are conditioned by textuality and literary imagination, but which might have larger consequences in the extra literary world.

(cf. *Selected Non-Fictions* 11)

The mirror in Borges, then, does not reflect the self so much as transform it. While Ubelaker Andrade questions the claim that Borges saw literature as a mirror which reflects the self, I argue that the Argentine author does in fact deploy the mirror as a motif in many short stories (which are analysed in this book) due to the possibility that it holds out for anagnorisis (Laraway, "The Blind Spot in the Mirror" 312). The classic text, "Borges and I" (1960), is a concise narrative which doubles the self of Borges into a private, unnamed person and "the other man" (*Collected Fictions* 324) whom the world recognises as the author "Borges." The speaker states, "I shall endure in Borges, not in myself (if, indeed, I am anybody at all), but I recognize myself less in his books than in many others', or in the tedious strumming of a guitar." Characteristically for Borges, the parenthetical remark in this statement casts doubt on the very concept of the self. But then the narrator asserts that he as a reader recognises himself in books and music, thus espousing the belief that art is a kind of mirror. Instead of "passively returning an image" (Danto 64), the work of literary art transforms the reader by enabling them to recognize "an aspect" of the self "at the moment that individual reads [the text.]" Thus, each act of reading involves interpretation.

Apropos of this conclusion, we may cite Laraway, who combines ideas drawn from Borges's essay "Kafka and His Precursors" (1951) and the concept of "artistic identification" from Danto to develop his argument. Borges's essay advances the idea that "from particular vantage points it may be possible to discern the unity of otherwise disparate texts" (Laraway, "The Blind Spot in the Mirror" 317), meaning that "literary works are in a deep sense constituted by the interpretations that are given to them" (Laraway, "The Blind Spot in the Mirror" 318). Danto believes that the philosophy of art "must come to recognize that artistic identification, in its interpretive character, is inseparably connected with the objects it analyzes." In other words, interpretations not only constitute literary works, but also enable the person engaging with them to acquire self-consciousness. While Borges is emphatic that the self is not a unitary whole, interpretation does enable "self-revelation" (Laraway, "The Blind Spot in the Mirror" 321). Thus, it is his readers who establish "the identity of 'Borges'" (Laraway, "The Blind Spot in the Mirror" 322) by completing his literary creations.

Danto formulates his theory, represented in capsule form in the long quotation above (64), as a corrective to the conception of literature 1) as that which by means of "fictive terms" refers vertically to "subsistent entities" in possible worlds (56–7), and 2) as text, which is defined as "a network of reciprocal effects" with merely internal, horizontal references (60–1). The latter concept is strikingly similar to that of the enigmatic writing found in the library's books. Thus, the overwhelming importance given by "the [imperfect] men of the Library" (112) to language and the books hides a grave lack in their culture, i.e., the near-complete absence of reflection on self-conduct. In fact, the narrator's presentation of the philosophical deduction made by the "librarian of genius" (114) concerning the books in the Library suggests the insufficiency of that conclusion. This is because it foregrounds only language and the extravagant character of the Library's contents without making any reference to the writers and readers of the books. The narrator's own understanding about meaning consists in the realisation that all speech and writing amount to "tautologies" (117)[14]: they are pointless because meaning is present not on the page but within ourselves.

On comparing "Tlön" and "The Library of Babel," we find that the two narratives share some striking similarities. The encyclopaedias in the former and the library, which contains all possible books and which is the universe in the latter, mirror each other. As we have seen, the ideal realms which they

---

14 This is so because any and all expressions in language already exist in the "divine library" (117). Due to this state of affairs, a person cannot say or write anything new.

reveal negate life,[15] which is based on corporeality, and is therefore formed by individual experience. By showing how people are spellbound by idealism, and by their misguided belief in the existence of meaning in books, respectively, the narrators suggest the extent to which this loss of the power of thinking for oneself and forgetfulness lead to enormous human suffering. This conclusion is supported by the loss of life, the past (77), and disintegration of this world reported in "Tlön" (81); and the occurrence in "The Library of Babel" of deadly quarrels, killings, fanaticism, "brigandage" (118), "suicides," and even the suspicion of impending human extinction. The narrator in the former narrative recognises the necessity of talking about the fragility of human life and mortality. Thus, at its close, we find him translating "Sir Thomas Browne's *Urne Buriall*" (81). However, he does not "intend to publish" his translation because people who have been habituated to Tlön will not read such a work. The blind librarian in the latter narrative also dismisses his narrative as pointless because the inhabitants of the realm will not listen to what he has to say about life and its contingencies, such as blindness[16] and old age. Like the people who look for "The Vindications" (115), and like other "fanatics" (116), he too has "squandered and spent [his] years" (117) searching for "perhaps the catalogue of catalogues" (112). However, it is evident from the narrative that he has come to realise the fruitlessness of such ventures. This recognition may be seen in his deep sadness, which is caused by the loss of life, the human cost involved in people's incessant search for supernatural books with the belief that they may help them solve personal and world problems. Thus, he suggests throughout the story that it is crucial to turn inwards, look for meaning there, examine one's experience, and become a writer instead of remaining a reader. This transformation may enable the person to gain self-understanding. In arriving at their respective insights, the narrators of the two short stories bring out the importance of memory in preserving an ethical perspective on life. The role of memory is unquestionably significant in other short stories by Borges, including "The Maker."

While in "Tlön" and "The Library of Babel" the narrators come to understand the importance of engaging with experiential reality, the narratives themselves do not, as we have seen in the foregoing pages, deal with it. In the narratives examined in the following section, a shift may be perceived with regard to this point; and "The Maker" represents a sea change in Borges's

---

15 In a conversation that Ubelaker Andrade and I had on July 10, 2014 via Skype, I realised that both of us had independently arrived at the reading of "Tlön" and "The Library of Babel" which exposes "the danger of withdrawing into such places," viz. the idealist realms which are the subject of the two narratives.

16 He declares in the second paragraph that he is "preparing to die" (112) because he is blind: "… my eyes can hardly make out what I myself have written… ." He gives in to this despair because he assumes that he cannot perform his duties anymore. It is worth noting in this regard that Borges was the director of the National Library of Argentina during the years of his blindness.

aesthetic approach to blindness. In that short narrative, the narrator tells the story of the Greek epic poet Homer becoming blind and realising through this experience his powers as a poet.

2.3 The Aesthetic Turn to the Experience of Blindness

The short story "The Secret Miracle" (156–62), first published in 1943, reflects on the responses of the writer and playwright Jaromir Hladik to the twin mysteries of time and the act of dying by dwelling on his efforts to complete his "unfinished tragedy *The Enemies*" (157). On March 19, 1939, the Gestapo arrests Hladik in Prague, and condemns him to die by gunfire on the 29th of the same month. During his imprisonment, he descends into the night of despair and, in the words of the narrator, dies "hundreds of deaths" (158) before remembering his unfinished play. Miraculously, God intercedes on behalf of Hladik, postpones his death, and *halts time* (161). Now the writer can complete his play in his mind. Thus, the narrative dramatises the difference between "real duration" and "spatialized time"[17] – a distinction made by Bergson in his book entitled *Introduction to Metaphysics* (1903). Bergson defines the former thus: "It is our own person in its flowing through time" (*Introduction to Metaphysics* 9). Duration is characterised by mental activity. Creativity is shown to be the power that sustains Hladik in the face of the destructive forces of time and death.

Borges says that blindness forced him to compose poems in "regular verse" (Laraway, "The Blind Spot in the Mirror" 307–08) forms because they could be worked on in the memory, without his having to look at a written page. In light of this biographical information, the reference to Hladik's working on his verse drama "without a manuscript" (160) may be considered as an allusion to blindness. Its aptness to the playwright's situation is remarkable. He is a prisoner who does not have access to his manuscript, which forces him to work in a sort of enforced blindness. Repeated use in the text of words such as "night" and "dark" are significant because they metaphorically allude to the loss of sight (Kristal ix). These words bring out Hladik's despair. Before he can complete his literary work, he is to be executed. The librarian of the Clementine Library in Hladik's dream is a character who has become blind looking for God. This points to the futility of trying to seek God visually. Although Hladik succeeds in reaching God by touching a letter on "a map of India" (160), his connection with the divine being is established through sound. First he speaks with God, and later God responds to him in like manner in a dream: "A voice that was everywhere spoke to him." Although blindness is used here as a metaphor, the short story deals with the

---

17 Merleau-Ponty refers to the distinction between "the flow of duration" (80) "in the Bergsonian sense" (47) and the impersonal, "objective time" (80). Although Merleau-Ponty builds a different philosophical system from that of Bergson's metaphysics, the former does draw upon the thought of the latter, for example, in discussing the subject's experience of time.

artist's creative work, which takes place in the mind in the spoken medium and the hexameter, without his having to rely on visual aids. Further, with an obvious reference to paralysis of the body, the narrator also uses the word "paralyzed" in order to describe the immobility of both Hladik and his executioners when God, answering the playwright's prayer for a year to complete his tragedy, halts time and freezes the physical world in order to postpone the execution (161).

Borges's friend, Estela Canto, links the short stories "The Aleph,"[18] "The Zahir," and "The Writing of the God"[19] to one another, and clarifies that they were composed in "the summer of 1945" (Núñez-Faraco 613). The three narratives explore a theme which increasingly troubled their author, viz. the tension between sight and its absence. The three symbols at the centre of narrative focus in the short stories embody this concern. In "The Zahir" (242–49), an occurrence appearing in a tableau of visible objects (each of which was the Zahir in its time) aptly symbolises this tension. The incident involves "a blind man in the Surakarta mosque" (242) who was the Zahir in Java. This man was "stoned by the faithful." The narrator of the story is named Borges, and he may be considered to be an alter ego of the author. He structures his narrative as a memoir of the Zahir. In Buenos Aires, the Zahir is "a common twenty-centavo coin." The narrative records his growing fascination with the coin. The Zahir gradually takes him from being obsessed with the visual appearances of the world to being solely occupied in thinking about that coin. His repeated descriptions of Teodelina Villar's images, especially her facial features (243); the rich trove of vivid images throughout the text of coins, a treasure of "red rings and gleaming gold" (246), various objects and creatures which were the Zahir in their time and country (242); and, finally, his declaration "Anything that is not the Zahir comes to me as though through a filter, and from a distance" (248) all bear significance for Borges the narrator. He eventually perceives the appearances of the world as being filtered or mirrored by the Zahir. The images catalogued above act as narrative indicators of a transformation in Borges's (that is, the narrator's) selfhood over five months – from June 7 to November 13 (242). Compelled by the power of the Zahir, he initially withdraws inwards from the visible, physical world, and engages in intellectual and imaginative pursuits. Further, in the course of time, his mind becomes absorbed in "the memory" (248) of the Zahir – since he has got rid of the coin by paying for a brandy with it. We may consider the Zahir to be a symbol of blindness because, once a person looks upon it, it influences their life completely like their own body, and they can never again think of or access the world except through its medium. Hull's conception of blindness as "the necessary avenue of communication between my interior and the world" (*On Sight* 136) captures the nature of this experience very well. Concerning the influence of the Zahir upon himself, Borges the narrator makes a couple

18 Borges dedicates "The Aleph" to Canto.
19 These short stories appear in the collection entitled *The Aleph* (1949).

of statements that are suggestive of the effects of blindness: soon "I will not know whether it's morning or night" (248), he says, and continues with a statement about his final relationship with the cosmos: "I will no longer" be able to "perceive the universe," but only the Zahir. He interprets the object of his continuous contemplation from a spiritual angle, and hopes that through concentration on it, he, like the Sufis, will find God (249).

The short story "The Aleph" (274–86) enacts a comparable journey from obsession with the seductions of the visual to an appreciation of imaginative activity through the mediums of tactile and auditory experience (Ubelaker Andrade "Against Seeing").[20] This journey is represented by the narrator's viewing the entire universe in a point called an Aleph; it concludes with his final assertion that the visible Aleph is false, and that the true Aleph is to be found buried in a stone column at a mosque in Cairo. If one puts one's ear to the stone column, he can hear "'the bustling rumour'" (285) of the universe.

The short story "The Writing of the God" (250–54) may be read in the light of a narrative image offered by Hull. He writes that "during the early months and years" (*On Sight* 42) of his blindness, there was "a persistent image" which bothered him to the extent of panicking him badly. This image is a mineshaft leading deep into a hill. In the imagined episode, Hull is being carried remorselessly "deeper and deeper into the hillside" "in a little coal-truck." He has no way of getting out of the mountain, and feels "trapped in an intolerable hiding place." Tzinacan is the priest of the god Qaholom, and the narrator of "The Writing of the God." The deep, oppressive stone cell in which he is imprisoned, and the smothering sand which buries him in a dream take on the significance of the loss of visual perception and the isolating experience of blindness. In his old age, the priest can still perceive the jaguar which is imprisoned in the adjacent cell in the light that "enters the vault" (250) of the prison, but he cannot see well. Further, his remark that he can no longer move suggests paralysis. Thus, although he "devoted [long years] to learning the order and arrangement of the spots on the tiger's skin" (251–52) with the objective of deciphering Qaholom's "secret text" (251), he can no longer see his jailer "whom the years have gradually blurred" (250). This statement is a clear indication of the gradual loss of eyesight. Phrases such as the following function as allusions to blindness: "my darkness," "each blind day" (252), as well as the rhetorical question, "between my days and nights, what difference can there be?" and the words appearing towards the end of the narrative, "allow the day to enter my night" (253). Thus, the priest/narrator serves as the alter ego of Borges.

Borges explores the theme of understanding in mystical terms by contrasting the following pairs in the short story: dream and reality, blindness and sight, physical sight and spiritual vision, and metaphoric blindness and vision. It is worth noting that a "bright light" (252) awakens Tzinacan from the nightmare

---

20 Se Ubelaker Andrade, *Borges Beyond the Visible* (2019), for an attentive reading of this short story (13–24; 35–7; 59).

and that, on waking, he sees all those things which define his life as a prisoner: "the face and hands of the jailer, the pulley, the rope, the meat, and the water jugs" (253). I suggest that he catches sight of these things in "an epiphany of sorts" (Laraway, "The Blind Spot in the Mirror" 310). In the poem "A Blind Man" (*Selected Poems* 357),[21] the speaker's yearning to see the world and himself is embodied in a sudden glimpse of "a lock of hair, the colour of ashes or perhaps gold" (Laraway, "The Blind Spot in the Mirror" 310) in an instance of "unexpected, synaesthetic vision." In "The Writing of the God," Tzinacan's sight of the familiar things in his prison after he emerges from the series of dreams heralds a profound spiritual transformation in him. This enables him to have a vision of the universe. He narrates that on waking from the "indefatigable labyrinth of dreams" (253) in which "the countless sand" (252) suffocated him to the point of death, he blessed the prison, its discomforts, and his own "old and aching body" (253) – in short, his whole, severely restricted world. At this point, he has a life-changing, mystical experience and states that "there occurred union with the deity, union with the universe (I do not know whether there is a difference between those two words)." This ecstatic experience is symbolised by the vision – he does actually use the words "saw" and "sight" here – of the great, "infinite" wheel. While the dark world within the prison symbolises blindness and isolation in Tzinacan's waking life, the sand that crushes him in the series of dreams that occur one within the other stands for blindness in his dream life or mind, which deals with metaphors. Further, his search for the god's writing, sustained through long, frustrating "years" (251) by the light entering the prison for an "instant" (252) every dark day, suggests a kind of blindness in terms of the lack of understanding. This metaphor takes on significance from the link between sight and knowledge evident in Borges's writings. Such a connection is also articulated by Hull:

> In situations of uncertainty, when I become a little panicky through being asthmatic or losing my way, then I usually have a very strong, even claustrophobic sense of darkness.... . I also feel plunged into darkness when I am emotionally involved in ignorance.
>
> (*On Sight* 20)

Besides, when Tzinacan "loses sight of himself just as [the] epiphanic vision is unfolded before his eyes" (Laraway, "The Blind Spot in the Mirror" 322), metaphoric blindness – in the form of losing sight of the self – and spiritual vision are brought together as the rationale for the narrator's decision not to speak the secret words of the god.

In a discussion about the journey of the protagonist to the underworld, viz. katabasis and his freedom from that trap as a literary trope, Ubelaker Andrade states,

---

21 The poem first appeared in the collection entitled *The Unending Rose* (1975).

[I] think that the journey to the underworld is actually quite full of earthly delights for Borges. Instead of being dark, it's filled with light: things to see, things to be excited by, things to possess, things to obsess over. Freedom, on the other hand, is full of darkness. Freedom can be the absence of sight, of desire, the empty hand that does not seek out anything to grasp. I feel that, for Borges, the underworld is not found in a place of darkness but instead in an amply lit museum, a perfect aperture like the Aleph, a perfect memory like that of Funes. All these modes of seeing, of remembering, of possessing with the mind are traps, whereas freedom is often constituted by forgetfulness, oblivion, absence, and blindness, especially in the case of "The Maker" where the gift of blindness allows discursive patterns to suddenly come into view in the mental realm.

These words point decisively to Borges's aesthetic turn away from the dominance of visuality towards a world without sight. As the quotation makes it clear, a self-conscious inversion occurs in his treatment of the underworld motif. Whereas in Virgil and Dante that region is dark and therefore available to touch, Borges conceives of it as well-lit and full of sensory delights that are available to sight. When the latter understands the visual as a trap, and thinks that its absence leads to freedom, he seems to indicate that blindness may be fruitful for the person.

The figure of Homer, the ancient blind singer of Greek epic poems, symbolically links blindness and creativity in Borges's work. The short story "The Immortal" (183–95) explores this theme by examining two sides of the coin of language, namely artistic potential and irony regarding the self. The unnamed narrator reports the princess de Lucinge's description of the protagonist – Joseph Cartaphilus – as "an emaciated, grimy man with gray eyes and gray beard and singularly vague features" (183). The narrator begins telling the story of "the rare book dealer Joseph Cartaphilus," and closes it with a postscript defending the authenticity of the manuscript containing Cartaphilus's narrative. It is this narrative that forms the bulk of the short story. The above words describe Cartaphilus, in Laraway's terms, "as others see [him]" ("The Blind Spot in the Mirror" 312). The phrase "gray eyes" is, I suggest, a hint that the man is blind. He is, as we learn later, also Homer. While the first allusion to his blindness appears in the opening paragraph of the narrative, two more veiled indications of his lack of eyesight are to be found in the middle and at the end, respectively. Part III of the narrative presents a third-person reference to the dead eyes of the Troglodyte who is Homer. The statement "there are no longer any images from memory" (195) from the postscript may be regarded as a first-person allusion made by Cartaphilus to his blindness. After centuries of not being able to perceive images, they have receded and eventually faded from his memory. Hull's observation about images sheds light on a significant effect of blindness on his mind. He writes that, in his case, images started becoming less and less important as time went by. Around three years after being registered blind, he finds it "more and more difficult to realise that people look like anything, to put any meaning into the idea that they have an appearance" (*On Sight* 19). A larger narrative movement is mirrored in Part III of the short story. Many years after the Roman tribune names Homer Argos after Ulysses's dog which appears in the *Odyssey*, the latter identifies himself as the person who is called Argos – a name found in a poem sung long ago by himself. Here we have an act of aesthetic self-recognition.[22] Thus, the narrative records a movement from a third-person, visual recognition of Cartaphilus to his re-discovery of his identity not through vision but aesthetically as the "man of letters" (194) Homer, and not as the Roman tribune Marcus Flaminius Rufus. He does this towards the end of Part IV by pointing out a number of anomalies – relating to the use of language and other aesthetic ones – which are present throughout the narrative.

Metaphoric blindness mirrors physical blindness, and both link up with the question of identity in the short story. As the narrator of "The Immortal" (who is Homer and Cartaphilus) shows through his narrative, language, with its power to evoke images, can be used to portray "the experiences of two different men" (193) as those of one man. What this seeming truism means in the context of this short story is that the poet, apart from describing his own experiences, has also represented those of Flaminius Rufus as his own. This he has done with the help of his memory and imagination. Since he is an immortal who has lived for several centuries, and thus has undergone the experiences of many men in his lifetime and also in his imagination, paradoxically, he "is all men" (191). This consideration of his insight into the experiences of different kinds of people calls to mind the blind prophet Tiresias, who symbolises blindness and insight. It effaces the protagonist's identity as a single man not only in the world, but also in his self-conception. Moreover, his narrative strategy of self-effacement, in the words of the narrator of the postscript, involves the use of "words taken out of place and mutilated, words from other men" (195) from centuries past. This ironic mode of self-presentation means that his identity is hidden from sight, behind the language used by others over the years.

The theme of the body and mortality, which forms a major thread in this narrative about immortals, is explored through converging and diverging patterns in the lives of Flaminius Rufus and Homer/Cartaphilus. When the former, a man of war who has killed other men, drinks from the river "*whose waters give immortality*" (italics as in the source, 192) and sees "the brilliant City" of the immortals after passing through "the blind realm" (187) of dark and utterly disorienting subterranean labyrinths, he becomes immortal, befriends Homer, and joins the community of Troglodytes on the bank of the same river. The "dark maze" and "the bright City of the immortals" (188)

---

22 See Laraway, "The Blind Spot in the Mirror" (312) for a discussion of self-identification in logical terms.

symbolise the man's difficult journey inwards, which results in his living for centuries "in thought" or in a state of self-absorption "scarcely perceiv[ing] the physical world" (190). A millennium before the Roman tribune comes to the river and the city, Homer also drinks from the immortal stream and joins the Troglodytes in their contemplative lifestyle after counselling them to build the bewildering city. Then, "at the beginning or end of the tenth century" (192), both men, like the other Troglodytes, set out to seek for the river that takes away immortality. While Homer/Cartaphilus finds this "spring" outside a city "on the Eritrean coast" in the twentieth century, tastes "its clear water" (193), and regains mortality, the reader does not learn anything further about the Roman tribune's life and fate after the two companions part in the eleventh century. Not only is the death of Homer in 1929 mentioned in the opening paragraph of the narrative, but we even read about other deaths and corporeal experiences throughout the text. Significantly, it is only after Homer regains mortality that he comes to re-discover his identity as the poet.

The opening paragraph of "The Maker" (292–93) portrays a man who "had never lingered among the pleasures of memory" (292), but had flitted from one "momentary and vivid" impression to the next – intensely experiencing objects of beauty that are available to sight, touch, taste, and "the nearness of the sea or women" – without dwelling on those experiences. This man, whom the reader comes to recognise as Homer, was sensitive, well-travelled, and courageous. He equally welcomed "complex stories [and] reality," but never gave them serious thought. However, all this changed when he started becoming blind, though the alteration was not immediate. As "the splendid universe began drawing away from him" (meaning that he became aware of the gradual dimming of his sight), he initially underwent a considerable period of great suffering – Borges's descriptive phrase is "Days and nights." The author employs the apposite expression "despair of his flesh" to bring out the visceral nature of the protagonist's grief and anxiety before he regained his "calm" as he settled into his new mode of existence 'in blindness.' This crucial moment in his life is marked by the use of a trope signifying both auditory experience and an act of remembering: "... the way one might feel upon recognizing a melody or a voice." These words herald both Homer's acceptance of a new way of experiencing the world, and his descent "into his memory, which seemed to him endless" (293). When he gained access to his memory, he recalled, with a sense of déjà vu, first the feelings that he had felt while embarking upon new adventures as a youngster – "fear but also ... joy and hopefulness and curiosity" – and then his early adventures themselves.

In "Who is the Narrator?" (1997), Richard Walsh demonstrates that "extradiegetic heterodiegetic narrators (that is, 'impersonal' and 'authorial' narrators,) who cannot be represented without thereby being rendered homodiegetic or intradiegetic, are in no way distinguishable from authors" (510–11). Following this narratological argument, I contend that the impersonal narrator in "The Maker" is indistinguishable from its author, Borges. This is so because, as Walsh asserts, "The narrator is always either a character who narrates or the author. There is no intermediate position. The author of a fiction can adopt one of two strategies: to narrate a representation or to represent a narration" (505). Since the narrative in question does not contain "a character who narrates," we may draw the conclusion that the author draws on autobiographical elements (Hagberg 135) to "narrate a representation," that is, to tell the imagined story of how a man in the ancient Mediterranean world discovers his poetic creativity through the experience of blindness. To put it in Walsh's words, "The one irreducible fact underlying the impulse to attribute [this narrative] to a narrator is that [this narrative is] fictional" (498). But a fictional work can hardly be said to suffer any diminution in its status of being imagined due to the presence in it of episodes from the author's personal history (Tomlinson). Therefore, in my critical interpretation, I refer to Borges as the narrator of "The Maker."

To return to our discussion of the short story, as a keenly sensitive man, Homer's experiences while being transformed by blindness necessitate sensuous expression throughout the narrative. Accordingly, a range of memorable language foregrounds Borges's aesthetic engagement with the passionate poet's history. The following words bring out the inexorable advance of blindness: "… the earth became uncertain under his feet" (292). Next, the author uses words which are a direct expression of Homer's feelings – important because they come from the character himself – on realising that he was losing his sight: "… *I will not be able to see the sky filled with mythological dread or this face that the years will transfigure*" (italics as in the source). Significantly, Hull also expresses similar regrets while talking about "a sense of cognitive dissonance" (*On Sight* 128; also see this book, ch. 3, p. 75; ch. 4, pp. 106, 110) about the self: "… I cannot witness the work of time upon my own face." This congruence between the experience of the fictional blind character and that of Hull bespeaks the clear impact of "autobiographical content" (Hagberg 135) on Borges's fictional practice. As Homer recollected his fight with the "boy who had insulted him" (293), what he wanted to recover "was the precise flavor of that moment," which then gave rise to the memory of his adventure with "the first woman the gods had given him." On recovering the intimate awareness of "the clumsy combat" and his search for the woman "through galleries that were like labyrinths of stone and down slopes that descended into darkness," he understood that blindness did not mean the end of his life, and that in the new life "love and adventure were also awaiting him." At this point of the narrative, an evocative expression metaphorically heralds Homer's new life[23] and indicates the mutability of the human body: "In this night of his mortal eyes into which he was descending." These words also signal a change in his attitude to blindness. He had

---

23 In doing so, it calls to mind his two youthful adventures which took place on two separate nights.

become aware of his memory. This discovery would enable him to recall the experiences that he had had in "the various world" (292), and the dramatic stories he had listened to. The maker's powers as a singer of great epics arise from this fundamental transformation in his selfhood. These memories would help him in the creative process of composing his epic poems. A remarkable phrase expresses the far-reaching influence on humankind of "the *Odysseys* and *Iliads*" (293) which was the maker's "fate to sing and to leave echoing in the cupped hands of human memory." The words "sing" and "echoing" signify auditory events, while the inspired metaphor "the cupped hands of human memory" refers to the Western literary tradition by means of a tactile metaphor. Forming an intimate part of a sightless person's experiential world, these sensory figures of speech appropriately describe the blind maker's work.

Taking up the turning point of the narrative when the recalled adventures of youth transform Homer, Ubelaker Andrade offers an absorbing reading of the short story. He avers that those significant experiences bring into view "the cultural foundations of the senses" (*Borges Beyond the Visible* 58):

> This is a moment in which his sensory experiences are revealed to have *always* been embedded within long-standing narratives of myth. It suggests the possibility that his previous experiences of the "immediate present" were, in fact, *only compelling* due to a set of stories that, at the time, remained both unperceived and unmentioned... .

> The story, in other words, describes how one blindness (the inability to see the cultural discourses that construct "immediate" experiences) is replaced by another (the inability to directly participate in visual sensory experiences).
>
> (*Borges Beyond the Visible* 58)

The question to which this explanation of sensory experiences gives rise is a familiar one, debated in the introduction to this book (14–18). If the senses – and, by extension, bodily experience – are constructed by cultural discourses, do the latter not nullify the personal nature of the former as comprehended by the individual? By the same logic, the experience of blindness also gets obscured by the said discursive forces. While Ubelaker Andrade's argument seems to espouse "strong constructionism" (Siebers 174–75),[24] a further statement indicates that the critic does resist the power of that theory to silence the voice of the individual. Words that closely follow the passage appearing in the long quotation above imply that Homer's body and will are

---

24 Siebers defines the concept thus: "Strong constructionism posits that the body does not determine its own representation in any way because the sign precedes the body in the hierarchy of signification" (174). Ubelaker Andrade's emphasis on the powers of Homer's (and Borges's) poetic imagination allows him to maintain critical distance from the strong constructionist stance. See *Borges Beyond the Visible* (56–60) for his explication of Borges's artistic reckoning with blindness.

not subsumed under cultural narratives. He emerges, according to Ubelaker Andrade, as the fount of Western cultural discourse: "Developing the second sight of imagination through language is made all the more urgent when it is revealed that the protagonist is, in fact, Homer: the writer that sits at the center of Borges's cultural tradition" (*Borges Beyond the Visible* 58). Taken together, these quotations suggest that "the personal nature of bodily experience is based on a combination of sensory, cognitive, psychological, cultural, and social experiences/contexts" (Ubelaker Andrade).[25] Responding to my critique of his reading, Ubelaker Andrade continues,

> I was not trying to suggest that experiences are solely cultural constructs. Though I suppose I would consider the category of the individual to be an unstable one, a provisional and relational/contextual phenomenon or process that is difficult to delimit…which might interfere a bit with the idea of 'the voice of the individual'.

Thus, we may conclude that the man who becomes the maker is shaped by the stories he has absorbed in the course of his eventful life, and he in turn shapes the epic poems which act as the source of the Western literary tradition. When he retrieves the memories of his youth while "descending" (293) into the "night of his mortal eyes," his creative powers are fired. He hears the "rumor" of the great poems which would spring from his imaginative effort. As Ubelaker Andrade demonstrates in his argument about the acts of reading and imagination,[26] Borges reveals through "The Maker" that "language, imagination and sensory privation work productively against one another" (*Borges Beyond the Visible* 58) in both Homer and himself.

The reader might well enquire How "The Maker" differs from "Tlön" and "The Library of Babel," since in the two latter narratives ideas and books bewitch inhabitants of their realms, and in the former Homer draws on experiences "embedded within long-standing narratives of myth." In other words, the stories which the protagonist of "The Maker" has absorbed along with reality rejuvenate him, and help him find meaning and purpose in his changed life. In turning to his cultural discourse to make sense of his personal experiences, does Homer not repeat the follies of those characters living in Uqbar and the library, respectively? It is crucial to recognise that he, like the blind librarian in "The Library of Babel," himself connects the threads of his varied experience to the stories in his memory. He thus exercises creative agency and re-shapes the narrative material available in his culture to produce his epic poems.

---

25 My book chapter appearing in the volume edited by David Bolt recognises how societal and cultural discourses of normalcy swamp the disabled individual. It tackles the junctures where the social constructionist explanation of disability and autoethnography intersect, thus retaining psycho-somatic experience as a valid subject of discussion for disability theory.

26 Which are presented in Chapter 1 of his book entitled "Borges's Literary Theology: Fiction and the Visible" (*Borges Beyond the Visible* 9–60).

The author's treatment of the experience that Homer has in the world undergoes an evolution in the course of the narrative in consonance with the changes in the man's selfhood. One who lived from moment to moment, immersing himself in all that life had to offer, without delving into his memory, was transformed by blindness into a person who reached back into his memory as an act of new awakening. (I will return to the theme of the maker's "memory" in greater detail in Chapter 3 [73–5].) At that moment, he remembered two adventures that he had had in "the dark." Those adventures had involved sensory experiences other than sight – hearing, touch, smell, and taste. When he reflected on those experiences that had taken place in his past, he recognised the promise of life as a blind man and as a great maker. Borges's use of the past tense from the beginning up to but excluding the last sentence, which is in the present tense, shows that "The Maker" is a retrospective narrative. This point becomes clear when we recognise that the author is telling the story from the situation of a blind person. Referring to Homer's realisation of hopes for the future, he says, "These things we know, but not those that he felt as he descended into his last darkness" (293). This mode of narration makes powerful use of figures of speech natural to a blind writer. We should recall here that Borges grappled with sight loss over a long period of time. As Manguel states, "His was a particular kind of blindness, grown on him gradually since the age of thirty and settled in for good after his fifty-eighth birthday" (15–16). "The Maker," thus, dramatises the discovery of poetic power after the self has been inserted in the blind condition.

On the evening of Sunday, June 28, 2015, I had a brief conversation about Borges with the writer and journalist, Selina Mills. We were attending the Blind Creations conference. When I remarked that Borges had a difficult time 'with blindness,' Mills responded with an insightful observation: "He must have been obsessed with the written word." I had occasion to refer to that remark the next day. After I had presented my paper, the blind artist, David Johnson, offered an objection: my argument that a dialectic of the ideal and the experiential characterises Borges's aesthetic of blindness is, he said, "too literary." He meant that it appears contrived. I disagreed, and explained that Borges did alternate between various positions with regard to his blindness throughout his career. Although in 1977, he states in his lecture on blindness that it is "a way of life: one of the styles of living" (*Selected Non-Fictions* 478), earlier in the same essay, he mourns the loss of his "reader's and writer's sight" (*Selected Non-Fictions* 475). He ends it by referring to "the slow process of blindness" (*Selected Non-Fictions* 483), which he experienced, and expresses mixed feelings about it: "… it is not a complete misfortune. It is one more instrument among the many—all of them so strange—that fate or chance provide." In an interview he gave in 1982, he laments, "Since I lost my sight in the fifties, I have not been able to exult in writing in this casual manner" (Heaney et al. 78), and be "a playboy of words." Thus, we can perceive a continual alternation between hope and despair with respect to blindness throughout Borges's writings. The dialectical movement in his aesthetic approach to blindness, evident in his reading and writing practices during the 1940s and 1950s, exemplifies this shift in attitudes.

In line with this shifting pattern of responses to blindness, the short story "Blue Tigers" (494–503), published in English in the collection *Shakespeare's Memory* (1983), portrays a blind character as somebody who liberates the narrator from a terrible fate. When the tiger enthusiast from Scotland, Alexander Craigie, goes in search of a blue tiger (which he has heard and dreamt of) in a village somewhere in India, he stumbles upon magical stones of the same colour – blue – "as the tiger of [his] dreams" (497). These stones breed and multiply, thereby violating the "essential law of the human mind" (500) relating to mathematics and bewitching Craigie. He is forced against his will to dream and think about the stones continuously, and is driven towards insanity. When he first arrives in the village which "squatted at the foot of a hill" (495), he senses that the inhabitants of the village are concealing a secret from him, which he conjectures is concerned with the blue tiger. One day, on proposing to climb to the top of "the wooded hill" (496) near the village, he is dissuaded by the villagers:

> The eldest of them said gravely that my goal was impossible to attain, the summit of the hill was sacred, magical obstacles blocked the ascent to man. He who trod the peak with mortal foot was in danger of seeing the godhead, and of going blind or mad.
>
> (497)

Just as thinking continuously upon the Zahir is recognised by the narrator of "The Zahir" to be a path to God, the magical blue stones in the present narrative, which are like "coins, or buttons, or counters in some game" (497), are linked to divinity. Thus, the stones that Craigie finds on the plateau which the villagers call "'blue tigers,'" are "the godhead" mentioned by the elder, or symbols of that deity. As indicated above by this same villager, the stones gradually drive the narrator insane, thereby forcing him to turn away from the world and withdraw into himself. The story ends with a blind beggar accepting the blue stones as alms and blessing Craigie: "'... You may keep your days and nights, and keep wisdom, habits, the world'" (503). However, the latter indicates in his narrative that even though the stones are no longer in his possession, they continue to exercise their power over him. This becomes evident from the words about the day on which he found the stones: "It may be that I have tried to forget the rest of that day, which was the first of a misfortunate series that continues even until now" (499). The village elder's words about the alteration in the person's corporeal make-up (in terms of his physical or mental condition) on viewing the godhead, and Craigie's subsequent experience of being mentally unmoored or reality being tampered with by the stones both suggest the idea that when the individual comes into contact with god or the divine being, their self and relationship with the world are altered radically forever. Thus, the blind beggar embodies the mystical power of god in the story.

Through a reading of a number of short stories covering Borges's writing career, I have outlined the phases of the author's literary engagement with the question of blindness. At the heart of this engagement may be perceived a dialectical movement that shapes his fiction-writing during the crucial decades of the 1940s and 1950s, when he became blind and had to change the ways in which he read and wrote. This aesthetic, as this chapter shows, is determined by an initial move into the ideal realm prompted by blindness which constitutes a withdrawal from the experiential world, and by an eventual turn to engaging with that experience itself in the fictional realm. My reading of "Tlön" and "The Library of Babel" details the ways in which people can be duped by idealistic systems of knowledge, and by the textual realm if they give up introspection. While my interpretation of "The Secret Miracle," "The Zahir," "The Aleph," "The Writing of the God," and "The Immortal" brings out the shift in the aesthetic of blindness, my observations on "The Maker" show how engagement with the experience of blindness and the life of the imagination go hand in hand for both poets – Homer, who is the subject of the narrative, and Borges, who is its writer. Having looked at the temporal dialectic that constitutes Borges's aesthetic of blindness, we will turn in the next chapter to the treatment of disability, including blindness and other bodily deformities in relation to time and memory, and their role in self-understanding.

3   Altered Sensation and Self-Understanding in Borges's Fictions

We saw in the previous chapter that a philosophically significant dialectical movement between the ideal realm and artistic engagement with experience informs Borges's aesthetic approach to blindness in his 'fictions.' Furthermore, it is evident that this dialectic possesses a self-constitutive power, and shapes the author's creativity. In the present chapter, I will show that Borges was keenly aware of various kinds of disability experience by interpreting six short stories which cover half a century of his fiction-writing career (1934–1983). I will focus, in these select 'fictions,' on instances of direct emphasis on disability experience such as paralysis and blindness, and will illustrate the point that being reflective about disability indicates a deepened awareness of, and interest in, the fragility of corporeal existence.

As already explained, Borges had conflicting feelings about being blind. His experience of gradually advancing blindness over many years contributed to his varying attitudes towards it. As Manguel states, "His was a particular kind of blindness, grown on him gradually since the age of 30 and settled in for good after his 58th birthday" (15–16). Borges himself treats blindness in all the literary genres which he practised – short fiction, poetry, the essay, lectures, and interviews. Manguel writes further, "Borges often talked about his own blindness, mainly with literary interest" (16). Borges's ambiguous attitude to his blindness is evident in the wry humour (Laraway, "The Blind Spot in the Mirror" 312) that the following words from his lecture "Blindness" express: "… it is not that perfect blindness which people imagine" (*Seven Nights* 86). He was conscious of how blindness could lead to creativity. This awareness is manifested in a number of his writings. For instance, in the poetic short story entitled "The Maker"[1] from the collection carrying the same title (1960), the narrator imagines what another great blind poet of the Western tradition, Homer, felt as he gradually became blind, and through the experience of blindness realised that he had the creative potential to sing great epic poems. In the poem "In Praise of Darkness," originally published in Spanish, the speaker, referring to the consequences of his blindness, tells of "reading and transforming" (line 29) texts "in my

---

1 This narrative occupies our interest in both Chapter 2 and Chapter 3.

DOI: 10.4324/9781003399667-3

memory" (line 28).² These words point to the vertiginous creative process in a blind poet. However, Borges expresses regret at the loss of sight and the difficulties he consequently faced in writing and reading in "Blindness" and the interview with Heaney and Kearney:

> Since I lost my sight in the fifties, I have not been able to exult in writing in this casual manner. I have had to dictate everything, to become a dictator rather than a playboy of words.... But I miss being able to read even more than being able to write.
>
> (Heaney et al. 78)

Here, Borges expresses a desire to see words on paper – a wish that blindness has made poignant for the author.

Borges's narrative on blindness is, however, not one of straightforward sorrow at the loss of his sight, but a nuanced one that recognises the multifaceted nature of disability experience. In "Poem of the Gifts" (*Selected Poems* 94–7), he writes of the supremely ironic experience of becoming the director of the National Library of Argentina in 1955, and losing his sight around the same time. He talks about the "splendid irony" (line 3) of God, who "granted me books and blindness at one touch" (line 4). When he articulates the realisation that for him being blind is not a complete tragedy, it becomes evident that he recognises the value of blindness and its consequences in his life: "It should be seen as a way of life: one of the styles of living" (*Selected Non-Fictions* 478). In contrast to the ironic gifts referred to above, he even speaks of owing "to the darkness some [advantageous] gifts." After he became blind, he learned new languages, namely Anglo-Saxon and Icelandic, and also wrote poetry. Thus he succeeded in creating a whole new world, replacing "the visible world with the aural world." In light of this discussion, it becomes clear that deformities are, in the lives of those who are disabled, one among the many aspects of experience which define their subjectivities.

The underlying premise and structuring principle of my argument in the present chapter is that bodily deformities affect self-conception in diverse, observable ways. Given his "literary interest" in blindness, Borges's 'fictions' manifest an intense awareness of this corporeal, sensory process of understanding the self. His engagement of senses is not restricted to representation of disabled characters in his fiction. Borges's experientially altered sense of the self and of the world conditions his many narrative choices, especially those related to voice, perspective, and time. Let us first consider the question of time in select short stories in his oeuvre.

While talking about his blindness in his lecture on that subject, Borges describes it in terms of the experience of time, of night descending slowly over the world, lasting more than three quarters of a century: "In my case, that slow nightfall, that slow loss of sight began when I began to see. It has

2 This activity reminds us of Borges's rich "remembered library" (Reid 5).

continued since 1899 without dramatic moments, a slow nightfall that has lasted more than three quarters of a century" (*Selected Non-Fictions* 474–75). This correlation of the gradual onset of blindness and the experience of time can also be seen in the short story "The Other" which appears in the collection entitled *The Book of Sand* (1975), where the narrator-protagonist says: "Gradual blindness is … like the slowly growing darkness of a summer evening" (417). I argue that the differential sense of time is a function of alternative bodily being. In the short stories I take up for this study, one can observe that when characters lose, in part or whole, the faculty of the senses, they come to acquire a different understanding of time; time slows down for many of them. The reasons for this novel sense of time are as follows. The character with the deformity is restricted in movement, and spends his time in physically non-active, but intensely contemplative ways. He has a heightened awareness of reality, and an expansive sense of time. He also begins to notice unmistakable similarities in experiences, perceptions, and memories from day to day. The disabled character's experiential homogeneity, thus, calls up the theme of repetition and the idea of circular time. My contention is that Borges pertinently foregrounds the consequence of bodily deformities in a differential matrix of sensations which, in these short stories, appears as a creative temporal consciousness.

Distinguishing between himself and people "who suddenly lose their sight" (*Selected Non-Fictions* 474), Borges says that his case was not "especially dramatic" because he had lost his sight slowly, over a long period of time. Thus, he had got enough time to adjust to his disability. (However, as is clear from the foregoing pages, even late in his life, Borges had difficulties accepting blindness and its consequences.) But those who become blind or acquire other bodily deformities suddenly, are plunged into a life with disability without any warning. In the short stories I have chosen for this study, Borges examines both experiential paradigms of disability. We should not fail to note how time plays a significant role in the above distinction among disability experiences.

3.1 Durée and Intuition

Before we move further into a discussion of Borges's short stories, let us turn our attention to Bergson's philosophy of time, or, as he terms it in the preface to *An Introduction to Metaphysics*, of duration ('durée') (Lacey 26). This brief digression will enable me to illuminate certain aspects of the argument pertaining to time and self-understanding. In the preface to *An Introduction to Metaphysics*, Bergson distinguishes between science and philosophy. He states that the subject matter of the former is "spatialized time and … space" (*Introduction to Metaphysics* 10), while that of the latter is "real duration." Imagining the self to be a sphere, he finds that its surface is composed of elements bound to one another – perceptions, memories, tendencies, and habits. Consequently, it is turned towards "the external world." But if we

penetrate this surface, and reach the depth of our person, we will find a "sol-
idly organized" (*Introduction to Metaphysics* 11), continuous flow of states
which Bergson calls 'duration.' A. R. Lacey describes it as "'concrete time'"
(28). It involves continuous change. This duration is "constitutive"
(*Introduction to Metaphysics* 15) of a person's "being." Thus, in this flow of
states that is truly the self, time is of paramount significance.

The durational flow is "profoundly animated with a common life"
(*Introduction to Metaphysics* 11). This unique "current of feeling"
(*Introduction to Metaphysics* 12), which runs through the temporal contin-
uum of the self, fashions the unique character of each person. Every state in
this "succession of states ... announces what follows and contains what
precedes" (*Introduction to Metaphysics* 11). Clearly, memory is central to
personhood. When consciousness attends to the flow in the depth of the person, both "the past and present" (*Introduction to Metaphysics* 23) of the self
are seized by it. Two conclusions follow from this claim: first, consciousness
acts in time; all its actions – the roles it plays in affections and intuition – are
temporal in nature. Therefore, it is not possible to have "a consciousness
without memory" (*Introduction to Metaphysics* 12). Secondly, 'duration' is
animated by memory.[3]

Bergson declares that the self can be comprehended in its flowing "from
within" (*Introduction to Metaphysics* 9) only "by intuition and not by simple
analysis." He understands intuition to mean a "sympathy" or spiritual power
with the help of which the person can enter an object and understand its essence
by coinciding with it (*Introduction to Metaphysics* 6). He illustrates the work of
intuition in the following statement: "When you lift your arm, you accomplish
a movement the simple perception of which you have inwardly" (*Introduction
to Metaphysics* 5–6). We know our body, which is a part of the external world,
not only by perceptions, but also by 'affections' (first-hand, internal experience). While the former give the person knowledge of his body from without,
the latter are a species of intuition which facilitate knowledge of the body "from
within" (*Matter and Memory* 1). It is our consciousness which, acting "in the
form of feeling or of sensation" (*Matter and Memory* 2), gives rise to affections,
and plays a role in all the actions we perform with awareness.

3.2 Disabled Characters and Variations in Subjective Time

Having taken this important detour into Bergson's process philosophy, we
come to Borges's fiction. I will first look at "The End" (168–70) in order to
examine the theme of time. This short story was first published in 1953. "The
End" has as one of its three main characters a disabled man, Recabarren, the
proprietor of a general-store-and-bar who is paralysed suddenly one day.

---

3 Bergson goes so far as to declare that "consciousness means memory" (*Introduction to
Metaphysics* 11). See Amanda Tink's essay as letter, "The Nuances of Memory," for a view
which challenges the valourisation of memory.

The occurrence that is central to the plot (in more ways than one) happened seven years before the short story begins, and is only summarised in the second paragraph of the narrative. This incident is "the payada, or song contest" (Fishburn and Hughes 98) between "a black man [a stranger in those parts] who had shown up one night flattering himself that he was a singer" (168) and "another stranger" who is the enemy of the former. The second man is a knife fighter called Martín Fierro. That the event took place seven years earlier is evident from the black man's words to Fierro that he had been waiting for that length of time (169). On that occasion, not only did Recabarren, who acts as a witness in the short story, first set eyes on the black man and Fierro, but the incident also prompts the reader to infer that the two antagonists were already acquainted with each other. It is noteworthy how the former directly "challenged" (168) the latter to the contest. The inference is proved to be correct when we learn that Fierro had killed the black man's brother seven years earlier. Further, the song contest prefigures the final encounter between them, the duel. Fierro, getting ready for the knife fight, says tiredly to the black man, "'Leave that guitar alone, now—you've got another kind of contest to try to win today.'" The same idea is hinted at in the following exchange between the two men. Referring to the approaching contest, the black man says, "'Could be this one goes as bad for me as the other one did.'" Fierro replies, "'It's not that the first one went bad for you ... It's that you couldn't wait to get to the second one'" (170). The song contest stands out in Recabarren's memory for one more important reason. It was the day after the event that he became paralysed: "[He] would never forget that contest; the next day, as he was trying to straighten some bales of *yerba*, his right side had suddenly gone dead on him, and he discovered that he couldn't talk" (168). The onset of his paralysis,[4] and the resulting speech disability are life-changing events for the man.

Recabarren is a contrastive figure in the tale. His disability sets him apart, literally and character-wise, from the black man and Fierro, and more generally from the rest of society. Before becoming paralysed, he was actively engaged in the day-to-day running of his establishment. This fact is implied when we are told that "he was trying to straighten some bales *of yerba*" when the disability set in. When the narrative commences, the reader finds him "lying on his back" (168), just waking from his sleep and in a contemplative mood. He does not rise from his bed throughout the short story, which suggests that his paralysis does not allow him to. His movements have thus been severely restricted for seven years by paralysis. In contrast, the black man and Fierro have been engaged in their respective activities: they are gauchos (Fishburn and Hughes 98). The former has been waiting for an opportunity to avenge his brother's killing by the latter, and the latter has been to see his children, as we learn from his words (169). Also, it may be

4 His condition may be described, in medical terms, as hemiplegia, that is, paralysis of one side of the body.

safely speculated that he has been carrying on with his knife fights. So, Recabarren before paralysis, and the two gauchos before and after their first encounter follow their respective routines, performing habituated actions in order to complete the day-to-day requirements of their respective livelihoods, living only to fulfil the various goals of their respective lives. In this mode of living, they experience time in terms of definite divisions. If one were to interpret this in Bergsonian terms, they think of time in its "symbolical representations such as hours, days, months and years, which are only its spatial concepts" (Kumar 8). Here, the reader of the short story will recall how the two gauchos constantly refer to the time that has gone by in terms of the number of days and years. In Bergson's terms, as indicated above, this sort of division of time represents an artificial abstraction (*Introduction to Metaphysics* 53–5). However, Recabarren, who is unable to walk or move many parts of his body due to his disability, experiences time differently, as a flow represented by natural processes and events. He is aware of the time – evening – by looking "up at the sky" (168) from his window. It may be said, then, that he has aligned his life to the natural rhythms of the earth. The narrator says that he is a "man in the habit of living in the present, as animals do." His experience of time is symbolised by an aural labyrinth, the music of a guitar, because music is temporal: "From the other room there came the strumming of a guitar, like some inconsequential labyrinth, infinitely tangling and untangling." In Bergson's terms, this means that Recabarren experiences what Shiv K. Kumar calls "la *durée* or psychological time" (7), "an immeasurable and multidirectional process" (8). Besides, the moon, which is noticed by Recabarren, symbolises cyclical time, meaning that time is measured in terms of lunar cycles.

In the course of the short story, the reader learns that the black man and Fierro are baying for each other's blood. Each man is waiting to kill the other and defend his honour. Therefore, to Fierro's subtle challenge to a knife fight the black man says, "'Fall's coming on, and the days are getting shorter'" (170). Fierro replies, "'The light that's left will be enough for me.'" Not a thought of the time that is given to them on earth enters their minds. The black man succeeds in avenging his brother's killing, and Fierro's life is brought to a bloody end. Ironically for Fierro, his words about the sufficiency of "'the light that's left'" turn out to be true. However, his killing proves, in a less measurable but nevertheless profound way, to be the end of the black man's life too: "His work of vengeance done, he was nobody now. Or rather, he was the other one: there was neither destination nor destiny on earth for him, and he had killed a man." Having accomplished the one goal which he had set for himself in his life, he had nothing more to live for.

As mentioned above, the narrator comments that Recabarren's attitude to life as a paralytic is animal-like: the latter lives in the present. According to Bergson, the present is not a single "instant in which [time] goes by" (*Matter and Memory* 176). The philosopher explains that such an instant is only "a pure conception," and states that "the real, concrete, live present" which is defined by our "present perception ... necessarily occupies duration." Since knowing the flow of duration includes the awareness of our physical existence, "[the] present is, in its essence, sensory-motor" (*Matter and Memory* 177). This statement means, then, that "my present consists in the consciousness that I have of my body." When Recabarren awakes fully, he is brought into the present by the reality of his situation: "Little by little, reality came back to him, the ordinary things that now would always be just these ordinary things" (168). This sombre statement calls our attention to his heightened awareness of the repetitive nature of the external world, given the restrictions imposed on his movements by his paralysis. Intensely aware of his body, he knows that he cannot go out into the world to seek the muchneeded variety in his life. Therefore, his ringing "the brass cowbell that hung at the foot of the cot" to call the "boy with Indian-like features" (169), and his enquiry as to "whether anybody was around" may be interpreted to mean that he wants people to be present, not only for the business, but also because there would then be conversation and stories about events occurring in the world at large. We see how "his left hand played awhile with the bell, as though exercising some power," as though by exercising this power, someone would arrive at the bar. As it happens, he gets to witness the murderous end of the rivalry between the black man and Fierro.

Recabarren's mind runs in another direction too: since, as indicated above, he knows the duration of his self (*Introduction to Metaphysics* 22), he is aware of the moving power of "the true memory of the past" (*Matter and Memory* 197). Bergson describes this "true memory" as "the memory of dreams" (*Matter and Memory* 199). Thus, the following observation may be understood as being partially "focalized through" (Genette 197–98, 209) Recabarren's consciousness: "The plains, in the last rays of the sun, were almost abstract, as though seen in a dream" (169). The following thoughts express, in some way, the paralysed man's understanding of what he witnesses:

> There is an hour just at evening when the plains seem on the verge of saying something; they never do, or perhaps they do—eternally— though we don't understand it, or perhaps we do understand but what they say is as untranslatable as music.
>
> (170)

With this evocation of music, the reader will recall that on waking, Recabarren hears the "infinitely tangling and untangling" labyrinthine "strumming" of the guitar from the adjoining room. In a half-wakeful state – here the phrase "little by little" is suggestive of the state – his consciousness is on the edge of dreams that are also untranslatable. Thus, while the black man's life has no future to speak of, which suggests that he experiences time as a linear succession, Recabarren's life holds some promise in terms of dreams and creativity. He is aware of the durational flow of his self, and experiences the concrete flow of time as a "multidirectional" process.

Bergson's words, "A human being who should dream his life instead of living it would no doubt thus keep before his eyes at each moment the infinite multitude of the details of his past history" (*Matter and Memory* 201), describe well Ireneo Funes, the disabled character portrayed in the short story entitled "Funes, His Memory" (131–37). Funes is a much more vibrant character compared to Recabarren. This trait may be the result of his young age, whereas the storekeeper is older and "perhaps" even has a son (169), the taciturn boy with Indian-like features mentioned above. Borges composed the narrative on Funes, which appears in the collection *Fictions* (1944), as a "testimony" (131) written by the narrator about the young man. The narrator was acquainted with Funes in his youth, and he writes this testimony nearly "half a century" (134) after the latter's death. He recounts his encounters with Funes, and the account covers, more or less chronologically but in an incomplete manner, Funes's life before and after his fall off "a half-broken horse on the ranch in San Francisco" (132) and the resulting paralysis. This is, then, a retrospective narrative about Funes and his remarkable memory. In this densely written tale, Borges sets up the narrator-character as a foil to Funes. The narrator also compares Funes with himself, indirectly, and with other people for the purposes of bringing out the differences in character, and highlighting the themes of the short story.

The reader learns early on in the narrative, when the narrator relates his "first recollection of Funes" (132),[5] that Funes had a very good sense of time: "Unexpectedly, Bernardo shouted out to him— *What's the time, Ireneo?* Without consulting the sky, without a second's pause, the boy replied, *Four minutes till eight, young Bernardo Juan Francisco*" (italics as in the source). Bernardo Haedo, The narrator's cousin, informed him that Funes "always [knew] what time it was, like a clock." The evocation of the clock is apt here[6] because, apart from being able to tell the time to the minute,[7] Funes before his accident and paralysis, along with the narrator-character and the rest of society as depicted in the short story, live according to time divided and measured by the clock. This is indicated by the above incident, and by the number of times the narrator gives references to dates in the short story. According to Bergson, it is the nature of reality to flow: "One recognizes the real, the actual, the concrete, by the fact that it is variability itself" (*Introduction to Metaphysics* 43). Thus, if we consider la durée or concrete time, recalling that it involves in its essence continuous flux, we can say that Funes succeeds in intuiting its flow. The rest of the characters, including the narrator, lead their day-to-day lives unmindful of the continuous change taking place deep within themselves and the world. This is not to say that they are not aware of change; it would be more appropriate to say that they do not recognise and accept it

---

5 This was the time he saw the boy "one afternoon in March or February of '84" (131), viz. 1884, running quietly along a raised brick sidewalk.

6 A second reference to the clock may be found later on in the narrative (136).

7 The narrator-character even calls him "'chronometric Funes'" (132).

as the primary reality. Evidence for this claim is to be found throughout the narrative. Take, for instance, the following passage:

> I was told he'd been bucked off a half-broken horse on the ranch in San Francisco and had been left *hopelessly crippled*. I recall the sensation of *unsettling* magic that this news gave me: The only time I'd seen him, we'd been coming home on horseback from the ranch in San Francisco, and he had been walking along a high place. This new event, told by my cousin Bernardo, struck me as very much like a dream confected out of elements of the past.
>
> (emphasis added, 132)

It is generally accepted that Funes's paralysis is a great misfortune. The phrase "hopelessly crippled," and the narrator's observation that "the iron-barred window" (133) behind which the young man lay on his cot "crudely underscored his prisoner like state" signify this attitude. On hearing the news of Funes's disablement, the narrator-character feels unsettled because the only time he had seen the former was when he and his cousin were riding horses, and the other had then been "walking along a high place." Now he could not walk due to his paralysis resulting from a fall off a horse. What is of significance here is the place where the accident occurred, namely the ranch in San Francisco, and the fact that the two cousins had been returning home from the same place on horseback when they saw Funes. The unsettling feeling that the same thing could have happened to either of them disturbs the narrator-character. As Schor declares,

> The relentless focus on ever greater sensual plenitude is pornographic, a denial of the frailty of the human body, of the weight of genetic destiny, of the play of accident and chance and of the vicissitudes of history. ... though that Body has been [understood to be] "tremulous," "in pain," in pieces, the site of torture, disciplining, discrimination, illness, and other forms of insult and injury, it has been regarded as drawing meaning from an implied healthy norm.
>
> (83–4)

Despite having come into contact with "the play of accident and chance" in the life of Funes; encountering references to two battles (133, 135) that caused widespread mutilation and death; and the recent death of his uncle Gregorio Haedo, the narrator-character did not, at the time, possess an intuition of "the frailty of the human body." This conjecture is strengthened into a conviction when we read of his unfeeling behaviour and lack of seriousness with respect to the news of his father's ill health. The telegraphic phrase quoted by the narrator "my father was 'not at all well'" (133) suggests that the man was nearing his end. The narrator's confession of his cavalier attitude towards his father's illness and likely death, his admission of being distracted "from any possibility of real pain" by his desire for recognition, point to the lack in him as a youth of any inkling about the profounder realities of life. He is candid about his character and motives in the narrative because he is narrating the events many years after they occurred.

However, the narrator seems to have moved in the direction of gaining some insight into the flux of life in the course of half a century. This change in his character is evident in his mode of narrating what Funes told him about his powers of memory, perception, dreaming, imagination, and about his number system connected to words. The narrator's incredulity, irritation, understanding, and awe – all come through in his narrative. Thus, he says, "Those are the things he told me; neither then nor later have I ever doubted them" (135). His sombre observation concerning the fact that not a single study was carried out with Funes on his memory shows that he has come to realise that time never stops flowing, and that change and death are everpresent realities. This deepening of personality may be seen in his words of understanding about Funes's unremitting experience of reality: "... no one in the populous towers or urgent avenues" (136–37) of the wondrous cities of "Babylon, London, and New York ... has ever felt the heat and pressure of a reality as inexhaustible as that which battered Ireneo, day and night, in his poor South American hinterland." However, it becomes evident from his characterisation of Funes as "such a proud young man" (133), and from the assumption "that he pretended that his disastrous fall had actually been fortunate" that the narrator shares the widely held non-disabled view of persons with disabilities as weak and unfortunate.

Describing the first occasion of his meeting with Funes, the narrator makes the following admission: "I am so absent-minded that I would never have given a second thought to the exchange I've just reported" (132). Funes cannot be said to be an "absent-minded" person even before his accident and paralysis, as is clear from the fleeting glimpse that the reader gets of him at the beginning of the short story. He tells Bernardo the exact time "without consulting the sky, without a second's pause" (131). The intensity of his awareness after his fall off the horse, and recovery of consciousness are symbolised by an image that the narrator offers at the opening of his story:

> I recall him ... holding a dark passionflower in his hand, seeing it as it had never been seen, even had it been stared at from the first light of dawn till the last light of evening for an entire lifetime.
>
> (131)

What is of interest here is the correlation between the act of perception and time. According to Bergson, "However brief we suppose any perception to be, it always occupies a certain duration, and involves consequently an effort of memory which prolongs one into another a plurality of moments" (*Matter and Memory* 25). Thus, we see the involvement of "an effort of memory" in Funes's perception:

Not only was it difficult for him to see that the generic symbol "dog" took in all the dissimilar individuals of all shapes and sizes, it irritated him that the "dog" of three-fourteen in the afternoon, seen in profile, should be indicated by the same noun as the dog of three-fifteen, seen frontally. His own face in the mirror, his own hands, surprised him every time he saw them.

(136)

As this quotation indicates, Funes's perception had become so extraordinarily keen after the accident that he could perceive all the variations in the external world and the moment-to-moment changes occurring in the creatures and objects around him as well as in himself. He, thus, had a heightened awareness of reality. We may draw three conclusions from this insight into Funes's perceptual capabilities: first, his awareness of change through time points unmistakably to the work of memory in perception; second, as a result of his awareness of this variety and of continuous change, he believed (1) that only particulars existed (137); and (2) that each individual, from moment to moment, should be referred to using different symbols; and third, his perception of all the details that characterise reality and the changes that it undergoes one moment to the next means that Funes had placed himself in "the flow of duration" (*Introduction to Metaphysics* 39).

As Funes was detached from action due to his paralysis, time had slowed down for him. To quote Bergson on duration,

May we not conceive, for instance, that the irreducibility of two perceived colours is due mainly to the narrow duration into which are contracted the billions of vibrations which they execute in one of our moments? If we could stretch out this duration, that is to say, live it at a slower rhythm, should we not, as the rhythm slowed down, see these colours pale and lengthen into successive impressions, still coloured, no doubt, but nearer and nearer to coincidence with pure vibrations?

(*Matter and Memory* 268–69)

Accordingly, when Funes woke up after the fall, he realised that "the present was so rich, so clear, that it was almost unbearable, as were his oldest and even his most trivial memories" (135). When he saw, for instance, a wineglass, he could perceive "every grape that had been pressed into the wine and all the stalks and tendrils of its vineyard." One look at, or one feel of, a thing was enough for him to remember it forever in all its sensory aspects. He could effortlessly manipulate all the images in his vast memory, combining them, comparing one with another, and so on. The narrator refers to Funes's awareness of each one of his dreams, and his ability to intuit the forms of complex things and creatures in their incessant process of becoming: "... anything he thought, even once, remained ineradicably with him." These remarkable powers are proof of an exceptionally creative mind.

In Bergson's terms, the narrator is a person who sets great store by "abstract ideas" (*Introduction to Metaphysics* 17), and shows a preference for the ability to generalise and think in terms of concepts (137). Thus, he excludes all other modes of viewing reality. Bergson intensely distrusts this kind of thinking. When the "variation" (*Introduction to Metaphysics* 48) of reality is "resolved" into "different concepts" by conceptual thinking, he avers, "the stable drives away the unstable" (*Matter and Memory* 269). Therefore, what we get are merely "so many stable visions of the instability of the real" (*Introduction to Metaphysics* 48). Reality, as mentioned above, is unstable and, by nature, variable. Funes intuitively knew this reality in its flowing, and was aided by his "perfect" memory and perception (135): "He saw—he noticed—the progress of death, of humidity. He was the solitary, lucid spectator of a multiform, momentous, and almost unbearably precise world" (136). Who was this person if not someone who knew the durational flow of his self and the world? Funes, then, "stretch[ed] out this duration, that is to say, live[d] it at a slower rhythm." Due to the slowed rhythm of time, he could actually perceive the incessantly varying shades of reality in its flowing. So, when the narrator voices his suspicion that Funes "was not very good at thinking" (137), and goes on to explain that he could not "ignore (or forget) differences," and "generalize ... abstract," he shows merely that he has not understood Funes's mind.[8]

When the narrator of "Hakim, the Masked Dyer of Merv" (40–4) opens his story with the statement "In the year 120 of the Hegira, or 736 of the Christian era, there was born in Turkestan the man Hakim" (40), he is placing Hakim in a temporal system different from the modern, scientific system wherein time is spatialised and thus understood to be a linear succession. The Islamic reckoning of time depends, firstly, on the date of the Prophet Muhammad's Flight (42) from Mecca to Medina in 622 A.D. and, secondly, on the cycles of the moon. Muslims rely on a lunar calendar. Here the reader must note that the narrator refers repeatedly to the moon to mean 'month' (41–3) while, at the same time, giving dates according to the Muslim calendar. This portrayal of time as a cyclical phenomenon parallels the representation of Hakim as a prophet. This religious phenomenon is a manifestation of repetition, because he plays the role of a prophet who comes just over a century and a half after the coming of the Prophet Muhammad. However, although the year is measured by the cyclical movement of the moon, and Islamic mythology displays an element of repetition, as the narrator of "The Zahir" remarks, the Islamic conception of time is rigid. He refers to "the hard, solid time of Islam" (245), which is the opposite of Bergsonian time.

8 Christopher Krentz advances what I think is a valid alternative reading, which is incidentally in line with the belief of the story's narrator, that Funes "has cognitive limitations" (44), that is to say, he is immersed in the plenitude of his memory to such an extent that he "cannot generalize, cannot think analytically" (45; cf. Quian Quiroga ch. 1).

I consider the narratorial statement "Hakim's voice attempted one final deception" (44), which comes towards the close of the narrative, to be a pointer to the career of Hakim the masked dyer of Merv. He leads a life of deception motivated by his ambition for power, deceiving the people and religious rulers of his land and, ultimately, even himself. We learn that "the people of that time and that region were to call [him] The Veiled" (40). This epithet is apt both literally and figuratively because he first wears a mask and later, with increasing power and wealth, "a fourfold veil of white silk embroidered with precious stones" (42). He does this in order to hide his face – which is disfigured due to leprosy (44), as also his designs from the world. As the narrator suggests at the beginning of the tale, Hakim is not a man who follows the dictates of religion. He was trained to be "a dyer—the craft, known to be a refuge for infidels and impostors and inconstant men, which inspired the first anathemas of his career" (41). This declaration seems to be a hint to the reader that he would go on to become one of the disreputable men mentioned in the quotation. This suspicion is strengthened when we read the narrator's quotation from "a famous page" of the book, *The Annihilation of the Rose*: "*Thus did I sin in the years of my youth, deforming the true colours of the creatures*" (italics as in the source, 41). Here, the suggestion is that he is a man who hides his "*true colours*" from the world.

When Hakim contracts leprosy, he immediately becomes an outcast and must disappear from his community. To understand the peremptoriness of this societal requirement, we need only consider the narrator's description of people with leprosy as "a band of loathsome lepers" (43), and his graphic description of Hakim's disfigured face. These narratorial statements clearly imply that the man is a monster. That the society of his times regarded lepers with hatred is shown when Hakim is assassinated for being a leper, and for deceiving the world and his followers by representing himself as a prophet while actually being a loathed outcast (44). The aforementioned points bring out not only the narrator's perspective on Hakim's illness, but also the attitudes prevalent in that age and society towards those having leprosy.

Thus, when Hakim is infected with leprosy and he progressively acquires bodily deformities, his life in society comes to an end. The regular, legitimate avenues of fulfilling his ambitions are closed to him. He is forced to abandon mainstream conceptions of what life means, and has to come to terms with a hard existence away from humanity and the comforts of society. He struggles for food and shelter along with other lepers, and comes to adopt a way of thinking according to which life appears to be a difficult daily grind. Time seems to stretch ahead interminably, the future bringing the same, never-ending struggles. We must note that the narrative is silent about the twelve years (146–58 Hegira) that elapse between Hakim's disappearance from Merv and reappearance as the Masked Prophet (41). During this long period, one imagines that he suffers from a consuming anger against society. Understandably, he cannot acquiesce to the degrading life imposed on lepers and other outcasts. Being one who possesses great cunning and knowledge of human nature, he conceives an audacious and ruthless plan to better his lot, and gain power and glory. He decides to make use of his illness and bodily deformities to achieve his ends, representing himself as The Veiled Prophet and placing himself in the cyclical history of the prophets. The narrator's choice to tell the last five years of Hakim's life in greater detail than the first 26 years, and to pass over a dozen harrowing ones affects the pace of the narration in a paradoxical manner. While it speeds up the narrative by narrowing the focus of the telling, it also accords with Hakim's slowing sense of time by drawing out the narration of his final years.

Hakim's cynical cosmogony is a reflection of his *self-conception*. The latter is to be seen in his obsession with hiding his body from the world (given prevalent attitudes towards those affected by leprosy and the resulting bodily deformities), and also from himself. This attitude leads to his being obsessed with his face, and investing it with divine power (42). His understanding of life is adequately captured in the following statement: "The earth we inhabit is an error, an incompetent parody. Mirrors and paternity are abominable because they multiply and affirm it" (43). Such a view may be explained by the fact that the former reveal to us ourselves – the broken brass mirror acts as a symbol of Hakim's cosmogony and self-conception (42) – and the latter prolongs life on earth. Significantly, to the person who is consigned to his mirror-like, symmetrically identical domains of hell, the Prophet says, "Here, in this life, dost thou suffer one body; in death and Retribution, thou shalt have bodies innumerable" (44). Thus, to have a body which is deformed in this world is, according to his experience, enormous suffering; to have innumerable such bodies in hell is incalculable suffering.

3.3 Memory, Cyclical Time, and Creativity

The next three short stories, viz. "The Maker," "The Other," and "August 25, 1983" (the last one was published in the collection entitled *Shakespeare's Memory* in 1983), variously dramatise the ideas of repetition and circular time. In these stories, Borges also deals with the theme of "gradual blindness." The following narrative statement is the key to elucidating "The Maker": "Then he descended into his memory, which seemed to him endless" (293). Before blindness, the protagonist was "keen, curious" (292), and sensitive: "He had never lingered among the pleasures of memory. Impressions, momentary and vivid, would wash over him [and] could flood the entire circuit of his soul," the author informs the reader. The man was someone who lived immersed solely in the present. This means that he "remain[ed] seated" (*Matter and Memory* 194) in the concrete present "in virtue of the fundamental law of life, which is a law of action." But, as Bergson states, each and every feeling "contain[s] the past and present of the being which experiences it" (*Introduction to Metaphysics* 23). So, it is evident that the protagonist was merely unaware of the life of the memory. His state of consciousness may be explained by invoking Bergson's differentiation between "two forms of memory" (*Matter and Memory* 195) "which are profoundly distinct": spontaneous memory, which "recalls differences" (*Matter and Memory* 201), and habit memory, which recalls "similarity." The latter is described as "habit rather than memory" (*Matter and Memory* 195) because it is orientated towards action: "it acts our past experience but does not call up its image." The former is understood to be "the true memory" because it truly moves "in the past," and records all the events that happen in our lives and our psychological states "in the order in which they occur." It is not surprising why, when the protagonist descended into his "true memory," it "seemed to him endless." He was a man who was accustomed to acting according to habit, and had not as yet plumbed the depths of his memory, "continually acting his life instead of truly representing it to himself" (*Matter and Memory* 201). His life of action, and his attitude of unquestioning acceptance of "complex stories [and] reality" (292) define his character. However, all this changed with the advance of blindness.

When the protagonist lived solely in the present by the "law [of] satisfaction and immediate indifference" (292), he led a life of busy activity, participating in battles, travels, and taking in the world and its stories. Time had passed quickly, unnoticed as it were. However, as "the splendid universe [gradually] began drawing away from him," and he realised that he was becoming blind, an unknown amount of time – "Days and nights" – of deep despair engulfed him. But, as the author states,

> ... one morning he awoke, looked (with calm now) at the blurred things that lay about him, and felt, inexplicably, the way one might feel upon recognizing a melody or a voice – that all this had happened to him before, and that he had faced it with fear but also with joy and hopefulness and curiosity.
>
> (292–93)

This quotation points to repetition and circular time. Waking up "one morning" and coming out of the "despair of his flesh" (292), the protagonist entered the vibrant life of his memory. It led him to realise his powers as a great poet. The two episodes which he recollects from the "vertigo" (293) of his memory help him recover the spirit of adventure through "the precise flavor" of power and love. They are youthful memories of two life-changing events that took place at night and "in the darkness of a subterranean crypt," respectively. The arising of these memories when he has become blind foreshadows "the present" (292). The following narratorial statement suggests repetition of experiences in his life: "In this night of his mortal eyes into which he was descending, love and adventure were also awaiting him" (293). The evocative expression in this quotation equating 'night' and 'blindness' alludes not only to the mutability of the human body, but also to a change in the maker's experience of time. Further, it signals a shift in his attitude towards his blindness. Through it, he becomes aware of his memory.

He succeeds in "giving himself the intuition of the duration constitutive of his being" (*Introduction to Metaphysics* 15). These words from Bergson illuminate the fact that the blind singer is on the cusp of his creative adventure.

The final passage of the short story describes the maker sensing the return of his creative powers. Further, it strongly suggests repetition and circular time. Apart from revealing that he has come to terms with his blind self, it also indicates that his sense of time has become expansive. Consider the following words:

> ... now he began to sense (because now he began to be surrounded by)
> ... the rumor of the *Odysseys* and *Iliads* that it was his fate to sing and
> to leave echoing in the cupped hands of human memory.
>
> (293)

The blind maker is destined "to sing" great epics which would continue to echo in the memory of humankind. The metaphor of "the cupped hands of human memory" conveys tangible power. Just as the short story "Funes, his Memory" deals with the extraordinary memory of the disabled character Funes, "The Maker" also revolves around the creative power of the protagonist's memory. The word "echo" signifies an auditory event, entirely appropriate because the poems that he composes are to be sung.

"... and living consists in growing old" (*Introduction to Metaphysics* 11), says Bergson in a crisp definition of living. In a case of sensory 'compensation,' Borges, old and blind, remembers how his self was as a younger man by creating paired characters who are auctorial doubles, significantly different in age, bodily abilities, and world view, in the fictional cosmos of the two short stories entitled "The Other" (411–17) and "August 25, 1983" (489–93). Here we may cite Hull's understanding of his doubled self to suggest that persons who lose their sight later in life tend to have this unsettling experience, and it derives from "a sense of cognitive dissonance" (*On Sight* 128):

> I have become separated from my own shadow, as in the cartoons. A quivering image of myself is left behind, while the real me has been blown away by a sudden explosion, which has split me into two images. Each one has a different expression and posture, and is doing different things. I have a double relationship with myself. ... I was confronted by the first twenty-four years, the childhood and youth of that sighted self, from whom I have now become divided because I am plunged into different ways of knowing my present self.
>
> (*On Sight* 128)

These words describe with poignant exactitude Borges's predicament. While Borges steadfastly held the belief that the self was an insubstantial entity which changed easily in the course of time (Wilson 8–12), blindness prompted him to conceive of his self as being split into two. Jason Wilson states that

Borges's famous parable about the doubled self, entitled "Borges and I," which appeared in the collection *The Maker*, was "first published in a magazine when blind in 1957" (8). Thus, Borges's creative response to the doubling of his self occurred during the shift in his aesthetic of blindness which I have dated between 1955 and 1960.

Let us first turn to the short story "The Other." "The essence of time is that it goes by" (*Matter and Memory* 176), says Bergson pithily. The narrator-character of the short story, who is "sitting comfortably on a bench beside the Charles River" (411) in the city of Cambridge, remarks in the same vein: "Large chunks of ice were floating down the gray current. Inevitably, the river made me think of time...Heraclitus' ancient image." The evocation of the river, whose waters are continuously flowing by, as an "image" symbolising the flow of time is important here because the theme of time is prominently dealt with in this short story. The narrative is replete with references to time. The narrator, who is seventy years old and blind, meets his eighteen-year-old self, a young man, different and not yet blind like his older self. The story brings to life a temporal loop wherein the older self of the man Jorge Luis Borges meets his younger self, who will grow old and will meet his younger self. We have here the ideas of repetition, the double, and the suggestion of never-ending circularity; the meetings between the two selves occurring again and again in cyclical time. Here, the river and, by extension, water can be considered as a symbol for circular time. The following are some points which show that the narrator suggests the same ideas: he has a "sense" that he "had lived this moment before" (411). The other man asks him pertinently how it was that he had forgotten meeting the older self of Borges as a young man in 1918 (415). The narrator's observation about the young man's whistling – "I have never been able to carry a tune" (411) – is a hint that "the other man" and "I" are two selves of the same person. He becomes certain of this when he hears the other's voice, which is a blind person's way of recognising people (412). Telling his younger self "'about my past, which is now the future that awaits you'" (413) – history, both personal and collective – he states:

> "As for history ...There was another war, with virtually the same antagonists... England and America battled a German dictator named Hitler—the cyclical Battle of Waterloo. Buenos Aires engendered another Rosas in 1946, much like our kinsman in the first one. In '55, the province of Córdoba saved us, as Entre Ríos had before..."
>
> (413)

In this revelation of the future of the world (for the young man), the narrator suggests that "history" is repetitive and "cyclical" in nature. Talking about books, he asks the other about the works of Fyodor Dostoyevsky, and reports that among the works by the Russian novelist the young man had read was *The Double* (414), surely a suggestive reference. At one point in their conversation, he declares, "'... *Yesterday's man is not today's*, as some Greek said. We two, here on this bench in Geneva or in Cambridge, are perhaps the proof of that'" (italics as in the source, 414; cf. *Selected Non-Fictions* 5). This statement shows that he acknowledges the flow of time and the ever-changing self of man (and woman). The implication is that the two selves of Borges could "perhaps" be two men with totally different personalities. However, he actually believes that they are two selves of the same man. When a difference of opinion about literature arises between them, he remarks, "A half century does not pass without leaving its mark" (416). Further, regarding the differences in their views on metaphors, he says,

> My *alter ego* believed in the imagination, in creation—in the discovery of new metaphors; I myself believed in those that correspond to close and widely acknowledged likenesses, those our imagination has already accepted: old age and death, dreams and life, the flow of time and water. I informed the young man of this opinion, which he himself was to express in a book, years later.
>
> (italics as in the source, 415)

Listening to what the other was saying, the narrator comes to the following conclusion: "There was no point in giving advice, no point in arguing, because the young man's inevitable fate was to be the man that I am now" (416). In Bergson's terms, the views expressed in the two quotations above attest to the fact that the narrator has intuitively grasped the duration of his self. The metaphors he "believed in" prove this. While being aware of the significant differences in their views, he recognises his past embodied in the young man who is his "*alter ego.*" The following remarks point to his awareness of the "survival of the past in the present" (*Introduction to Metaphysics* 41): "We were too different, yet too alike" (416), and "We haven't changed a bit, I thought. Always referring back to books." Here, the narrator recognises, contra Heraclitus, that although the self is in flux, something fixed remains in selfhood. We may then say in Hagberg's words that Borges's "selfhood displays aspects both of fluidity and of fixity that are ungeneralizeable, unsimplifiable" (132). Both narratives featuring doubles of the author demonstrate this understanding.

In the fictional cosmos of both the short stories, the narrators exist in dreams. First, we should observe the following narrative statement from "The Other," which justifies the above claim: "The other man dreamed me, but did not dream me rigorously" (417). Casting our minds back to the opening paragraph of the narrative, we recall that the narrator began by confessing that he has decided to "write about what happened, [because] people will read it as a story and in time I, too, may be able to see it as one" (411). Since the encounter with his younger self led to his realising that he was dreamt into existence, he desperately wants to convince himself that "what happened" was merely a story and not true. As he remarks to the other man, who has just asserted that he is *"'dreaming you,'"* if their encounter is a dream, "'then each of us does have to think that he alone is the dreamer'" (412). Thus, the narrator wants to believe that he "'is the dreamer,'" and not the young man. His words "I spoke to him while I was awake" (417) may be understood as arising from this desire. Each believes, then, that he "alone" exists in reality, and is therefore in his 'own time.' However, it is important to note that the narrator does not possess the silver piece that the other man gave him. So he cannot prove to himself (and to the reader) that he really does exist. In the case of "August 25, 1983," the key statement is: "Outside awaited other dreams" (493). The fact that the narrator-character is not, at the end of the short story, in "the hotel in the town of Adrogué," as he asserted earlier in his conversation with his older self,[9] shows that he exists in a dream. Further, the title of the short story, which refers to the present – "today" (489) – of the older self of the man, Jorge Luis Borges, that is, August 25, 1983, indicates that the dream was dreamt by this man on that date. What constitutes the most telling evidence that this is so is the fact that the older self, who is blind, recognises his younger self as soon as he opens the door to his room and stands in the light (490). The older self knows that his younger self is standing at the door because he is dreaming him.

Dreaming, then, is an important theme in both "The Other" and "August 25, 1983." In the former, the narrator says, "'... when one wakes up, the person one meets is always oneself. That is what's happening to us now, except that we are two'" (413). They are different but alike. It is in this light that the older self indicates thrice in "August 25, 1983" that they "'are two yet ... are one'" (490–91). This phenomenon is significant because self-recognition is the question at issue here. It is for this reason that there are so many things in both the short stories which act as mirrors, things that reflect. In Bergson's terms, we may say that memory, dreaming, and books of literature play the role of mirrors in the two short stories, showing an ever-changing self and reality. In "The Other," the narrator states, "'My dream ... has already lasted for seventy years'" (413). Life is described metaphorically as a dream in this statement because the person attempting to understand the ever-changing nature of reality and the self undergoes a dream-like experience. Therefore, Bergson insists that "an absolute [such as reality and the self] can only be given in an intuition" (*Introduction to Metaphysics* 6). That dreaming is related to intuiting the self becomes evident in "August 25, 1983." There the narrator-character states that on opening the door to Room 19 in the hotel in Adrogué, he encountered himself, older and disabled: "In the pitiless light, I came face to face with myself. There, in the narrow iron

---

9 The temporal loop seen in "The Other" is also present in "August 25, 1983" because in it, as in the former short story, there is a meeting between two selves of Borges. The idea of circular time is expressed by the older self when he declares "the conviction of having already lived each day" (492). Further, both stories contain references to existence in "two times and two places" (417, 493), a highly suggestive narrative feature.

bed—older, withered, and very pale—lay I, on my back, my eyes turned up vacantly toward the high plaster mouldings of the ceiling" (489). In directly grasping his self in the dream, Borges realises that he is old and blind. Thus, the process of understanding the self involves recognising bodily deformities, and coming to terms with them.

I have attempted in this chapter to examine how Borges deals with blindness and other deformities in his literary creations with the objective of showing the complex ways in which disabilities play a role in self-understanding. Bodily deformities are a concrete reminder of the fragility of the human body, and of the continuous change that characterises reality and the self. With the help of Bergson's insights such as "intuition" and "duration," I have explored what it means to experience life, which is temporal in nature, in the world as a disabled person. It emerges from the study of the short stories that to "know the duration of the self" in the case of the disabled characters portrayed therein is to accept their disabilities and to fashion new lives. Bergson distrusts concepts (*Introduction to Metaphysics* 48–9). I have endeavoured to illuminate Borges's short stories by means of presenting characters and metaphors, thereby attempting to deploy Bergson's philosophy in a creative manner. As we have seen, Borges experiments with a variety of narrative positions in order to problematise the process of self-comprehension and self-presentation. Fictional narratives must necessarily take into account the physical, sensory world. Faced with the paradox of personal loss and artistic imperative, he invents an alternative narrative dynamics based on a creative, tropological use of bodily sensations in acts of recall and imagination. With this, we move on to the next chapter, where I present an interpretation of two diaries which record the growth of the self in Hull into blindness.

4   The Everyday Experience of Growing Blind

Narrative Subjectivity in Hull

In writing about the narrative subjectivity of John M. Hull (1935–2015) as a blind person in two chapters, I shall explore a movement in his self, and in his understanding of it as evident in his two diaries – or two editions of a single diary – *Touching the Rock: An Experience of Blindness* (1990), and *On Sight and Insight: A Journey into the World of Blindness* (1997). The latter is "an enlarged and revised edition" (*On Sight* xi) of the former diary. He developed the books out of recordings he had made "on cassette [of his] daily experiences" (*Touching the Rock* ix) over a period of "three years" (x) as stated in *Touching the Rock*, and "three or four years" (xi) in the case of *On Sight and Insight*. As the words (addressed directly to the reader), "In reading this book, you ... want to know what it is like to go blind, and to be blind" (*Touching the Rock* ix) suggest, the diarist describes an evolution in his selfhood over the period covered by his diaries. He characterises it as a "transition from being a sighted person who could not see to being a blind person." These words signify a shift from one way of being-in-the-world to another, and understanding that change in his reality. Comprehending "the truth of being blind," that is to say, one's existence, is tied up with reflecting on one's "daily experiences." This fact demonstrates the dynamic connection existing between Hull's maintaining the cassette diary and realising his condition of being blind. Recording his daily experiences[1] not only plays a therapeutic role, enabling him "to monitor [his] own reactions to blindness, and thus to keep some sense of balance and control in what was a deeply disturbing period of [his] life" (*On Sight* xi), but also leads to the development of the self and self-knowledge, or in Bruce Merry's words, "discovery of self" (4) as a blind person.

However, as Hull states, this process of self-discovery is neither straightforward nor easy for him:

> Interpretation takes time. This process of reinterpretation is piecemeal; sometimes there are moments of dawning realization; often there are long periods of apparent stagnation. Sometimes the wound of the

---

1 This means that he maintains an audio diary, an important medium for a blind person.

DOI: 10.4324/9781003399667-4

original loss seems never to heal. At other times one feels that the terrible gift has been received and assimilated.

(*On Sight* xii)

This uncertain psychological process, which does not have a pattern as such,
is complemented by or necessitates the fragmentary form of the narrative
sections that make up the two diaries. In talking about a movement in Hull's
being and self-conception, then, we should pay adequate attention to the
fragmentary form of the narrative. This commonplace recognition in literary
criticism carries special significance for the chapters on Hull because he has
used the said narrative form to record and deal with the gradual nature of the
movement in his selfhood, with its alternating gains and setbacks.

4.1 The Narrative Form of the Diaries

Hull describes a person's entry into the world of the blind with a self-constitutive statement: "… those who live in that world have a new consciousness"
(*On Sight* xiii). Thus, when people who have sight lose their vision and
become blind, there is a movement in their selfhood: "Entry into this consciousness, for those who lose sight," says Hull,

is experienced as a fall. At first, the fall is out of consciousness, into the
dreaming life, into the darkness. Later on, in my own case at any rate,
the fall was discovered not to be out of consciousness but into it.

(*On Sight* xiii)

The form of his diaries, with their cumulative effect, is well suited to describe
and examine this process of leaving one kind of consciousness and experiencing the birth of a new consciousness. Thus, he states, "I can only describe
that consciousness and the way to it through the presentation of a series of
fragments. The thing itself is not fragmented but the path to it is experienced
fragmentarily" (*On Sight* xiii). These words provide an answer, at least in
the case of Hull, to Jochen Helbeck's question "Which mechanisms bring an
individual's reflections about self and time into place and account for the
very fact of his/her diary?" (623). Thus, the narrative sections of Hull's
diaries dwell on his daily experiences, and reflect on what it is to lose one's
sight and become blind. They show the difficult process of growing into the
self of a blind person. My analysis will draw from two interpretative texts
by Hull on Christian scripture, namely *In the Beginning There was Darkness:
A Blind Person's Conversations with the Bible* (2001) and *The Tactile Heart:
Blindness and Faith* (2013), which are written from a blind person's
standpoint.

In the foreword to *On Sight and Insight*, Hull says, "I had the recorded
diary turned into a print transcript, and arranged it into chapters" (xi). The
task was accomplished by gathering, assembling, and editing the recorded

fragments on blindness (xiv).[2] The book was published in order to further one of the main objectives of maintaining the cassette diary, as Hull states in the following words:

> I kept the diary ... partly in an attempt to communicate with sighted people. For me, going blind had been an experience of isolation and marginalization, and I wanted to explain myself to the sighted world. I wanted the changes which had come over me and my life to become intelligible to my friends by helping them to have insight into blindness.
>
> (*On Sight* xi)

It becomes evident from these statements about Hull's objective in both maintaining the diary and creating the manuscript that 'ātmakathana,' or narrating the self, which introduces retrospection as a feature of the text, is important in his narrative sections.

I adopt the Indian term mentioned at the conclusion of the previous paragraph from a brief discussion I had with Professor D. Venkat Rao about the concepts of knowing the self and narrating the self as elaborated in Indic philosophical literature in saṃskṛtam. This exchange followed Professor Rao's lecture on J. M. Coetzee, which he delivered on Monday, 24 February 2014, at the English and Foreign Languages University located in Hyderabad, India, as part of a workshop entitled "A Day Seminar on J.M. Coetzee: Pain, Body, Society, Desire, and Animal." While the two above-mentioned concepts regarding the self are clearly distinguished in the Indian philosophical tradition, post-structuralist thought conceives of the self as being constituted by 'writing.' On 5 October 2015, Professor Rao explained this concept of writing as follows:

> Jacques Derrida does not use "writing" in the colloquial sense of the term. His notion of archi-writing, or foundational writing if you like, is not reducible to the colloquial sense of writing. Archi-writing precedes and constitutes both speech and writing as we understand them colloquially... . The structure of writing is identical to the structure of speech... . So there must be something that enables these colloquially differentiated communicative forms to be constituted... . Whatever you may want to talk about, be it memory, intelligence, or intellectual capability, you can do so only through the intervention and mediation of a "communication system" [that is to say] only if you articulate it or give

---

2 The only change the author and editors effected in the text when they converted the cassette diary into a manuscript was to arrange the recorded and dated fragments in titled chapters and narrative sections. From the point of view of genetic criticism, unlike other texts such as long fiction, short stories, or even autobiographies, a diary does not have an "avant-texte" or previous versions of a finished text.

it a form, either verbal or scribal. Derrida calls those finite ["concatenated chain" of] markers elements of archi-writing. Without archi-writing intervening, communication itself is unthinkable... . As far as the relation to the self is concerned, you can understand that any conception of self or any attempt to figure out self is inescapably enmeshed with "communication systems," whether it is visual or verbal, scribal or oral. The conception of self or figuration of self is contingent upon the materiality of communication.

Thus, language is the limitation and condition of knowledge, and therefore of subjectivity. This view may be characterised as representing "a language-dependency position" (Hagberg 122) on selfhood. While I do not adopt Derrida's strong position on language, I concur with the conception as cautiously articulated by Hagberg, viz. that self-descriptive language is "self-defining" or "self-creative" (149). Therefore, I recognise that the creative use of words allows the authors whose works I study in this book to conceive of the self in the process of articulation.

The fragmentary form of the narrative sections constituting Hull's diaries not only draws the reader's attention to the elements of retrospection and "immediacy and the fragmentary character of this experience" (*On Sight* 232), but also lays emphasis on the reflective nature of the books. In the introduction to his translation of Aristotle's *Poetics* (2006), Joe Sachs highlights the importance of imaginative reflection in relation to action or "praxis" (2):

> ... the worth of poetry is even greater if action can become visible nowhere but in an image. An action is stretched out in time, so that even in life, we can comprehend it nowhere but in the imagination. And its origin, in the act of choice, is interior, and never available to us in another person except by an act of interpretation. Even our own choices are not always recognized when they are made, but only evident to us retrospectively.
>
> (3)

This statement serves as a commentary on Hull's reaction to blindness, which encompasses reflections on his experiences as recorded in the diaries.[3] Thus, in each of the narrative sections (all of which constitute an imaginative, interpretative response to blindness), he reflects on an experience or experiences that he has had in the recent past in dreams and in waking life. Moreover, these fragments record a slow and halting transformation in his self-conception, as is clear from his words about the difficult process of interpreting newly acquired blindness, and of understanding himself as a blind person (*On Sight* xii). Further, he states, "In this book I have gathered together a

---

3 They also illuminate the interpretative exercise undertaken in this book.

number of aspects of the life of this particular blind person so as to form a sort of mosaic which seeks to interpret the blind condition" (*On Sight* xiii). This quotation attests to the fact that he (and the editor) prepared the book manuscript in such a way that the narrative as a whole would constitute an interpretation of "the blind condition."

The "Preface" (ix–x) to *Touching the Rock*, and the "Foreword" (xi–xiv) to *On Sight and Insight* demonstrate why the retrospective character of the diaries is important: the two opening sections may be read as the latest in the narrative entries forming the diaries. Hull writes (or more correctly, dictates) the former in July 1989, the latter in April 1997; that is to say, just before the manuscripts went to press. The dates recorded at the end of both entries make it clear that the author has written them with the publication of the books in mind after turning the diary on tape into "a print transcript," and arranging the recordings in clear-cut chapters. From the wistful character of the words concerning blindness (which are from the "Preface") "It would be nice to be able to say that there was a happy ending, that a miracle happened, but it didn't" (*Touching the Rock* x) we may infer that Hull experiences blindness as a loss and a cause for sadness. This state of his mind means that even after he has made the (difficult) transition from the conception of himself as "a sighted person who could not see" to that of a blind person, he still regards blindness as an undesirable condition. In the "Foreword," on the other hand, we see that he has settled into blindness:

> ... the life of a person who is blind is experienced as a whole. Losing one's sight is not quite like losing a limb. The blind person does not always remain conscious of something missing. The personality regroups; there is a process of healing and reintegration which leaves the life of the blind person complete and entire although smaller than it was before... . A new consciousness was born.
>
> (*On Sight* xii–xiii)

This passage presents a self-conception that wholly incorporates blindness.

Hull begins *Touching the Rock* by saying that a "couple of years" (ix) after losing his sight, his interest "in blindness" was aroused. Prompted by his scholarly bent of mind, he read many first-hand accounts of blindness. His objective in reading the books was to learn about life in the blind condition, and about how it would affect him. Those blind people's stories amazed him because "they were often full of humour, courage and ingenuity." However, he says, "I did not find what I was looking for: an account of blindness as I knew it." As he read those stories, "focusing on a coherent collection of described characteristics to the exclusion of others" (Hagberg 131), asking himself as a reader "to what extent, and in what precise ways" he was "similar to and different from them," he increasingly came to realise that the books did not speak to his experience of blindness. He found them unsatisfactory because he did not, as Danto would put it, recognise any aspect of the self in those novelistic autobiographies.[4] As metaphoric mirrors, then, those works did not show Hull "the aspects of blindness which were more significant to [him]" (*Touching the Rock* ix). Therefore, he found it necessary to fall back upon his own resources to figure out, in a way that corresponded to the uniqueness of his self and experience, "what it [was] like to go blind, and to be blind." These observations clarify the intellectual source and route of Hull's cassette diary, to wit: the (unsatisfactory) reading on blindness that he engaged in, and the desire to represent to himself his conscious and unconscious responses to visual loss by means of "verbal descriptions and expressions" (11) because, to quote the pragmatist philosopher Richard Shusterman, "uttered or written formulation gives thought an exterior expression that enables the subject herself to experience it in a different way, allowing for more critical distance." Hull could "play the tape back to [himself]" (*On Sight* 203), listen to himself as an observer, and process his experiences in blindness.

Contrasting his book on blindness with the "more than twenty autobiographies of people who had gone blind" (*Touching the Rock* ix) which he read after losing his "own sight" in the early 1980s, Hull says that those books were literary in character: "they had a beginning, a middle and an end. They were like novels, with an interesting style, a climax or a resolution." Clearly, those accounts of blindness were fashioned according to Aristotle's precepts about the dramatic structure of a literary work which consist in "the inherent connections that constitute a well-made story" (Sachs 3). Writing about the "common structure" (133) typically followed by memoirs that deal with "psychological problems like addiction" – which are similar to illness narratives or memoirs about disability experience, Abigail Gosselin criticises such works for adhering to "a plotline that has a clear beginning, a dramatic middle, and a tidily resolved ending." Such narratives, she continues, "offer sensationalistic drama that safely contains the pain, messiness, and monotony of actual experience, and they often provide moral lessons as well." Her objection to this narrative aesthetic is that it simplifies experience and "does not reflect the lived reality of most people" (cf. Fludernik 23–4). Hull shares this concern, which is seen in his words about the literary autobiographies that failed to speak to him: they did not offer, as he puts it, "an account of blindness as I knew it.... . All I can say is that the books I did read did not write about the aspects of blindness which were more significant to me" (*Touching the Rock* ix). So he decided to maintain his own cassette diary and publish it as a fragmentary narrative, a form which he favoured as most suited to record his changing condition. Thus, his assertion that his "book is not like that," that is, like the literary accounts on blindness which he read finds support in the fragmentary form of his

---

4 Here, I draw upon ideas that Danto deals with in the essay entitled "Philosophy and/as/of Literature" (52–67).

diaries, and in the statement, "It [his book] has no particular ending, because blindness has no ending" (*Touching the Rock* x). In the words of Jibu Mathew George, this quotation foregrounds "the non-terminal character of subjectivity." Hagberg indicates the rich potential of this kind of subjectivity when he writes on the necessity of continuously extending our effort to understand the self: "And it is literature that affords an opportunity to reflect upon, to extend, to reweave, and ... to create those self-constitutive relations of psychological association and meaning-contributing connotation" (136). As Hull grapples with his blindness, he achieves understanding only gradually, with repetition in the issues that he faces and continual reversals. He says, "If there is repetition, it is because the same problems and the same experiences went round and round, interpreted from many aspects" (*Touching the Rock* x). Thus, the reflection on and extension of "relations of psychological association and meaning-contributing connotation" play a central role in the very process of constituting the self.

Hull uses the words "sub plot" and "plot," where "plot" is a common translation of Aristotle's term "muthos," to refer to the entries which deal with dreams in the diaries: "The dream narratives form *a sort of sub plot, if it can be called a plot,* since the conscious material shows how the unconscious mind struggled with the problem" (emphasis added, *Touching the Rock* x). These words show Hull's uncertainty about the use of the term "plot" to describe the narrative sections that deal with "the unconscious life of dreams" (*On Sight* 59). Sachs criticises the rendering of the Greek word "muthos" as "plot" in English translations of the *Poetics* because this practice diminishes the critical importance of "story" which, according to him, is the correct translation of the word (3). He explains, "The word 'plot' may suggest a skeletal framework of events onto which a poet can impose an illusion of life, but stories are genuine wholes that already have a life of their own" (Sachs 4). The translation of the word "muthos" as "story" (rather than as "plot") helps us consider the dream narratives in Hull's diaries as forming a subsidiary part of the main story which sheds important light on his emotions and activities in conscious life.

4.2 Life and (Diary) Text

In his "Introduction" (*On Sight* 1–9) to both diaries, Hull gives a brief autobiographical account of himself, covering in a few pages his life from his birth "on 22 April 1935 in Corryong, a town in North Eastern Victoria" (*On Sight* 1) to the point when he knew that he had finally lost his eyesight. He "registered blind" (*On Sight* 9) in 1980. He says that he found himself facing "a curious situation" one day in September of that year. When he returned from the eye hospital to his office at Birmingham University where he taught, he was confronted with a host of problems relating to his blindness. These included a fast-approaching, new teaching term at the university, and "files of notes representing years of work, all of which was now inaccessible."⁵ He goes on to say:

> The solving of these problems occupied the years 1980 to 1983, and might be the theme of a book in itself. *Touching the Rock* does not describe these years but deals instead with the years 1983-86. In 1983 the last light sensations faded and the dark discs had finally over-whelmed me. I had fought them bravely, as it seemed to me, for thir-ty-six years, but all to no avail. It was then I began to sink into the deep ocean, and finally learned how to touch the rock on the far side of despair.
>
> (*On Sight* 9)

Thus, the transition in Hull's selfhood actually consists of two movements covering three main conceptions of the self: an initial movement from the first state of being a sighted person to the second one of "being a sighted person who could not see," and then a further movement from the second position to the third state of "being a blind person." As is clear from this discussion, the two diaries deal, to a large extent, with the second movement. Although in 1970 Hull "began a decade of failing vision" (*On Sight* 8) and lost his sight almost completely by 1980, he began maintaining his cassette diary only "In June of 1983" (*Touching the Rock* ix). This passage of two and a half years between recognition of blindness and the commencement of recording accounts for the retrospective nature of the diaries. The reasons for this delay are clearly stated in the previous long quotation: first, it was in 1983, when "the last light sensations faded and the dark discs had finally overwhelmed [him]," and his fight against advancing blindness in the form of medical care and a series of surgeries over "thirty-six years" had failed, that he finally started to realise the nature of the blind condition and "began to sink into the deep ocean ... of despair." Secondly, he was kept busy for "about two and a half years" (*Touching the Rock* ix), from 1980 to 1983, solving many of the problems that he confronted as a blind person. In light of this discussion, we can describe Hull's cassette diary as "an expression of being" (Helbeck 626), which was motivated by "the existential urges ground-ing the act of writing," where for a blind person "the act of writing" means the act of recording. Helbeck's words show the personal importance to the diarist of writing (or keeping) his diary, and suggest that there is a "direct, substantive interaction [between life and text]" (626–27).

---

5 This situation in which Hull cannot read (or visually access) any written material is strikingly similar to the one faced by Borges in 1955 when he lost his sight and was made the director of the National Library of Argentina. Borges remarks, "There I was, the center, in a way, of nine hundred thousand books in various languages, but I found I could barely make out the title pages and the spines" (*Selected Non-Fictions* 475). As mentioned in both Chapter 2 and Chapter 3, the "Poem of the Gifts" speaks of this irony.

When Hull reflects on blindness and his experiences in the entries of his diaries, he is narrating the self in the sense that he is reflecting on the recent experiences that he has had. As George explains, "That one experiences something is not necessarily an evidence of some core identity, but when there is a subject which reflects on the past, the reflecting self can be cited as an evidence." This observation leads to the conclusion that when Hull records his diary, it is the present position from which he is creating it through reflection that constitutes the evidence of the self. This statement amounts to articulating the idea that the narration begins from an initial position of what the self means to the author:

> There is a provisional understanding of the self with which one begins
> ... and of the assumptions on which one bases judgements about the
> past... . There is very less focus in literary criticism on the dynamics of
> writing. Writing is a temporal process, and many things happen in time;
> there is something artistically critical about the very dynamics of writ-
> ing which cannot be underestimated.
>
> (George)

This passage acts as an accurate description of what happens to Hull's self-conception in the course of the two diaries and his books on the Bible, as I intend to show in this chapter and the next. He starts off with an initial notion of the self as a sighted entity in his diaries. He has lost his sight when he begins keeping the cassette diary, but he still conceives of himself as a sighted person who cannot see. The diary records with a deep sense of loss, repeated setbacks, and understanding achieved along the way a slow evolution towards a conception of himself as a blind person.

4.3   Dreaming and Waking Life

As suggested earlier, the life of dreams forms a major theme in the diaries, reflecting on which Hull makes sense of his blindness. The importance to him of interpreting dreams in relation to his journey into the blind condition may be understood from the words, "I was interested in what would happen to my dreams" (*Touching the Rock* X). It is also clear from the fact that he begins the book with a narrative section dealing with dreaming. "Dreaming 1 June 1983" (*On Sight* 10–11) continues to reflect on the idea articulated in the above quotation. The diarist asks the pertinent question, "How long do you have to be blind before your dreams begin to lose colour [and pictures]?" (*On Sight* 10). He contrasts a few significant experiences (where his vision is rather tenuous) which he has had over the last three years as a family man with his dreams during the same time, and wonders about the vivid visual character of the latter. He uses the phrase "colourful freedom" to describe his sense of freedom while dreaming, which indicates his attitude to his blindness. It cuts him off from the world, and forces him to feel imprisoned within himself. So he narrates a visual dream[6] he has of his two-and-a-half-year-old son, Thomas, and then describes his birth, which took place soon after his own "final eye operation": "A lot of the time I did not know what was happening." He is puzzled that although he has been "a registered blind person for nearly three years," and "totally blind" for a few months, his dreams continue to be colourful. This feature presupposes utilisation by the dreaming mind of images stored in Hull's memories. So, there is a conflict between the conscious and unconscious states of the self, which is brought out by the question, "Has blindness, then, made any impact upon my dreams at all?" The relationship between waking and dreaming is, therefore, the theme of this entry.

"Dreaming of the White Cane 3 June 1983" (*On Sight* 11–12) sharpens the focus of the issue concerning the relationship between Hull's blindness and his dreams when he says, "This is the first time I have dreamt of myself as being a blind person" (*On Sight* 11). We have seen above that he treats his dreams as subsidiary narratives (*Touching the Rock* x). This particular narrative portrays him as forgetting his "white cane on the train" (*On Sight* 11), and then "using [a long metal tube] to explore [his] path," thus demonstrating that his unconscious mind recognises him to be a blind man. However, he points out a number of "unresolved contradictions" in the dream, such as the following one: when he is walking along near the station, sweeping the metal tube from side to side in order to make sure that the path is safe, he notices "that the people in the area around the station were looking at [him] curiously." Since Hull is a blind man who has to tap his cane as he walks, it is indeed curious that he is able, as he states, to "see the reactions of the people around me" to his presence. He also "examine[s] the map to see where the station was." So, in representing a blind Hull who is "dependent upon a [substitute] cane" to find his way, but who can nevertheless see things (or perceive images), the dream evidences a gap in the diarist's unconscious mind. This gap may be perceived between his present reality of total blindness (portrayed as a blind man in the dream narrative), and his mode of dreaming in the medium of images.

In "Dreaming 1 June 1983" and "Dreaming of the White Cane 3 June 1983," Hull is able to vaguely connect his dreams to experiences (which he only alludes to) he has had about "six months ago" (*On Sight* 10), and about "a year or so before our wedding" (*On Sight* 11),[7] which makes it five years earlier (1978), respectively. By contrast, in "I Can Still Manage 8 June 1983" (*On Sight* 13), he is able to say with fair certainty that "My dreams seem to be lagging about six years behind reality" (*On Sight* 13). This statement comes after he describes a dream "in which [he] was walking along a river

---

6 I mean by this a dream where the self portrayed in the story experiences the sequence of incidents as being visual in character.

7 Hull and Marilyn got married on "1 November 1979" (*On Sight* 9) just a few months before the former "registered blind."

valley" while "on a walking holiday.." In it, he is represented as being a partially sighted man who "found that [he] could get a sufficient sense of the
place to move freely and to enjoy the scenery." This statement suggests that
although Hull's unconscious mind has recognised him as a blind person in
the dream recorded previously, blindness has not yet sufficiently influenced
the representation of experiences[8] in his dreams. When Hull characterises the
dream under discussion as being "a beautiful, refreshing dream," he is talking about the vivid, colourful freedom that he experiences as a still-sighted
person who cannot see. He goes on to relate the words "'can still manage'"
to his identical waking thought, which he says he has "been having ... for at
least ten years." This period of time roughly corresponds to the "decade of
failing vision" (*On Sight* 8) that he began in 1970. This narrative shows that
the loss of Hull's eyesight was gradual, like that of Borges.[9]

The diaries contain complementary pairs and, sometimes, even a cluster
of entries that deal with one idea or a similar topic. This is the case despite
the fact that days, months, and, in a couple of cases, even years intervene
between one entry and another. This sustained reflection upon a theme
means that it receives the diarist's attention from various perspectives over
the period of time that it interests him. This narrative practice, in turn, lets
the reader mark the changes in Hull's self-conception. One pair of dreams
narrated in two recording sessions that are separated by twenty days may be
read in the entries entitled "Sinking 16 September 1983" (*On Sight* 28–9)
and "The Waterfall 6 October 1983" (*On Sight* 35). Hull interprets both
dreams as metaphorical stories of how he is coping with blindness. In the
former entry, he narrates a visual dream where he sinks into the dark ocean.
So this dream may be linked with the words that Hull employs at the end of
the introductory chapter to indicate his first confrontation with blindness:
"[I] began to sink into the deep ocean" (*On Sight* 9). First, he finds himself
"struggling towards the stern" (*On Sight* 28) of an ocean liner with another
person (from the beginning, he uses the plural pronoun "we"), possibly a
woman, because he says that "it could have been Marilyn." Marilyn is Hull's
second wife. The dreamer receives no explanation for being forced to make
his way along with his companion, with difficulty, to the rear of the ship.
Since for Hull this "ship that moves away with its light and speed [repre-
sents] the world of the sighted" (*On Sight* 29), his exit from the visual world

8 I refer to comprehending objects through touch, recognising voices, and identifying objects
   through the sounds they produce, all of which the blind typically do when they are awake.
9 As mentioned in Chapter 2, Manguel states that Borges's "blindness [was] expected since his
   birth" (16). Coincidentally, in Hull's case too, as the following words show, his blindness
   was expected long before he lost his sight totally: "The curious thing is that I myself at the
   age of nineteen, having conceived a desire to enter the ministry of the Methodist church, was
   enormously distressed to find that the church authorities were reluctant to accept me because
   of the poor state of my own sight, and the threat of blindness which was already hanging
   over me" (*On Sight* 116). This incident would have occurred in 1954. It would be another
   twenty-nine years before he started grappling with the reality of his blindness.

may be interpreted as something meant to occur. Thus, as the diarist continues to narrate, both he and his companion were "transported over the stern of the ship and now I found myself with two [unknown] women on another ship" (*On Sight* 28). This second ship is sinking in a sea that is not wild but sullen, while the other ship is "going away, leaving us further and further behind." He finds that they are "clearly marooned" in the vessel which is sinking fast. He interprets the dream by enlarging on the collective impact of blindness upon not only himself as a blind person, but also upon his family:

> My family, my loved ones, and I are pushing our way through it [the first, well-lit ship which is departing]. We are stranded, increasingly cut off. We are immobile, waterlogged. I am being dragged down and down into something unimaginable from which there will be no return. One world will disappear. The world into which I am being dragged with my loved ones will engulf us. There will be no return. Blindness is permanent and irreversible.
>
> (*On Sight* 29)

He realises that his sighted self will cease to exist along with the disappearance of the world of sight, and that he and his "loved ones" will be engulfed by the "unimaginable" world of blindness. The passage makes it clear that blindness deeply affects not only the person who is (becoming) blind, but also their loved ones. This realisation brings to the fore the fact that we are members of a social group (or groups), and are all affected by something that happens to each one of us. Hull understands this dream – which fills his mind with a "terrible sense of dread and hopelessness" (*On Sight* 28) – to be an indication that his "dreaming self is, after all, not deceived" (*On Sight* 29). Hull's dreaming self knows that momentous changes are taking place in his consciousness. Here, the phrase "after all" perhaps alludes to the visual character of his recent dreams despite his total blindness for many months.

In the visual dream, strikingly different from the previous one, narrated in "The Waterfall 6 October 1983," Hull finds himself and Marilyn "in a religious house, some kind of retreat centre ... high in the mountains" (*On Sight* 35). From a "very lofty, very peaceful" chapel, they view "a majestic waterfall" consisting of a "great bank of water ['reddish brown ... with silt'] shooting over from the top." Then they walk "beside the sea," and watch "mighty ['brown'] waves" pounding upon "the seawall, along the promenade" beside (or at the base of) which is dug a "huge moat." The diarist says that the "atmosphere of this dream was peaceful and refreshing." The powerful waters forming the towering waterfall and the mighty sea, instead of washing him away or submerging him under their terrible weight, appear to him as visions of great beauty and sublimity. Comparing his previous and present dreams, Hull says:

> I awoke with a sense of having received a revelation, of having been in
> an awe-inspiring presence. Could this dream *be a foil to* the ominous
> one about the sinking vessel? There, the waters were sullen and heavy.
> Here, although no less powerful, they are cascading with movement,
> energy and control. In one dream I am being submerged. In the other, I
> am being elevated and renewed. I feel that these are big dreams.
>
> (emphasis added, *On Sight* 35)

This passage shows the direct connection between dreaming and waking, in
that Hull wakes from the dream refreshed because it leaves him "with a sense
of having received a revelation" from God. This religious interpretation is
supported by his presence in the dream in a beautiful, peaceful chapel. In
fact, in the dream, he and Marilyn discuss "the possibility of spending a
longer time there, or even living there" (*On Sight* 35). The diarist acknowledges the link between the dream related in "Sinking 16 September 1983,"
and the one dealt with in the present entry. He even feels "that these are big
dreams" in his journey because he gets motivated to go on despite facing
difficulties and occasional despair.

The entry entitled "Playing the Recorder 30 November 1983" (*On Sight*
39–40) is of significance to the diaries as a whole for two reasons: first, in it,
Hull introduces a principle of analysis that can be applied to his dreams
throughout the text. And secondly, through the "musical dream" (*On Sight*
39) narrated here, he shows that his dreaming self recognises for the first time
the disruptive impact (he uses the phrase "the cause of a crisis") that blindness has on his life. Therefore, the dream "marks an important step." He
describes two visual dreams in the entry. In the first dream, he is a musician
who plays the recorder in "a small orchestra." The orchestra is about to
begin playing the music, and he finds himself, as he states,

> in a terrible state because I could not read the music. I was blind. I had
> no idea what I should play. There was a part for the solo recorder, and
> I was very nervous about what I would do when it came to this part.... .
> For the first time I am in a situation where blindness is recognised to be
> the cause of a crisis.
>
> (*On Sight* 39)

Phrases such as "a question of competence" (*On Sight* 39), "a public disgrace
and ... letting one's colleagues down," and "a terrible panicky feeling of
helplessness" all make it clear that he interprets the dream as representing the
negative effects that blindness has on the performance of his duties.

However, despite not being able to "read the music" (*On Sight* 39) due to
blindness, he does "have a very distinct visual impression of the photocopied,
handwritten transcript of the words, the lyrics which somebody was to sing,"
and (in a second dream) even has "the most vivid impression of his [Thomas's]
features. [Hull sees] his face with the utmost clarity." It is from this

discrepancy between being blind in the dream, and nevertheless being able to see things vividly therein, that the diarist derives a principle or method of analysing his dreams. He distinguishes "between the way that blindness affects the process of dreaming and the way it affects the contents of the dream." This distinction serves to explicate how his "personality regroups" (*On Sight* xii) after he loses his sight. In the dream dealt with in this entry, blindness influences "the contents of the dream" because the dream pictures him as being blind. Thus, it is an example, as Hull puts it, of "the way in which the actual story of the dream recognises blindness, whether in the dream I encounter the problems of blindness, or know myself as being blind" (*On Sight* 40). However, a gap exists between the contents of the dream, and the way he dreams about people and places for which he has no visual images and details like colour. Despite his inability to "make anything out at all of the music itself" (*On Sight* 39) due to blindness, he perceives some vivid images in this dream. Tracking this distinction (and gap) through the successive dream narratives of the diaries will give us a sense of the changes in his selfhood over time. In *Touching the Rock*, he articulates such an understanding: "I was interested in what would happen to my dreams... . The relationship between dreaming and waking, and the nature of consciousness itself, is one of the persistent themes of the book" (x). Thus, he believes that, by means of this rigorous interpretation of his dream life, he can gain a fuller understanding of the blind self which was once sighted.

The next two entries concerning dreams (separated by three months) which I am going to write about deal with Hull's blindness in relation to his family members. The first of the two follows two months after the entry last discussed. "Loss 2 February 1984" (*On Sight* 49–50) relates a vividly visual nightmare in which Hull's daughter Elizabeth, who is nearly two years old, is dead and buried. This is unknown to the dreamer. As Hull reports in the following words, he is broken and furious: "I grabbed her [Marilyn] by the shoulders, and shook her fiercely, shouting out, 'What do you mean? How dare you! Is she not only dead but buried, and I not even told?'" (*On Sight* 50). He even sees the "slow" funeral procession moving over a "grassy plot" as well as "people's clothes, the green of the grass and the bright colours of the flowers." Analysing the dream narrative according to the distinction "between the way that blindness affects the process of dreaming, and the way it affects the contents of the dream" (*On Sight* 39), it may be perceived immediately that it displays "no trace of blindness" (*On Sight* 50). It is clear that, on both counts ("the process of dreaming" and "the contents of the dream"), it does not refer to Hull's altered sensory life. However, he does connect it to this theme through the experience of loss. In the process of portraying a story of terrible loss, the dream combines in Hull's reflection "the many faces of loss" (*On Sight* 50), including those that he considers to be brought about by blindness, and the ones resulting from his first, broken marriage: "Was it Imogen who was dead, lost first through divorce and distance and lost again through the isolating effect of blindness?" Thus, blindness makes it necessary for Hull to grapple not only with the consequences following from the lack of sight, but also with other sorrowful events in his life.[10]

"Making Love in the Pub 1 May 1984" (*On Sight* 74) continues to dwell on the theme of loss, because the dream narrated in the entry presents a situation where "his [Hull's] wife and daughter have been involved in an accident" (*On Sight* 74), and he cannot "get to them fast enough." More specifically, the dream emerges from Hull's "fear of losing Marilyn through blindness," which is allayed at its end. The statement which closes the entry, "This is a dream about blindness as well as a blind person's dream," clearly shows that the distinction between the way that blindness influences the mode of dreaming, and the way it affects the story of the dream is of significance to this dream narrative as well. When Hull says that it "is a dream about blindness," he means that "the contents of the dream" (*On Sight* 40) figure him as a blind man; that is to say, "the actual story of the dream recognises blindness." He explains, "In this dream I hear myself described as a blind man, I see myself holding a stick, I once again sense the panic of not being able to get quickly enough to loved ones in distress" (*On Sight* 74). The words "a blind person's dream" suggest "the way that blindness affects the process of dreaming" (*On Sight* 39). Although the diarist uses the words "scene" (*On Sight* 74) and "image" to describe a shift in his dream from the couple making love in the pub "to the crowded bar" and himself, respectively, none of these details are significantly visual. Instead, he first hears himself "*described as a blind man*" (emphasis added), and then has "an image of [him]self, holding the white cane, hearing the notice, stupefied with anxiety." The description is dominated by auditory details such as the repeated notice about the accident, "a scream" of anguish from Hull, and his relieved talk in the dream with his wife and daughter, Imogen, at the end of the distressing experience. Thus, the gap between the story of the dream and the process of dreaming is small, in that blindness does shape both elements.

I have had occasion before to note that Hull uses the metaphor of "sink[ing] into the deep ocean" to talk about starting (in 1983) to grapple with the reality of being blind. In fact, he makes use of the sea or ocean as a symbol in several successive entries throughout the books, in the course of which its symbolic meaning gradually morphs. Following the use of the symbol through the text of the two diaries may serve to throw light on the movement in the diarist's selfhood. His words in the entry "Darkness is as Light with Thee 27 February 1984" (*On Sight* 56–60) illustrate this point by correlating blindness, the sea, and the "world of the unconscious depths": "I may, perhaps,

---

10   I am grateful to Dr Ravi S. Bhat, who is a psychiatrist, for this insight. Hull does make the link between different kinds of loss. But the following psychological experience, which Dr Bhat explained to me, helped me understand this entry better: when a person becomes blind late in life, they grapple not only with the shock of the disability, but also with other losses that they have suffered in life. The latter return to such a person's mind with a renewed power to cause suffering.

live beneath the sea, in that world of the unconscious depths" (*On Sight* 58). "Above and Below the Sea 2 March 1984" (*On Sight* 60–1) explores these interconnected issues when it presents "[a] most powerful, frightening and impressive dream" (*On Sight* 60) which is set at sea. The action takes place "on board a huge ship," which is in the process of being overwhelmed (or sunk, which is significant in the case of Hull) by "[g]iant waves," as well as on a submarine which is deployed "on some kind of mission" (*On Sight* 61). The narrative is striking for the vivid visuality of the imagery used to describe the experiences that Hull undergoes in the dream. The words "Above and below blindness" show that the adventure he has (along with known and unknown others) above the sea alludes to his past sighted life, and the one that he has "under the water" acts as a symbol of blindness. Further, the words that end the entry, namely "loss," "failure," "incomprehensible," and "irresistible," are all used to express the diarist's grief and shock both at going blind, and at having the frightening experiences in the dream. So the dream narrative has only a symbolic connection to Hull's blindness.

The entry which appears under the title "Submarine 13 August 1984" (*On Sight* 108–10) narrates an entirely visual dream in which Hull sees "no trace of blindness" (*On Sight* 109) but a cinematic narrative display "in beautiful, impressive colour." He closes the entry analysed in the previous paragraph, namely "Above and Below the Sea 2 March 1984," with a question: "is there to be a meeting with something down there [in the ocean]?" (*On Sight* 61). The dream in the present narrative, which is "set entirely in the depths of the ocean" (*On Sight* 108) with nothing "above the surface" being shown, suggests an answer to Hull's question at least on three metaphorical levels. First, it depicts a huge underwater vessel which is "rather like a gigantic, elongated, flying saucer equipped with jet engines" (*On Sight* 109), a craft possessing "vast power" "travelling through the depths of the ocean" (for which two-fold reason the title "Submarine" is appropriate). The situation portrayed in the dream, with "the crew trying to interpret their instruments" and not knowing "whether the craft was travelling forwards or backwards," leads us to understand that the submarine is to all purposes blind. The fact that the dream is "divided between scenes of the outside of the submarine and those of the inside" heightens the impact because, despite its detailed visuality, the dream's power to depict is contained by the ocean's depths. Hull actually recognises this when he writes that both the submarine and the ocean symbolise his blindness. While the process of dreaming does not recognise the dreamer's blindness (the images projected are vividly visual), the content of the dream does so only metaphorically. Hull interprets the dream to mean that his difficulties 'in blindness' are understood by "the depths":

The submarine is blind, and sees as I do. But the ocean is also blind, and the submarine moves through it, trying to find direction and contact. Now I am the ocean; now I am the submarine. I am also the submarine and the ocean at the same time. The dream is me and yet it is greater than me.

(*On Sight* 109)

Here, he declares his oneness with the ocean. His words suggest that he thinks of the ocean, which "is also blind," as God and life at the same time. Both of these, it is clear, are "greater than me [i.e., himself]." There is, in the entry, an element of deep mysticism, expressed especially in the words, "my lifelong love affair with God" (*On Sight* 110). This sense is strengthened when we read what Hull has to say about his filial connection to his parents:

> Visiting my parents always makes me aware of the connection between my faith in God and my relationship with them. I have no doubt that my lifelong love affair with God is, at least partly, an expression of my lifelong attempt to know and love my father, and to be known and loved by him.
>
> (*On Sight* 110)

This mystical reflection suggests that the "meeting ... down there" is with his blind self, which is nourished by his God.

The two words "direction and contact" (*On Sight* 109) in the passage (quoted in the previous paragraph) about the blindness of both the submarine and the ocean lead us to the second and third levels of meaning that emerge when the dream is analysed. Describing the dream as a visual treat (which he compares to a film), Hull observes, "The outside world seldom comes home to me with such vividness." This statement points to a major problem that he faces after losing his sight. He feels – for a long time *finds that he is* correctly describes his view – cut off from the outside world because he cannot see all that surrounds him (more about this later [115–17]). Take, for instance, the following statement from the entry appropriately entitled "A Body without a World and a World without a Body 5 February 1985" (*On Sight* 136–37), which expresses his view not only about the state of his knowledge, but also about the ontological status of the blind person: "I, as a blind person, tend to be enclosed within my body, to be conscious primarily of it, and to be cut off from the world" (*On Sight* 137). He has this thought more than a year and a half after beginning the diary. The indication here is that he, at the time of recording this particular entry, regards his blindness as a condition that separates him from the outside world. This state of affairs means that he has not yet realised fully, despite having reported in earlier entries experiences of doing so, that he can establish meaningful contact with his surroundings through the other sense faculties.

When we consider another statement, this time one that the diarist records eight years after starting to grapple with his blindness, we see that he still believes that he is severed from the conversational flow taking place in the sighted human world. In the entry strikingly entitled "Can Sighted and Blind People Understand Each Other? 15 June 1991" (*On Sight* 209–11), as Hull reflects on conversations that sighted people engage in "'around the dinner table'" (*On Sight* 209), he says, "I am necessarily cut off from almost all of this. It happens through facial expression, body language" (*On Sight* 210). So he experiences alienation when he finds himself in social gatherings. He does not seem to consider it possible for him to participate in conversations with sighted people by relying on the skills of speech and audition because, as he points out, not each and every spontaneous feeling in the flow of conversation can be expressed vocally: "Not everything can be turned into an 'ooh' or an 'oh', a grunt or a laugh." Curiously, he uses the figure of a submarine to describe his situation on these occasions: "I am like a submarine, remorselessly ploughing along, having surfaced or just about surfaced especially for this occasion." The phrase "remorselessly ploughing along" reminds us of the submarine (appearing in the dream recorded on 13 August 1984) moving with great power in the depths of the ocean without its crew knowing the direction of its passage. As it happens, he makes a statement about his alienation from people in that entry as well: "I still find the experience particularly difficult and distressing, to be cut off in this way from the people one loves most" (*On Sight* 109–10). Although he may be present at a family or social gathering, he cannot be an active member of the group and, therefore, cannot help his wife in dealing with the reactions of sighted persons to his own blindness.

The third strand of meaning that we can follow in the dream recorded in "Submarine 13 August 1984" relates to the author's visit with his family in the summer of 1984 (during the months of July and August, inferring from his diary entries) to his childhood home in Melbourne, Australia. (In fact, he makes this diary entry when he is staying in that city.) He writes, "Melbourne is where my childhood lies. Here, I always have a strange experience of encounter with that past" (*On Sight* 110). He describes the visit in minute detail in the entry (recorded a few days before "Submarine") called "Visiting Melbourne 29 July 1984" (*On Sight* 101–5). Coming to the country that was his boyhood home as a blind man gives rise to a harrowing conflict in his mind between the "visual memories" (*On Sight* 102) of well-loved sights, remembered views of important landmarks, memories of the people of his youth, and his current blindness. He confides, "To be suddenly plunged back as a blind person into a world so full of remembered visions made me feel most unhappy." He also fears having to face mobility problems because he would be "deprived of my routine for so many weeks." A little later in the entry, he yearns to interact with loved people through the modality of sight:

I longed for a more immediate recognition of loved ones than the rather slow, day-by-day building up of impressions, histories and voices which blindness seems to require.... . I want to be in the immediate presence, to have the same person again. I want to be greeted by the person I love in his or her remembered form. Not being able to experience this is a cause not only of frustration but of grief.

(*On Sight* 103)

In this passage, the diarist deals poignantly with the way blindness confounds him, prevents him from coming directly and spontaneously into contact with his loved ones. We must also note his recognition that the self existing in the blind condition has to build a world separate from that of the sighted ("the rather slow, day-by-day building up of impressions, histories and voices"). In the same entry, he reports a dream set in a "beautifully furnished old college" (*On Sight* 104) in Cambridge, which is called Gonville and Caius College. In the dream, he is required to take an examination which he should not actually have to sit for. He interprets this situation as suggesting the 'blameworthiness' of his blind self:

> [I] was being judged in a context full of associations of a beautiful past which was, however, misunderstanding me, and to which I could probably not now gain access. I am blaming myself for being blind, accusing myself of being on the margin, critical of myself for not doing more for my parents, my wife and my children.
>
> (*On Sight* 104)

All this exposes him to deep anguish at a time when he has been coming to terms, however gradually this might be, with the loss of his sight.

The alternation of narrative sections that deal with dreams, and entries which reflect on events, activities, knowledge, and relationships in the diarist's conscious life is noteworthy. This formal feature of the diaries suggests, first, that a deep, subtle interaction takes place between the two realms of human existence, namely conscious and unconscious life (*Touching the Rock* x). Secondly, this narrative alternation records a gradual, halting change in Hull's selfhood. Both these themes animate the two following entries, which are recorded on the same day (the only time this happens in Hull's diaries), namely 21 August 1984. The first one is entitled "Seeing Lizzie" (*On Sight* 113), and it narrates a vividly visual dream; and the second one, which is entitled "'Can't You See Colours'" (*On Sight* 113–14), reports two incidents where Hull and his young son, Thomas, have exchanges relating to blindness. The former entry deals with the psychology of a dream, wherein the diarist sees his little daughter, Lizzie. He reports,

> In the dream, I knew that I had been blind, and that this was the first time I had been able to see her. I stared at her, full of wonder, taking in every detail of her face as she stood there wreathed in smiles, stretching out her hands to me. It was like a revelation.
>
> (*On Sight* 113)

Clearly, he regards the loss of his sight as being responsible for cutting him off from his loved ones. So he says,

I had a wonderful sense of a renewal of contact, as I felt that she was amazed as she realised, in some way, that there was something different about me, that I was responding to her in a new sort of way.

(*On Sight* 113)

In fact, not being able to exchange smiles spontaneously with others is something that gives Hull great pain, and he repeatedly returns to "the breakdown which blindness causes in the language of smiles" (*On Sight* 184), as in the entry entitled "'Between You and Me, a Smile 21 March 1986'" (*On Sight* 184). There he gets a rare opportunity to share a smile with the four-year-old Lizzie. The little girl remarks on this fact, and her father records,

I cannot describe my emotions as I reflected upon the fact that she had had so many experiences of smiling at me, but that the in-between smile was, for her and me, not only a great rarity, but a puzzle.

(*On Sight* 184)

While the story of the dream in "Seeing Lizzie" recognises that the adult person portrayed in the situation – the "I" who gazes at Lizzie – had been blind – the diarist's words are "In the dream, I knew that I had been blind" (*On Sight* 113), he is no longer so, and the process of dreaming offers a vivid, colourful image of the toddler who is "radiant with grace." Hull cites "the archetype of the divine child" (more about archetypes later [108–13]), which is investigated by Carl Jung. According to Jung, this archetype is "a kind of dream [that comes to the dreamer] when a new self was at the point of birth" (*On Sight* 113). Although Hull debates the significance of the dream, the words just quoted suggest his thought that it indicates the emergence in him of a new self.

The second entry mentioned in the previous paragraph, namely "'Can't You See Colours,'" presents the significant question asked by the little boy, Thomas. The contents of the two entries recorded on 21 August 1984 offer a sharp contrast between the unconscious and conscious parts of Hull's self. While "Seeing Lizzie" portrays a dream in which a sighted Hull who has been blind before but is not so anymore and can see his daughter, Lizzie, in vivid colours, "'Can't You See Colours'" depicts the blind man in conscious life, interacting with his young son on the subject of colour in relation to blindness. The contrast between the two entries made on the same day is, in this respect, noteworthy. Until his father explains it to him, Thomas does not realise that being blind entails the inability to see colours. Hull clarifies,

The concept of being unable to see has so many fragments. The child does not put these together into one global idea, any more than the adult does. Many adults do not immediately grasp the fact that it is no use saying to a blind person that something is over there. The words 'here' and 'there' have to be used in a different way with blind people. We may say that such an adult has not realised the linguistic implication of blindness.

(*On Sight* 114)

This occasion is by no means the first time in the diaries that Hull deals with the "many fragments" that constitute the "one global idea" of the "concept of being unable to see." In the entry entitled "Rapunzel Revisited 31 March 1984" (*On Sight* 68–9), which is recorded over four-and-a-half months before the present entry, Thomas asks his father, "'Can't you see the pictures?'" (*On Sight* 68). This question comes up when the boy is trying to understand the fact that Hull is blind.

Regarding the question of language – linguistic misunderstanding – as it relates to communication between the blind and the sighted, entries such as "Nice Day? 5 June 1983" (*On Sight* 12–13) and "'I See What You Mean' 1 September 1983" (*On Sight* 25–6) are good examples. In the former entry, Hull says, "Sometimes when I greet people by saying 'Nice day!' they remain unresponsive or even appear surprised" (*On Sight* 12). This is because he (as a blind person), and the sighted whom he greets do not share the same conception of a nice day. The description of what a pleasant day is has changed for Hull after losing his sight: "... the wind has taken the place of the sun, and a nice day is a day when there is a mild breeze." He explains, the wind not only "brings into life all the sounds in my environment," but it also feels good "in my hair and on my face, in my clothes." For the sighted, however, usually "[t]he idea of a nice day is largely visual. A nice day occurs when there is a clear, blue sky. The sun will be shining and it may be reasonably warm." Since Hull bases his appreciation of a nice day on whether "a mild breeze" is blowing or not, and the sighted rely on the sun and a blue sky, the possibility of a misunderstanding between the two is high. In order to close the gap in communication between himself and the sighted, Hull has to abandon conventional greetings. Instead, he has to be more specific in his use of language.

In the entry called "'I See What You Mean,'" the diarist draws our attention to the daily use of language, and an annoying kind of linguistic misunderstanding that he experiences while talking with some of his sighted friends because that language is burdened with "images drawn from sight" (*On Sight* 25). So when he uses expressions such as "'Nice to see you again'" or "'I see what you mean,'" his friends reply in surprise that surely he does not mean that, since he cannot see them. Although their attitude annoys him, he recognises that the problem arises from the nature of everyday language use:

The whole structure of our ordinary, everyday conversation presupposes a sighted world.... So when the sighted person draws attention to a little oddity in the use of a visual metaphor by a blind person,

beneath this lies a subtle shift in the whole character of communication
between sighted and blind people.

(On Sight 26)

This recognition suggests that when a blind person converses with the sighted,
the very "structure of our ordinary, everyday conversation" highlights the
former's corporeal difference. Hull believes that the disabled should nevertheless use all the resources of language, even if those resources should include
metaphors "of the disability from which they [disabled people] suffer" (*On
Sight* 26) in order to prevent the imposition of "a new, linguistic disability
upon people already disabled." This reflection upon language use demonstrates Hull's keen awareness of the modalities of human interaction.

The next entry about a dream, "A Secret Door 4 February 1985" (*On
Sight* 136), comes nearly five and a half months after the previous dream
narrative, viz. "Seeing Lizzie 21 August 1984." Hull begins the present narrative on a gloomy note with the words, "Trying to work in my office one
weekend I fell into a heavy, depressed sleep" (*On Sight* 136) because difficulties relating to his (lack of) knowledge of what is going on around him, and
interactions with his children weigh heavily on his mind. This mood contrasts
with the "strange and deeply moving" dream he has while sitting in his office.
He interprets the dream as follows:

> ... the dream describes the various kinds of frustrations and possibili-
> ties which blindness, the necessary avenue of communication between
> my interior and the world, poses. There is a strange hope in the myste-
> rious, tightly closed but previously unnoticed door. There is always
> more to a familiar place than you realize. In the most intimately loved
> situation, if you look closely, there is often another door.
>
> (On Sight 136)

This dream is set in Hull's office, which is also its subject. Therefore, that
familiar space, which – as described in other entries (*On Sight* 21, 46) – he
regards as a sanctuary, symbolises "the most intimately loved situation."
If we read the dream narrated in this entry as being connected with the
difficulties he faces in interacting with his children, and having a fulfilling
relationship with them – a matter dealt with in the entry immediately
preceding this one (*On Sight* 133–6), the mysterious door which he has
never noticed before holds the promise of "a strange hope." This hope
somehow lies in his blind, sensate body, which not only causes "various
kinds of frustrations," but also holds "possibilities." His recognition of
blindness as the necessary avenue of communication between himself and
the world is a self-constitutive thought. He connects the story of the dream
to the question of his blindness through the idea of "the relationships
between various kinds of interiors" (*On Sight* 136), which are alluded to
in the dream.

While in the previous entry, both the process of dreaming and the contents of the dream deal with Hull's blindness only metaphorically, the next dream narrative – coming more than six months later – offers Hull a deeply unsettling connection between himself and the self portrayed in the dream. For this reason, the two narratives form an unusual pair. In "Waking Up and Going Blind 8 August 1985" (*On Sight* 158–60), when the diarist falls asleep in his office one weekend, he dreams "that [his] colleague, Michael, knocked on [his] door to tell [him] that he was finishing work and going home" (*On Sight* 158). This occurrence, which opens the dream, is auditory in character. Michael's knocking on his office door, his spoken words, and finally his closing the door and walking away are all heard by the self portrayed in the story of the dream. Then the latter regains his sight. Hull writes:

> Then an unbelievable thing happened. My room was flooded with light. With incredulity, I gazed at the walls and saw the rows of books, filing cases and labelled boxes, all in bright colours and standing out clearly and neatly with an amazing simplicity of line, form and colour. I couldn't believe my eyes. The whole room was aglow with objects. I daren't blink in case it should disappear. I got to my feet, terrified lest the change of position should suddenly make me realise this was a dream.
>
> (*On Sight* 158)

Thus, we see that the dreaming self knows that he has been blind but has now regained his sight. This self also recognises that the vivid world he is experiencing may, at any moment, fade away, leaving him blind. As the narrative progresses, he does, in fact, wake up and go blind. As the diarist observes, the awareness of his blindness haunts the dream narrative:

> Within this dream there is a consciousness of being blind, since I am a blind person who, in the dream, regains sight and loses it again. The curious feature is that, although the regaining of sight is part of the dreamed story, the loss of sight is not, so to speak, something I dream about.
>
> (*On Sight* 159)

This consciousness of being blind appears in the "dream story" as the anxiety of the protagonist expressed in the closing words of the previous long quotation (*On Sight* 158).

Further, blindness leaves a strong trace in the psyche of the sighted self who walks in the dream, as Hull's words vividly describe the situation:

> As I hurried towards the lift, I was moving my hands side to side as if I was waving my stick... . The thought crossed my mind, 'There's no need for me to do that now. Now that I can see. But how hard it will be to throw off that habit of moving my hand from side to side.'
>
> (*On Sight* 158–59)

Clearly, although he wonders about this sudden recovery of sight, he is very happy about it. His thought about his no longer having to use the white cane to walk suggests his mood. So, as he walks, he thinks about the effort needed to switch from a blind person's mode of doing things to that suitable for a sighted person. When he wakes up, the full force of being blind, which is strengthened by the ironic state of affairs in the dream that prompts the thought just quoted, numbs him:

> The reality of it all was completely overwhelming, and the movement back from the dream-reality to the actual reality left my mind numbed, as with a blow. It was not merely the realization again that I am blind, but the strange sense of passing from one reality to another, as if my mind had become derailed.
>
> (*On Sight* 159)

The power of the dream narrative "Waking Up and Going Blind" lies in representing to Hull, in reverse and with irony, the radical nature of his transformation in actual life from being a sighted person to being a blind person who uses the cane.

The above narrative, and Hull's reflection on the dream forcefully highlight his desire not to be blind. The dream narrative communicates this wish despite his awareness that he is "a blind person who, in the dream, regains sight and loses it again." We may infer one of the main reasons for the strength of this desire from his observation about the state of his knowledge. He remarks sadly,

> The vivid distinctness of perceived objects was now exchanged for the feel of my body and clothes on the armchair, the smooth edge of the desk at which I was sitting, the knowledge that all I knew was confined within the reach of my fingers. Everything else had gone again.
>
> (*On Sight* 159–60)

Thus, it is clear that in the face of the beauty of the world available to sight, all else fades into something less appealing. This concern about knowing the world as a blind person runs persistently through the text of the two diaries.

The next two dream narratives involve the sea, and form a pair because of the contrast in the stories they portray. The first, "Lost Children 3 October 1985" (*On Sight* 166–67), tells the story of the sea taking away two of the diarist's children – Thomas and Lizzie – by means of a "huge wave" (*On Sight* 166). Another consequence of the flood is that the depths of the sea swallow up Hull's former, sighted life. He interprets the dream thus:

> The dream is basically about the loss in family relationships which blindness causes. Thomas and Lizzie, who are just learning to understand blindness, are drowned beneath it. Imogen was born before the

shock and Gabriel after it. The dream also suggests that fragments of my old life, my conscious, sighted life, are sliding and crashing down all around me into the all-engulfing world of blindness.

(*On Sight* 166–67)

It will be clear to the reader that the dream presents the sea as a symbol of Hull's blindness. It is with this understanding of the all-engulfing waters that the diarist interprets the drowning of Thomas and Lizzie. He also recognises that whatever fragments are left[11] "of [his] old life, [his] conscious, sighted life" are being shattered and swallowed up by "the all-engulfing world of blindness." This tumultuous sequence of images suggests his irrevocable journey into the blind condition. The concern that blindness has resulted in "the loss in family relationships" runs through the diaries. Another important feature of the narrative is the language in which Hull records it. Although it is a visual dream, full of action and vivid with despair, we find few images which can be thought of as being exclusively appreciable through sight. This narrative feature constitutes the link between the blindness of the narrator and symbolic blindness in the dream.

The second entry in the pair, "Navigating through the Storm 3 March 1986" (*On Sight* 183–84), narrates "a sea dream" (*On Sight* 183). It offers a contrast to the previous one – as mentioned above – in two ways. First, the experience that the dreaming self has in the dream thrills Hull, and makes him happy. Secondly, the character of the dream is refreshingly visual in his view. He describes it as "a beautiful night of dreaming ... a long series of most exciting adventure stories, all in full technicolour" in which his "mind had been renewed, had been on holiday, had been in open spaces, knowing the freedom and excitement of living in a visual world." Thus, he experiences for a little while in dream reality the 'exhilarating freedom' of being sighted. He regards the dream, then, as a "blissful" escape (*On Sight* 184) from "the all-engulfing world of blindness." As we saw above, the previous dream symbolically presented blindness as overwhelming him.

According to the diarist, a sighted person lives "in the world" (*On Sight* 184) as against the blind person, who always lives "in consciousness." He deals with the latter state of existence in the earlier entry entitled "To Accept or not to Accept 8 January 1984" (*On Sight* 45–7). In it, he explains the way in which blindness imposes an "inflexible kind of life ... upon people" (*On Sight* 46) by restricting them to a rigid routine:

Familiarity, predictability, the same objects, the same people, the same routes, the same movement of the hand in order to locate this or that: take these away, and the ... world which remains [to the blind person] is then one's own body, the introspective consciousness.

(*On Sight* 46)

11 This recalls The line "These *fragments* I have *shored against* my *ruins*" (line 431) from *The Waste Land* (1922) by the prominent modernist poet, T. S. Eliot.

He experiences this enclosed, blind life "in consciousness" as a trap because he does not have access to the wide expanses of the world he used to have as a sighted person. In this regard, another dream narrative may be mentioned, viz. "Two Daughters 22 June 1986" (*On Sight* 192–93). In it, he records "two separate dreams" (*On Sight* 192). Each of these involves "a recovery of sight, and each a daughter." This pair of vivid dreams in which the "I" portrayed regains "perfect vision" expresses "'[a] fantasy of perfect vision'" (*In the Beginning* 45). Hull says in *In the Beginning there was Darkness* that persons who have lost their sight late in life, and who can, therefore, "remember vividly the colour and movement, the excitement and spontaneity of that [earlier] life" (*In the Beginning* 46), inevitably have the hope that one day their sight might be restored.

"Town Hall 26 July 1986" (*On Sight* 193–95) is an important entry because it narrates a dream, and gives a holistic interpretation of its visual character. It records a shift in Hull's understanding about the self through the comprehension of the unconscious life of dreams. It describes a dialectic from language to imagery, or expressed in logical terms, from sentences about the blind subject's abstract knowledge in conscious life concerning his surroundings to vivid images in the unconscious that his dream portrays. The transmutation that the dreamer performs of linguistic statements into "symbolic or image-like impressions and snatches of memories" (*On Sight* 194) succeeds in encompassing Hull's past sighted life and his present blind life.

I wish to recall here a distinction which Hull makes concerning the relation between blindness and his dream life in the earlier entry called "Playing the Recorder 30 November 1983." As mentioned earlier in the chapter, there he distinguishes "between the way that blindness affects the process of dreaming, and the way it affects the contents of the dream" (*On Sight* 39). Since Hull acknowledges himself to a great extent "as a blind person in these recent dreams" (*On Sight* 194), he accounts for the visual nature of "the contents of the [present] dream" by distinguishing between the dream as well as the dreamer, both of which see everything, and the blind "I" seen by them:

> It is not I who see the auditorium, but the dreamer... . The sleeping dreamer, who is sighted, admits that the waking person, who is dreamed about, is blind. This does not mean that my subconscious does not acknowledge my blindness, for one always dreams of what one knows, what one senses, or images... . In the dream ... the sequence of sentences, the running tide of thoughts expressed in language, which more or less fills waking time, is suspended in a series of images, events and emotions in which what is known is directly experienced, not mediated through the abstractions of language.
>
> (*On Sight* 194)

When the diarist offers this elegant interpretation of his knowledge and dream life, he integrates the contradictory facets of his selfhood. However, in stating that he "cannot remember having dreamed about people's faces for a long time" (*On Sight* 194), and wondering if one day "the dreamer will discover ways of knowing that people are scattered around in space, here and there, without representing them bodily, as blobs of coloured presence" (*On Sight* 195), he does retain the earlier distinction between the process of dreaming and the contents of the dream. He is curious to know if, one day, the influence of blindness will close the gap between the two. This state would mean that he would, at that point of time, have become a profoundly blind person whose dreams represent no visual images, and also recognise him as being blind.

Towards the close of the entry entitled "Your Image on the Far Side 13 October 1984" (*On Sight* 126–28), Hull reflects on knowing the self in its journey through time by means of visual memories, which he expresses as "my relationship with myself" (*On Sight* 128). The question of visual knowledge of the self results in the diarist having (what he calls, drawing from psychology,) "a sense of cognitive dissonance" about himself: "On the one hand, I know that I am such and such a person, with certain features. On the other hand, I know myself as someone who probably no longer looks like that." The asymmetry between the memories he has of himself and his present appearance troubles Hull. So he says, "... I cannot witness the work of time upon my own face." This conflict (based on visual knowledge), which is brought about by the passage of time, produces in him (to quote his words) "a double relationship with myself." The following two dream narratives may be read in the light of the conflict in Hull's relationship with himself through time.

Interestingly, the dream narrative entitled "In the Public Library 23 December 1983" (*On Sight* 40) succeeds the entry "Playing the Recorder 30 November 1983," which plays an important role in Hull's hermeneutics of the relationship between dreaming and waking life. "In the Public Library" presents a remarkable division of the self into two blind men. It is noteworthy that although the observing self in the dream is blind, and that he faces a few difficulties in the library due to his blindness, he observes the other blind man, reads with his eyes, and sees the rest of the library vividly. However, the fact that the observed man cannot see is clear from the narrative. A more telling difference between the two is that the former reads printed books, while the latter listens to recorded books. Thus, while the observing blind self infers, "I could tell he was blind because he was carrying big boxes of what appeared to be books on tape" (*On Sight* 40), somebody watching the first blind man might mistakenly infer that he is sighted because he reads printed material. This point is crucial since just in the previous entry, Hull has recorded a dream where for "the first time ... blindness is recognised to be the cause of a crisis" (*On Sight* 39). So the present entry may be interpreted as an occasion in which the diarist's unconscious mind generates a dream where the blind person who can see has an encounter with a self (in his future) that lives and works comfortably in the blind condition. Thus, although the dream recognises Hull to be blind, it is full of colourful images. This makes for a contradictory reading experience.

Hull builds the narrative entry "A Fall into Consciousness 12 March 1991" (*On Sight* 197–98) from a dream which contrasts with the one analysed in the previous paragraph. In it, one man witnesses the death of another man who throws "himself through the window and [falls a long way down] to his death on the coast" (*On Sight* 197). It may be inferred from the last statement of the entry (see below) that the "living consciousness" that watches the "sheer descent" on to the seashore of the "border-line consciousness" is Hull's blind self; and that the observed consciousness which is falling and gets extinguished is his old self, namely "a sighted person who cannot see" (*On Sight* 36). The reason for the demise of the old self is that "it fell upon the border" (*On Sight* 197) "between the earth and the ocean, the world of light and air, and the world of depth and darkness." Therefore, he calls that man "after all, someone else" (*On Sight* 198). The diarist interprets the two men pictured in his dream as doubles of his self. He suggests this point in the "Foreword" when he says with clear reference to the dream under discussion, "I was prompted to start collecting new material when I had a dream in which I was falling from a high tower and landing on the shore, crushed between the land and the sea, yet alive" (*On Sight* xi). The fact that in this dream he is "crushed between the land and the sea" due to his fall "from a great height" (*On Sight* 197), but is still "alive" shows the doubled character of his self. Through his reflection in the entry, he paradoxically suggests that a new self is born. So he closes the entry by saying, "Losing sight has meant a fall into consciousness" (*On Sight* 198). The expression "a fall into consciousness" indicates Hull's awareness that he can live happily and without fear of the unconscious as a blind man.

Hitherto in the diaries, the ocean has symbolised the dark, smothering world of blindness, as well as Hull's unconscious mind that teems with images and the visual memories of his past, sighted life. However, in this dream, he explicitly states that his unconscious "is no longer an abyss, an oceanic depth into which I sink, endlessly and remorselessly, a border upon which I must be crushed and lost" (*On Sight* 198). These words allude to the "someone else" who threw himself to his death from a great height, his double who is now dead on the margin of the dark deep. The image presented in the above quotation also reminds us of the scenario described in the dream narrative, "Sinking 16 September 1983." His other self, the living consciousness, is blind, alive, and well. The dream is, however, vividly visual. This contrast may be understood in accordance with the distinction[12] between the sighted dreamer and the blind waking person "who is dreamed about" (*On Sight* 194). Therefore, the following statement is valid for the dream narrated in the present entry:

12 Hull makes this distinction in the entry "Town Hall 26 July 1986" which was recorded more than four and a half years before "A Fall into Consciousness."

The fact that I am seen by the dream, and, indeed, that everything in the dream is seen by the dreamer, is no failure to acknowledge that I, who appear as part of the content of the dream, am blind.

(*On Sight* 194)

The confident knowledge that he can live life as a blind person is symbolically presented by his unconscious in the form of a dream story in which the birth of a new self is recognised through the death of an old one. Thus, his unconscious has been transformed, to express it in his own words, into "my refreshment space which I fill; it is the proportions of my body, no larger than my body" (*On Sight* 198); and it is made up of "warm waters" passing through which he is "reborn" and baptised.[13] The phrase "the proportions of my body" leads directly to Hull's description of his unconscious, which refreshes him, as "my coffin, made for my body," of which he is "not afraid." In this paradoxical wise is Hull's living, blind self born. The figuring of his unconscious as a coffin may suggest the dissolution of this self and the possible birth of another, new one, an acknowledgement of the changing nature of the self.

4.4 The Self-Constitutive Power of Archetypes

I will now turn to a matter which is closely related to the life of dreams and its impact on conscious existence, namely potent images and archetypes of blindness and religion which possess self-constitutive power. Coming twenty days after the early dream narrative "The Waterfall 6 October 1983," the entry entitled "Reaching into Clouds 27 October 1983" (*On Sight* 36) presents "a sort of daydream" (*On Sight* 36) or "fantasy" which forces Hull to acknowledge his blindness, and abruptly alters his self-conception. He imagines that a veil of sooty smoke covers first his children, then his wife, eventually his house, and thereafter even the world, thereby taking all these from his sight and veiling them with "a black cloud." When he discovers that friends of the family "can see through these black clouds," and that only he cannot do so, he realises, as he puts it, that "The black clouds are in me," and are not simply an external phenomenon which hides the world. This experience metaphorically presents to Hull his own blindness, and drives him to record it as a "mysterious curse" afflicting him. This daydream compels him to acknowledge (to quote his words) that the

fantasy troubles me. I have been thinking to myself that I am not a blind person, but a sighted person who cannot see. In this fantasy I have to realise that the blindness is inside me. The black cloud is in my brain. It surrounds my consciousness.

(*On Sight* 36)

---

13 A statement in *Planet of the Blind* expresses a similar liberating acceptance of blindness: "When one is returned to life" (175) after having grown up "wearing chains like Houdini, trying to pull off a magic trick" (178), Kuusisto observes, "everything is compelling" (175).

These words may be understood as echoing his reference to the "passage over the frontier" (*On Sight* xi) between sight and blindness. In this entry, he begins to make the transition, which is prompted by the realisation that his self-conception of being "a sighted person who cannot see" is no longer tenable.

The fantasy presented in the previous paragraph connects with the narrative of Hull's being trapped deep in a mineshaft under a solid mountain.[14] The diarist discusses this "persistent image" (*On Sight* 42) in the entry entitled "Panic in a Mineshaft 6 January 1984" (*On Sight* 40–2). When he has an asthmatic attack, the difficulty in breathing leads, in his own words, to a powerful feeling "that I was being strangled, suffocated by the blackness" (*On Sight* 42), and gives rise to the oppressive image. It dramatises his experience of going blind in terms of a spatial movement, where he is remorselessly carried "in a little coal-truck ... deeper and deeper into the hillside" further and further from the fast-diminishing "round window of light at the end of the tunnel." This image represents Hull's journey through time, away from his past, sighted life (*On Sight* 125).[15] Thus, he is thoroughly isolated by his blindness. Then the mountain "hides the light, the day, the air" (*On Sight* 42), and he knows, to quote him on his despair, "that between me and the world there lies this mountain of rock, or this impenetrable mass of smoky veil which is heavy and hot like the rock itself." The "impenetrable mass of smoky veil" which oppresses Hull is akin to the "inky-black cloud" (*On Sight* 36) that engulfs his world in the fantasy discussed above. The important point to note with regard to this series of images is their power to fill the subconscious and conscious parts of Hull's mind with a pervasive sense of despair. However, in the late entry "Can Sighted and Blind People Understand Each Other? 15 June 1991" (*On Sight* 209–11), the diarist remarks as follows about the image of the tunnel: "The dark tunnel under the mountain holds no fears for me anymore; I am nestled within it like a bat that has learned to hang upside-down in this subterranean cavern" (*On Sight* 209). This statement expresses his state of being accustomed to the world of blindness. Nevertheless, he and Marilyn are only too aware of the radical difference between their respective worlds. This is to say that Hull as a blind man, and his wife as a sighted woman possess different consciousnesses.

It is important to emphasise at this point that the image of the tunnel appears repeatedly in Hull's diary entries as a narrative device. The diarist describes "the dramatic realization of the remoteness of [his] visual past" (*On*

---

14 I introduce this image in Chapter 2 (49) while opening my discussion of Borges's short story, "Writing of the God."

15 Hull reports in the entry "'It's Like Going Down and Down' 20 April 1986" (*On Sight* 184–85) that his little daughter Lizzie achieves an impressive "insight into the blind condition" (*On Sight* 185) when she compares going blind with the experience of "'going down ... to the bottom of a very ... deep well where you can never get out... .'" He recognises her remarkable insight into his traumatic experience of great loss.

Sight 125), which he comes to on his visit to Melbourne, by using the image of "turning the corner in a tunnel." He also represents the experience of going blind "as a journey into a dark tunnel" (*On Sight* 126) to dramatise "the strange poignancy and confusion" (*On Sight* 127) he experiences "in the presence of loved people whom once [he] saw but now no longer see[s]." This conflict consists in realising that, as he grows older in the blind condition, he moves further and further away from the remembered images of loved people. This reality means that he cannot hold on to their looks even though he might wish to do so because, as those people grow older, their appearances change. This state of affairs generates in Hull's mind what he calls "cognitive dissonance" (*On Sight* 127). Besides illustrating the psychological power of the tunnel image, this discussion foregrounds the importance to Hull of human relationships.

In "To Accept or not to Accept 8 January 1984," the diarist dwells on "experiences of panic" (*On Sight* 45) from a religious standpoint. He considers his blindness to be "a kind of religious crisis." As a result, two disturbing images come together in his mind:

> The sense of subterranean or subconscious weight oppresses me, and I link in my mind the dream image of the huge, water-soaked hulk being dragged down into the depths with my waking reverie about the little coal-truck being driven remorselessly deeper and deeper beneath the infinite weight of the mountain. The common feature is irresistible heaviness.
>
> (*On Sight* 45)

This mental response involving the conjunction of oppressive symbols reveals the origin of Hull's agony as lying in his being forcibly removed from the midst of the world he has known until now as a sighted person, and being plunged into the alien world of the blind. He theorises his experience by drawing on Merleau-Ponty's explanation of why people who have lost their sight or the use of their limbs continue to live in past time, when their bodies were 'whole.' Not recognising their present reality, wherein their physical make-up does not include sight or (the use of) limbs, makes it very difficult for them ever to accept their selves completely. The distinction (or gap in the disabled person's corpo-reality) between "the ordinary, habitual body" (Merleau-Ponty 95; *On Sight* 175) and "the actual body" results in conflicts in the person's self-conception. Moreover, this dilemma generates the "poignant tension between past and present time" (*On Sight* 176), which Hull describes as "the real heart of the emotions of disability." So he regards blindness as a calamity. He states that continuous work is what enables him to stave off the sense of helplessness experienced by him in the blind condition: adopting "tiny techniques which help one to do tiny things step by step" (*On Sight* 45) provides his brain with a ceaseless series of tasks to perform (*On Sight* 46). Thinking about the above symbols gives rise in Hull's mind the archetypes of light and darkness, which in turn brings him to the archetype of blindness (*On Sight* 54).

Hull devises an hourly timetable in order to accomplish meticulously planned tasks which enable him to battle "a sense of pointless desolation" (*On Sight* 45). This strategy is defined by a realisation akin to that of John Milton's speaker in the poem "On His Blindness," namely that he is "not expected to solve the problem of blindness" (*On Sight* 46). So Hull surrenders his work to God with the words, "If I can take one step, it is yours." Thus, he occasionally experiences peace in the state of blindness. However, depression frequently threatens him. In "Blindness as an Archetype 23 February 1984" (*On Sight* 54), he explains that blindness is not thought of simply as a physical condition, but is in fact converted into a metaphor which is applicable to humanity as a whole: "Blindness is the archetype of the loss of consciousness.... . In the blind person, one confronts the symbol of the loss of the ordered, intelligent life" (*On Sight* 54). So the blind person is reduced from his or her individual self to being a symbol of unconsciousness. Such a psychological response has its origins in the metaphoric linking of light, knowledge, and consciousness. Since darkness is the opposite of light, it stands for ignorance,[16] which brings in its wake the other associations that trouble Hull. They recall the oppressive image of a mineshaft along which he is inexorably carried deep into a solid mountain (*On Sight* 42). The following quotation explains the shift in self-conception which a person facing blindness undergoes:

> The sighted person who goes blind confronts in his or her own person the actual presence of the archetype which had been dimly feared. The archetype will now be activated, not by being confronted in a stranger, but by being a fact of one's own daily experience.
>
> (*On Sight* 54)

With the advance of blindness, thus, a person embedded hitherto in the sighted world is brought face to face with the archetype of blindness. As a result, they are likely to succumb to depression.

The entry "Fighting Depression 24 February 1984" (*On Sight* 54–6) narrates the effects that the archetypes of blindness and light produce on Hull's current self-conception. Although he dwells mainly on depression, he connects it to panic: due to these forces of his struggling mind, he goes "to pieces" (*On Sight* 55) and says, "I am dissolving." These experiences threaten him when he is grappling with social responsibilities, particularly while trying to play "with the children" (*On Sight* 54). In such situations, the oppressive archetype of blindness batters his selfhood. Hull's inability in blindness to see his body and know his image (*On Sight* 55) leads to self-dissolution. Although he briefly considers "the Aaronic Blessing" (*On Sight* 56) as it offers spiritual succour in the form of the archetype of light, which dispels the darkness generated by the archetype of blindness, he comes to the conclusion

16 The reader will find indications of a de-symbolisation in Chapter 5.

that the biblical passage in question is ultimately deceptive because the world of light is beyond the blind person. So he says, "By obliterating the darkness, it obliterates me." This realisation heralds Hull's imminent transition to a new comprehension.

The change takes place in the entry "Beyond Light and Darkness 26 February 1984" (*On Sight* 56) when Thomas's words, "'Thomas needs the light. Daddy doesn't need the light'" (*On Sight* 56), inspire an epiphany in Hull: he is reminded of Psalm 139.12, which states that for God, light and darkness are equal. (The diarist meditates on this psalm in two further entries which succeed "Beyond Light and Darkness.") Thus, he discovers the archetype "which transcends and unifies at a higher level" the archetypes of darkness and light. Both negate his life as a blind person: one by making him "feel as if [he has] become nothing" (*On Sight* 54), the other "by the brightness of its contrast" (*On Sight* 56). However, Psalm 139 describes, in a way that profoundly moves Hull, "the religious experience of the blind person" (*On Sight* 58). It clarifies that "God does not need the light to know and the darkness cannot prevent him from knowing" (*On Sight* 59). Similarly, 'in blindness,' Hull moves beyond light and darkness, thereby becoming like God (*On Sight* 56–9). Therefore, he states that God knows him, and makes "himself known to me in the manner which suits my condition" (*On Sight* 58). "He will not show himself to me," the diarist continues and then concludes with a statement of faith, "He will remember my blindness." So God will take Hull by the hand and guide him. Hull feels blessed because he is known by his God (*On Sight* 58–60). Accordingly, he says a few years later, "in the state of being beyond light and darkness, one is brought into a strange intimacy with the divine" (*In the Beginning* 132). Thus, Hull's blindness enables him to achieve fresh contact with, and nearness to, the divine being.

Closing his second diary, *On Sight and Insight*, Hull informs us in the entry entitled "Postscript: The Meaning of Blindness" (232–34) that he has tried to interpret, in the course of the fragmentary entries, how he encountered the despair brought into his life by blindness, and how his consciousness was transformed by the struggle. He avers that his vulnerability as a blind man opened him to the realisation of the social and spiritual potential inherent in disability. Through the medium of books on his experience of blindness as an individual, he brings to our notice the broader matter concerning human weakness and mutuality in the contemporary despiritualised world:

> My interpretation of blindness has led me from archetypes to socio-economic phenomenology. The first phase of the interpretation was regression into the archetype; the second phase of the interpretation was a return with the archetype into the present and future of our society.
>
> (*On Sight* 233)

While in the beginning the archetypes of light, darkness, and blindness fill him with despair, he gradually comes to realise that "blindness can offer a sort of archetype of the future" (*On Sight* 233): it not only increases his similarity to – and intimacy with – God, but also helps him to identify with the struggles of people facing various kinds of hardships (*On Sight* 233–34). Continuing his engagement with the wider world in *The Tactile Heart*, Hull states,

> Facing every day a dozen frustrations and little humiliations, continually aware of my dependence upon others, alienated at the same time from any easy rapport with other people, I became increasingly conscious of the way that marginalized and disabled people experience the world.

> (10)

Thus, we see that Hull recognises the biopolitical dimension of blindness even as he pays close attention to personal experience in his books.

I will conclude this chapter by stating that Hull's dream narratives, coming at regular intervals, and entries dwelling on archetypes in the diaries illustrate his interpretation of links that he considers to exist between his conscious and unconscious life. He asserts this view in the following words, just before the manuscript went to press: "… it is through the dreaming life that the changes in the relationship between consciousness and unconsciousness are first realized" (*On Sight* xiii). Further, I have attempted to indicate the major issues that powerfully inform his evolving thinking about his blindness. This critical commentary allows the reader to follow the movement in Hull's selfhood through time by means of his diary entries recorded over four years and spanning eight years' experience, from June 1983 to August 1991. In the next chapter, I will examine the interlinked issues of how Hull, as a blind person, knows the world and the self as he reflects on his interactions with his family, friends, and surroundings.

5   Self-Knowledge through Interaction with the World

In this chapter, I examine Hull's reflections on the twin questions of knowledge and social relationships as they impact his selfhood. The diaries show why knowledge is fundamental to the day-to-day living of life, and how this fact necessitates reflection on one's experiences, thereby producing self-knowledge. What impact does blindness have on Hull's knowledge? How does his ability to gain knowledge in the blind condition affect his being-in-the-world? It is clear from his reflections that the ways in which he knows the world exercise a formative influence on his existence in, and passage through, it. To start with, I want to illustrate how the ways in which Hull knows the self are inextricably linked with the modes of being with others. We have already seen in some of the entries discussed in the previous chapter that he highly values "human relationships." The extent of their significance for his self-conception becomes clear when he remarks decidedly in *On Sight and Insight* that "it is in the interaction with others that we know ourselves" (xiii). It is no surprise, then, that early in the diary he presents a reflection upon the change brought about by blindness in the nature of his relationships with sighted people in "Eye Contact 19 June 1983" (*On Sight* 13–14). There he talks about the loss in his relationships with others of "playful details" (*On Sight* 14) such as smiles, "winking, sticking out your tongue, exchanging mocking glances, raising the eyebrows and so on" which infuse interactions between people with a lightness of mood and a subtle character. What troubles him is "the inability to reply to all the fleeting nuances of the face, and especially the eyes." "Blind people," he adds, "also lose communication through general body language, since although they can speak using gestures they cannot receive the body language of other people." It becomes evident from the tone of the entry that light-hearted conversations used to delight the diarist when he had sight. It is with the convivial nature of his personality (*On Sight* 103) as the background that the opening statement of the entry gains its significance: "The relationship between blind and sighted people can become rather serious" (*On Sight* 13). The reason for this change lies in the modes of communication that the two parties must adopt. Interactions need to take place either through words that "are often too abstract" (*On Sight* 14),

DOI: 10.4324/9781003399667-5

or through touch that "is often too concrete." He suggests that this constraint imposed on the blind leaves him impoverished.

The entry "Faces 21 June 1983" (*On Sight* 14–15), as its title suggests, deals with the topic of Hull's knowledge pertaining to the looks of people whom he knows. He reflects on how one recognises other people. Furthermore, this question has to do with his conviction that knowledge is always better than ignorance. The point arises when he dwells on his desire to know Marilyn as she gets older in their shared process of aging as man and wife (*On Sight* 15), and on the situation where a blind person lacks information "to form certain impressions" (*On Sight* 16) when they meet somebody new. The entry that follows this one, "Does It Matter What People Look Like? 23 June 1983" (*On Sight* 15–19), continues reflecting on the themes raised in the first entry. It fleshes out the changes in Hull's selfhood over three years, from his registration as a blind person in 1980 to the present (the time when he is recording these entries).

In his "sighted days" (*On Sight* 15), Hull used to relate to others visually, relying on the appearance of their faces, as the sighted usually do (*On Sight* 16). However, now, as a person who has become blind recently, he distinguishes between two groups of acquaintances, friends, and family members: "The people I knew before I lost my sight have faces but the people I have met since then do not have faces" (*On Sight* 14). This statement concerns his perception of people. He remembers the ones he "knew before [he] lost [his] sight" as those whose faces he can recall and relate to. However, he cannot access the faces of the ones he has "met since then," that is, after becoming blind. This state of affairs worries him: "I knew how I knew the first lot – by their faces. How could I ever feel that I really knew the second lot?" He is concerned about the means available to him of engaging with people in the blind condition, wherein he must learn (as time passes by) to cope with the absence of visual information. Talking about this issue in the context of making "a new acquaintance" (*On Sight* 16), he observes that we constantly form "hypotheses about a new acquaintance" throughout the duration of our relationship with them. Since the blind person "has a lot less information to go on when forming these hypotheses … it takes [them] longer to get to know somebody" (*On Sight* 17). Due to not being able to form "first impressions" (*On Sight* 16) about the new acquaintance on the basis of visual information, the blind person needs to rely on "the voice, the touch of the hand and so on" to form an idea about the person they are meeting for the first time. For this reason, says Hull, he takes more time than a sighted person to "get to know somebody" and adds, "perhaps I am not a very skilful blind person" (*On Sight* 17). This statement articulates a tentative conception of the self, and indicates his struggle to live optimally as a blind person who is able to respond well to people and situations.

The diarist reports that vivid images began flashing in his mind about "a year after I was registered blind" (*On Sight* 15). They "went on" flashing "for six or twelve months" almost as if he was hallucinating. He recognises the sharp divide evident between these images and the visible world. He records that he would come back [out of the "absorbed" state of mind in which he gazes "upon these images"] with a shock, realising that there was nothing to indicate which of these images was closer to reality. There was simply nothing there at all.

(On Sight 16)

The problem that Hull faces – and he returns to this issue repeatedly in the diaries – is one of relating his mental images of people to what they really look like, given the fact that he cannot verify the truth of the images due to blindness. This uncertainty, or gap, is articulated in terms of the unascertainable question of correspondence between these memory-images in the mind and "reality." This question clearly pertains to epistemology.

As is well known, Descartes, Berkeley, and Hume raised "sceptical challenges" (Kitcher 418) for philosophy. Descartes expresses the problem of scepticism in his *Meditations on First Philosophy* ([1641] 1996) thus:

I will suppose therefore that not God, who is supremely good and the source of truth, but rather some malicious demon of the utmost power and cunning has employed all his energies in order to deceive me. I shall think that the sky, the air, the earth, colours, shapes, sounds and all external things are merely the delusions of dreams which he has devised to ensnare my judgement. I shall consider myself as not having hands or eyes, or flesh, or blood or senses, but as falsely believing that I have all these things.

(15)

Thus, Descartes resorts to the method of radical doubt, pretending to deceive himself about the very existence of the external world and his own body (xiii) in order to avoid being cheated by "any falsehoods" (15) in his quest to achieve certain knowledge. These falsehoods pertain to perception. Kitcher elucidates the sceptical challenge as the problem where a "'veil of perception' [stands] between knowers and objects" (418). Early modern sceptics grapple with the question of certain knowledge because they recognise that perception is limited to qualities of objects, and that it fails to grasp objects in themselves (Beiser 20). Thus, it became difficult to establish that the external world exists independently of the perceiver. Grayling states that "our possession of the best evidence for claims about the world is always consistent with the falsity of those claims ... so that we cannot regard ourselves as ever being justified in making those claims" (*The Refutation* 2). This impasse "undermines our common-sense beliefs in the reality of the external world, other minds, and even our own selves" (Beiser 18). The uncertainty in the subject's mind about the reality of the external world severs them from the latter. Noteworthy here is the parallel between this state of affairs and the problem that dogs Hull. Since as a sighted person he had relied heavily upon sight to the extent of excluding other sensory modalities, the question confronting him now is: how can he know the world as a blind person? Thus, blindness is a veil separating him emphatically from the visible world. He puts this fear into eloquent words in the entry "Blindness as an Archetype 23 February 1984" (*On Sight* 54):

> In my own case, the feeling of being bricked up inside comes into conflict with the fear that there is no reality outside, and that one is trapped on the borderlands between the real and the unreal, where all is confusion and darkness. Perhaps part of the panic is the desire to get outside in order to reassure oneself that there is something there.
>
> (*On Sight* 54)

This quotation conveys Hull's stark separation from the world, and his fear of being "trapped" in "'a formless void'" (*In the Beginning* 1), to quote from the description of the earth in the *Book of Genesis*.

To be sure, the two states of affairs explained above form an asymmetric parallel: the former is a metaphysical problem, while the latter involves reorientation in the phenomenal world. The connection between them is metaphorical since, as Hagberg states, "A metaphor ... cuts with a fine epistemological disregard across the distinction" (147), here, between different orders of philosophical problems. I wish to direct the reader's attention to the radical nature of the challenge facing Hull. The epistemological uncertainty precipitated by scepticism resembles the inability to access the world visually 'in blindness,' and both experiences may be captured by the metaphor "darkness." On extending the above asymmetric parallel, a crucial point becomes evident: the blind are considered to be ignorant because they do not have sight,[1] whereby one faculty of perception, namely sight, is unconsciously linked to knowledge. This leads to (1) sight being the dominating concern in philosophy of perception; (2) the other perceptual modalities garnering little attention in philosophical inquiry;[2] and (3) the world of blind people being regularly misunderstood.

I explicate the phrase, 'the world of the blind,' as the creation of "acquired worlds" (Merleau-Ponty 149) from "a primary world." Merleau-Ponty explains how "the actual subject" comes to "have a world or be in the world, that is, sustain round about it a system of meanings whose reciprocities, relationships and involvements do not require to be made explicit in order to be

---

1 This matter becomes clear when we examine metaphorical uses of the word "blind" in its various forms in common statements such as "Don't follow them blindly," "The authorities turned a blind eye to ...," "He went on a blind date," and so on. We may note that in the sentences quoted here, the word "blind" connotes ignorance. Hull suggests that "the use of visual metaphors" (*On Sight* 25) that imply blindness in such expressions dealing with the lack of adequate knowledge exposes the widely-held view that "an intimate connection [exists] between seeing and knowing." Also see Kuusisto's *Planet of the Blind* (65) for his view on the matter.

2 See Gatzia and Brogaard, *The Epistemology of Non-Visual Perception*, for cutting-edge research which remedies this lack.

exploited." This interrelated "system of meanings" constitutes an acquired world. Here, the subject, in the course of living their life, fashions out of the primary world where they exist secondary (or acquired) worlds. Drawing upon this thought, the world of the blind and that of the sighted may be described as acquired worlds which confer upon the respective persons' "experience its secondary meaning;" and these are "carved out of a primary world which is the basis of the primary meaning." Merleau-Ponty defines the latter as the "one world [which] is ... antepredicatively self-evident" to the subject who shapes the world that they inhabit as a human.

I mentioned above Hull's problem of reorientating himself as a blind person in the world. Both entries ("Faces" and "Does It Matter What People Look Like?") talk about how he has adapted[3] to the blind condition. The former entry reflects on states of mind and changes that occur over three years. In it, he says, "As time went by, the proportion of people with no faces increased" (*On Sight* 14). As his time as a blind person lengthens, he increasingly interacts with people on the basis not of their looks, but of speech and voice, sound, touch, and the situations they have jointly been through. He confirms this conclusion when he states,

> Increasingly, I am no longer even trying to imagine what people look like. My knowledge of you is based upon what we have been through together, not on what you look like.... . I am beginning to lose the category [of what people look like] itself.
>
> (*On Sight* 19)

This development indicates that he is making a transition from a reliance on visual information to a state of mind and corporeal awareness where information gained through means other than sight becomes important. So he affirms an aesthetic of listening:

> The crucial thing in any new acquaintance is the sound of the voice. I am continuing to learn more and more about the amazing power of the human voice to reveal the person. With the people I know very well, I find that all of the emotion which would normally be expressed in the face is there in the voice.... . My impressions based on the voice seem to be just as accurate as those of sighted people.... . The capacity of the voice to reveal the self is truly amazing. Is the voice intelligent? Is it colourful?
>
> (*On Sight* 18)

We see here that Hull is acquiring a blind man's abilities of getting to know people, and of recognising their moods with the help of their voices. He is gradually shifting from a visual criterion of recognition to establishing the link between self and voice. However, much later in the diaries, he records

3 This is for now: the same problems recur, as indicated earlier.

experiences of not being able to recognise people by their voices (*On Sight* 148, 174). As he notes in *Touching the Rock*, "… the same problems and the same experiences went round and round" (x) in his life, which he interprets "from many aspects."

5.1 Knowing the Body, Knowing the Self

I will now turn to an important question for Hull as a blind person, viz. the links he perceives between the face, body image, and self-knowledge. The entry "Does It Matter What People Look Like?" ranges over a period of two years, tracing the changes in his mode of existence. In it, he describes one of the results "of not knowing what people look like" (*On Sight* 17) as follows: "the face no longer has the central place for me which it has in normal human relationships," because he cannot recognise people or relate to them by means of what their faces look like. So people have come to be defined for him by their voices, not by their faces. The significance of the face now lies for him in the fact that it "is merely the place from which the voice comes." This state of affairs vividly brings out the change that blindness has effected in Hull's being-in-the-world. It becomes clear that the kinds of information available to him, that is to say, the sorts of perceptual information he can acquire and use, impact the existence of the self. As explained above, he must now interact with people on a completely new basis, that of voice and touch.

All this has a deeper meaning for the diarist. In the entry entitled "What Do I Look Like? 25 June 1983" (*On Sight* 19), he raises a concern about "the loss of the body image" (*On Sight* 52). He "discover[s] with a shock that [he] cannot remember [his face]" (*On Sight* 19) and muses, "to lose one's own face poses a new problem," namely that of self-knowledge. So he continues,

> To what extent is loss of the image of the face connected with loss of the image of the self? Is this one of the reasons why I often feel I am a mere spirit, a ghost, a memory? Other people have become disembodied voices, speaking out of nowhere, going into nowhere. Am I not like this too, now that I have lost my body?
>
> (*On Sight* 19)

The theme of the reflective entry is therefore visual awareness of one's self, the visible body. He conveys a sense of despair in the following categorical statement about the theme: "… the horror of being faceless, of forgetting one's own appearance, of having no face. The face is the mirror-image of the self" (*On Sight* 48). At this juncture, he starts "feeling [his face] with [his] own hands" in order "to regain the assurance that [he has] got a face." Tactile exploration of the face helps him anchor his self to a physical body. This desire to feel his face helps explain the speaker's act, in his own words (line 6), of feeling "the contours of my face" in Borges's poem, "A Blind Man" (*Selected Poems* 357). In both writers, the face serves as the emblem of the self. Therefore, Hull connects not knowing what his own face looks like, and not being able to remember his appearance with losing "the image of the self," that is, the visual appearance of the (corporeal) self, and construes himself as being merely a disembodied voice. Curiously, Hull does not talk about proprioception, a "nonvisual sixth sense" (289) which Swan describes as "our ongoing, barely conscious awareness of the position, orientation, and movement of our bodies and limbs in space." The critic observes further that "if Descartes had recognised it [i.e., proprioception], we might have been spared a lot of trouble about the mind/body split." The thought of this perceptual modality has not occurred to Hull due to his preoccupation with the sight of himself. So he says that he often feels as though he is "a mere spirit, a ghost, a memory." This feeling is similar to his perception of people as having "become disembodied voices, speaking out of nowhere, going into nowhere." This statement points to a serious epistemological problem for Hull. Due to visual loss, he has the experience of being dissociated from other people and the world. Thus, it is not a coincidence that he talks about a "deterioration of the process of knowing" (*On Sight* 25) and "the death of the old self" in "recently blinded people." This conclusion means that the process of knowing exercises a direct impact on the self's existence.

We now come to two entries separated by a year and a few days which highlight a fresh point of view on the blind person's selfhood in relation to the environment. For this reason, the entries constitute a pair. I see them as representing a new way of knowing, which Hull comprehends by means of occurrences in the natural world. It is in this context that we must read his statement in *Touching the Rock* about the two persistent themes of the diaries: "the changing perception of nature [and] the transformation in my understanding of what a person is" (x). The two themes are intimately connected, and "Rain 9 September 1983" (*On Sight* 26–8) brings out this link very well. Towards the close of the entry, the diarist states that while the rain falls, "I feel as if the world, which is veiled until I touch it, has suddenly disclosed itself to me. I feel that the rain ... has granted a gift to me, the gift of the world" (*On Sight* 27). These words derive their force from Hull's sense that when his environment produces only "various broken [or intermittent] sounds," the world is veiled from (or made invisible to) him. With the loss of visual access to the world, and having to rely upon touch and audition in order to know, he feels isolated. This experience of being cut off from the external world (by the veil of blindness) is highlighted in his wish, "If only rain could fall inside a room, it would help me to understand where things are in that room, to give a sense of being in the room, instead of just sitting on a chair." So the rain allows him to comprehend "the contours of everything" (*On Sight* 26) through the varied sounds it generates when it comes into contact with objects and structures in the environment. The spontaneous "acoustic experience" of rain, therefore, brings him out of a state of self-absorption into immediate and continuous contact with the outside world. He emphasises the truth and power of this experience when he says,

I am no longer isolated, preoccupied with my thoughts, concentrating upon what I must do next. Instead of having to worry about where my body will be and what it will meet, I am presented with a totality, a world which speaks to me.

(On Sight 27)

So he contrasts a life 'in blindness' of dogged action and a mode of being where aesthetic appreciation is possible.

I will briefly examine these two modes of existence available to Hull at this point of time and stage of his evolution as a blind person. The first mode is represented by the following statement (found in the passage quoted in the previous paragraph), which suggests that he often concentrates "upon what [he] must do next" (*On Sight* 27). In a later entry entitled "To Accept or Not to Accept 8 January 1984" (*On Sight* 45–7), he explains this conception of work further: "Each hour must have its particular skills, its various techniques, its little routines which enable something to be accomplished successfully. Otherwise, I will have a sense of pointless desolation" (*On Sight* 45). This careful timetabling of his life constitutes a strategy he adopts to cope with the consequences of blindness. The strategy lays emphasis on planning, doing things, and accomplishing goals. It enables him to stave off the sense of being left helpless by blindness.

The aesthetic realisation that Hull achieves of his being-in-the-world may be gathered from the following excerpt:

When what there is to know is in itself varied, intricate and harmonious, then the knowledge of that reality shares the same characteristics. I am filled internally with a sense of variety, intricacy and harmony. The knowledge itself is beautiful, because the knowledge creates in me a mirror of what there is to know. As I listen to the rain, I am the image of the rain, and I am one with it.

(On Sight 27–8)

This passage is remarkable for its presentation of a mode of knowing the self which is radically different from the visual comprehension of it, as treated through most of the entries, "Does It Matter What People Look Like? 23 June 1983" and "What Do I Look Like? 25 June 1983." In this auditory identification of self with the world, where the former mirrors the latter or resonates with it, Hull does not hanker after his visible face or body image, but recognises his oneness with the rain-filled world. Explaining phenomenology, and distinguishing his thought from Kant's critical philosophy by relating them to each other, Merleau-Ponty writes, "What distinguishes intentionality from the Kantian relation to a possible object is that the unity of the world, before being posited by knowledge in a specific act of identification, is 'lived' as ready-made or already there" (xix). This point is illustrated when the diarist reports at the start of "Rain 9 September 1983" that, on opening "the front door" (*On Sight* 26) and discovering that it was rain-ing, He "stood for a few minutes, lost in the beauty of it." Thus, he lives (or is lost in the beauty of) "the unity of the world ... as ready-made or already there" before he conceives his "knowledge of that reality" as creating "in [himself] a mirror of what there is to know." It is only when Hull compares[4] his auditory experience of the falling rain with what "a sighted person feels when opening the curtains and seeing the world outside" (*On Sight* 27) that he articulates the following realisation. To express it in Merleau-Ponty's words, "... in experiencing the beautiful ... I am aware of a harmony between sensation and concept, between myself and others, which is itself without any concept" (xix). This aesthetic dynamic reveals "the hidden art of the imagi-nation ... which forms the basis" of subjectivity.

We see that blindness has altered Hull's bodily relationship with the world. Concerning this epistemological question about self and world confronting the diarist, Swan explains,

> He understands acutely the effect of no longer being able to visualize space or visualize himself in space, and he looks forward to moments when the wind is blowing or when it rains. In wind and rain, sound performs the role of light in shaping a three-dimensional space where usually there is no space.
>
> (291)

Thus, in this early entry, Hull experiences the beauty of rain with the loss of sight as a constant presence. With this point in mind, it would be fruitful to compare "Rain 9 September 1983" with "Rainfall and the Blind Body 21 September 1984" (*On Sight* 118–20). The former entry describes, using a few auditory metaphors, the beauty that the diarist finds in the sounds of "steadily falling rain" (*On Sight* 26), and reflects on what it reveals to him. However, at important points in the entry, the language used displays a reli-ance on visual figures of speech:

> ... it throws *a coloured blanket over previously invisible things...* . Over the whole thing, *like light falling upon a landscape* is the gentle background patter gathered up into one continuous murmur of rain. I think that this experience of opening the door on a rainy garden must be similar to that which a sighted person feels when opening the cur-tains and *seeing the world outside.*
>
> (emphasis added, *On Sight* 26–27)

While the imagery in the above passage can be interpreted as Hull's attempt to explain his auditory experience to sighted people, it also carries the

---

4 The act of comparing may be described as being an overtly conceptual exercise.

emotional force of loss. By contrast,[5] the latter entry significantly harnesses sensory qualities of sound and touch, eschewing images:

> There is *a slow, steady drip, drip, drip*, and *a more rapid cascade*, against *the background of the pitter-patter* of the individual drops on the window pane. These vary in speed as the rainstorm itself ebbs and flows, and some *patterns of sounds overtake others*, a bit like the *music* of Steve Reich... .

> ... There is *the high-pitched drumming staccato* as the drops fall on metal, *the deeper, duller impact* on brick or concrete, and I notice that *the note being struck* differs slightly even from one window pane to another... . On the window pane, it is *very loud*. The panes of glass *vibrate on my forehead*. The sounds diminish, *layer upon layer*, receding into the faint distance as the rain falls on nearby trees. I wonder how far away I can hear it falling.
>
> (emphasis added, *On Sight* 119)

In presenting a detailed, precise description of the intricate sound of the rain, this passage makes it amply clear that the blind diarist has come to acquire a keener, even musical, appreciation of the auditory world since 9 September 1983, when the entry entitled "Rain" was recorded. Standing at his study window, Hull gains a comprehensive picture of his surroundings through the various qualities of sounds as the rainwater "*swishes, gurgles, pelts along* in a fury, comes and goes" (emphasis added, *On Sight* 119). While he deals with common themes – such as the blind body and perception – in both entries, "Rainfall and the Blind Body 21 September 1984" goes further than the first one because in it, he "complicates the usual understanding of the way bodies are located in an environment, describing the relation as an intermingling of self and space evoked by sound and suggesting a special ecology of existence in a landscape" (Swan 292). So, in the latter entry, Hull conceives of the self in a distinctly different way from the visual mode of the body image.

As we have seen in Chapter 4 (110), in "To Accept or not to Accept 8 January 1984," Hull discusses the way in which the blind person can be enclosed within their self. He describes this state of being thus:

---

5 The late entry "Thunder Over Koster 13 August 1991" (*On Sight* 220–22) represents Hull's rich experience of Sweden's natural world through the medium of dramatic sounds generated by a thunderstorm. This narrative section presents a contrast between sighted sensory experience and Hull's multisensory appreciation of the same natural occurrences by describing how his daughter, Imogen, and his wife, Marilyn, wonder at the beauty of the thunderstorm even as he immerses himself in the same event through the medium of sound. The diarist articulates an aesthetic of listening in the entry, thereby producing a prose composition comparable to Kuusisto's essay "Harbor Songs" appearing in *Eavesdropping*. The action of the essay is set in Finland, a country located in Scandinavian climes.

The span of attention, of knowledge, retracts so that one lives in a little world.... Only the area which can be touched with the body or tapped with the stick becomes a space in which one can live. The rest is unknown.

(*On Sight* 47)

He experiences life as being starkly restricted by blindness and its modes of dealing with the world. Thus, the entry offers two ways of being-in-the-world: first, of being trapped in the "world [of] one's own body, the introspective consciousness" (*On Sight* 46); or secondly, of engaging in constant work, "to get on with some little piece of work which would keep my brain ticking over." Both modes of living do not facilitate fruitfulness because they express a kind of despair.

Just over five months after recording "Rain 9 September 1983," Hull talks about the extremely depressing non-availability of the body image in the entry, "Fighting Depression 24 February 1984" (*On Sight* 54–6). In the following passage, he explains the impact that this fact has on his self-conception:

I feel as if I want to stop thinking, stop experiencing. The lack of a body image makes this worse: the fact that one can't glance down and see the reassuring continuity of one's own consciousness in the outlines of one's own body.... There is no extension of awareness into space. So I am nothing but a pure consciousness, and if so, I could be anywhere. I am becoming ubiquitous; it no longer matters where I am.

(*On Sight* 55)

Here, Hull describes the dissolution of the self in states of depression, when the "lack of a body image" produces in him a sense of having "become nothing" (*On Sight* 54).

By contrast, in "Rainfall and the Blind Body 21 September 1984," he arrives at a new, creative understanding of the blind body. He not only questions his previous conception of self, but also finds a solution to the problem of scepticism 'in blindness' discussed earlier in this chapter (115–17):

Is it true that the blind live in their bodies rather than in the world? I am aware of my body just as I am aware of the rain. My body is similarly made up of many patterns, many different regularities and irregularities, extended in space from down there to up here.... Nothing corresponds visually to this realization. Instead of having an image of my body, as being in what we call the 'human form', I apprehend it now as these arrangements of sensitivities, a conscious space comparable to the patterns of the falling rain.... My body and the rain intermingle, and become one audio-tactile, three-dimensional universe, within which and throughout the whole of which lies my awareness.

(*On Sight* 119–20)

This passage unequivocally declares an expansive conception of self which embraces the world around the blind person. Whereas in "Fighting Depression 24 February 1984" Hull links not having a body image with disintegration of the self, in this entry he conceives of the state as opening a door onto a fresh way of understanding himself. This non-visual conception expands his consciousness much beyond the confines of his body, and transcends the body image as a representation of the self. His consciousness contains layered "arrangements of sensitivities, a conscious space comparable to the patterns of the falling rain." This shows that, for the first time, the diarist does not crave for his body image. Thus, in Swan's words, "A remarkable outcome of Hull's reflection on his experience is the possibility of imagining the body in a manner unaffected by the visual" (291). Hull's new selfhood may be symbolised by the comprehensive awareness of "one audio-tactile, three-dimensional universe." Clearly, then, the entry is a meditation on self and existence itself in relation to blindness. The questions that close it are important. I list some of them here: "Where do thoughts come from? Upon what do they depend? Into how many worlds am I inserted? What is blindness?" (*On Sight* 120). The last question suggests, in light of the discussion presented in the whole entry, and of the question preceding it, that blindness is only one aspect that may define a person's selfhood. If the person is inserted into "many worlds," the former's existence is fed by many rich sources. A corollary of this conclusion is, in Swan's words, that

> Hull can be understood as exploring versions of perception and relatedness available to sighted experience but usually hidden under the dominance of the visual. It may be from this vantage that he begins to think of blindness not as a lack or an absence but as a new existence, a gift.
>
> (292)

Thus, by elucidating his experience of the "audio-tactile, three-dimensional universe," the diarist undermines conventional ideas about bodily, perceptual, and cognitive normalcy.

In what follows, I will further examine the importance of knowledge for Hull's selfhood, and for the task of building the world of blindness. In an early entry significantly called "Darkness Within 10 July 1983" (*On Sight* 19–21), the diarist says that ignorance generates a "sense of darkness" (*On Sight* 20) in his consciousness. He explains that such situations arise "when I become a little panicky through being asthmatic or losing my way," when he does not know his children's playful activities, or when he becomes anxious, and (in his own words) "when I am emotionally involved in ignorance." When he compares the current state of his self 'in blindness' with sighted others, and with his own sighted self in the past, he experiences deep anguish: "For me, consciousness is an experience of internal darkness, in that it is no longer illuminated by colour, shape and movement." At this juncture, the modalities of touch and hearing do not fulfil his desire for "the precision, complexity and detail of the actual world" in perception. These words suggest his (mis)understanding that sight alone can provide access to these qualities. The entry, "What Blindness Does to the Brain 4 August 1983" (*On Sight* 24–5), highlights the acuteness of the dilemma concerning knowledge. It dwells on how blindness impacts "the process of knowing" (*On Sight* 25) in "recently blinded people," and brings about a profound transformation in their personalities. The lack of visual information suffocates the brain, and negatively impacts selfhood. Such persons may be said to experience "the death of the old self." However, Hull does state,

When I am engaged in something which gives me a sense of intimate and accurate knowledge, like taking part in a discussion on a subject that I know a lot about, reading an interesting book or making love, the sense of darkness diminishes. (*On Sight* 20)

These activities create in him a sense of fulfilment. Further, when he knows "the content of the relationship" (*On Sight* 21) while interacting with loved people, and also knows his environment accurately, he does not experience darkness. So knowledge is crucial for him to be at home in the self.

Now that the diarist is inserted in the blind condition, he is impelled to explore the tactile and auditory senses. However, he sets up a comparison between the two modalities from the start. In "Touching 12 July 1983" (*On Sight* 21–2), he explains with examples why he considers that "Sounds are abstract, but touch puts body on things" (*On Sight* 21). While walking around a museum or cathedral, the oral descriptions that he receives from others help him to form a picture of the place. But it is only when he touches "a statue or a piece of machinery," or explores "with [his] fingers some of the intricate carvings on the screen," or when he runs "the palms of [his] hands over the roughness of the stone" that he regains "something very vivid" in experience. Thus, he describes the tactile modality as "earth[ing] the words." He feels that bodily contact with the world through the sense of touch affords him a more intimate knowledge.

By contrast, in "Acoustic Space 27 April 1984" (*On Sight* 71–4), Hull recognises that audition makes possible a wide "range and depth of … contact points between [him]self and something created by sound" (*On Sight* 71), while the "tangible world sets up only as many points of reality as can be touched by [his] body." So, the former modality allows him to become aware of the wide world, and the latter is useful to him as a means of exploring minute, delicate details characterising reality. The reference to "space" in the title is significant because, as Hull explains in the entry entitled "Nice Day? 5 June 1983" (*On Sight* 12–13), sounds moving through the space around him create the world for him: "… the sound of the wind in the trees … creates trees; one is surrounded by trees whereas before there was nothing" (*On Sight* 12). Expressed another way, he is "thinking of the way in which sound places one within a world" (*On Sight* 72). Kuusisto's words from the essay entitled "Harbor Songs" (*Eavesdropping* 3–6) about how sounds created the world for him as a small blind boy elaborate this modality: "I put such great faith in sound: sound was this tree and that grass; this man; this dimension of light and shade" (6). As this quotation vividly expresses the point, for the boy, the world is the sounds it produces. Similarly, Hull relies on sounds to reveal the world to him. The phrase "the world of sound" (*On Sight* 71), thus, acquires the twofold meaning of acoustic phenomena and the phenomenal world which is brought to the subject's awareness by sounds, more particularly the phenomenon where objects are created for the blind subject by sounds emanating from their environment. Hull alludes to this idea when he refers to "something created by sound." The entry also shows that the diarist is experiencing a change in his outlook on life 'with blindness.' However, the transient nature of sounds leads him to conclude that he is a passive receiver: "The creatures emitting the noise have to engage in some activity... . They must take the initiative in announcing their presence to me. For my part, I have no power to explore them" (*On Sight* 73). As is clear from this quotation, the blind person who is ready to hear the world has to wait for the world to announce itself to them. Such a subject cannot "discover" creatures and objects "without their active cooperation." This feature of sound explains Hull's philosophical conclusion about his world: "When there is rest, everything else passes out of existence. To rest is not to be. To do is to be. Mine is not a world of being; it is a world of becoming." When objects in the world do not produce sounds, they simply do not exist for him. So a gap is evident between existence and knowledge in the case of the blind person when there is no sound to tell them about the former. We may, therefore, conclude that Hull exists in the world in action.

Now I come to the phenomenon of echo location, which is, in Hull's words, a "much-discussed blind experience" (*On Sight* 22). In "Facial Vision 14 July 1983" (*On Sight* 22–4), Hull records that after he became totally blind, he "gradually realized" (*On Sight* 22) that he "was developing some strange kind of perception," that is, echo location or facial vision. "This is the obtaining of information about the animal-environment system" (182), Thomas A. Stoffregen and John B. Pittenger explain, "from relations between a pulse, a perceiver-generated wavefront coming directly to the perceiver's ear from its source, and its echo, that same sound arriving at the ear after reflection from the object or surface." In this perceptual modality, then, the blind person senses the presence of objects close at hand through becoming aware of sounds being reflected off their surfaces (*On Sight* 23–4). "The sense of pressure" (*On Sight* 24) created by the echoes, Hull clarifies, "is upon the skin of the face, rather than upon or within the ears." This perceptual journey indicates the slow and sure changes taking place in the self that has been inserted in the blind condition. The shift from the past tense to the present tense employed by the diarist also indicates the temporal extension of the process covered in the entry. The following passage illustrates this point because it incorporates the shift:

Not only have I become sensitive to thinner objects, but the range seems to have increased. When walking home, I used only to be able to detect parked cars by making contact with my cane. These days I almost never make contact with a parked car unexpectedly. Nearly always, I realise that there is an obstacle in my path before my stick strikes against it. This is in spite of the fact that I am now using the very long cane.

(*On Sight* 22–3)

Besides his growing confidence in using echo location for mobility, it is also noteworthy that Hull carries the white cane which is very useful to the blind person "as an extension of his perception" (*On Sight* 33). The cane serves "as an instrument of sense perception, as a way of gathering information about the world" (*On Sight* 34) through the sense of touch.

In "Less Space, More Time 17 April 1984" (*On Sight* 69–71), Hull explores with examples of his own, and of other disabled persons' lives, how a contraction in space and an expansion in time occurs for the disabled (*On Sight* 70). This experience may be understood with the help of the "notion of lived body" (Toombs 10), as elucidated in phenomenology. Toombs explains that the lived body is the basis of the embodied subject's existence in the world, and that its disruption throws light on "the meaning of disability": "… my body *as I live it* represents my particular point of view *on the world*" (italics as in the source). It may therefore be said that I experience the lived body not as another object in the world of objects, but as the locus of my (the self's) orientation in the world, and "of my intentions" (Toombs 11). This means that I exist in the world, organise it, and perform actions in it "through the medium of my body." So, when the body is impaired, and the subject's ways of performing actions are disrupted, their experience of space and time is transformed. Due to "loss of mobility" (Toombs 15), the space that the disabled person can traverse shrinks (cf. Toombs 15; *On Sight* 70). Conversely, since it takes much more time for such a person to perform actions than it would have without the disability, time expands for them (Toombs 19; *On Sight* 70–1). Accordingly, Hull clarifies, the sighted and the blind understand time differently. Daily tasks and activities also take on a different significance for each. He concludes, "It is because of the space-time co-ordinates within which the blind person lives that his or her life becomes gradually different from the lives of sighted people, particularly in a time of high technology" (*On Sight* 71). Hull's striking analysis of why the lives of the blind are different from those of the sighted goes to the root of the matter in giving importance to space and time, which are fundamental categories in the fashioning of worlds.

Hull realises via Merleau-Ponty's phenomenological thought that blindness is significant not just because it makes it necessary for the subject to acquire a different kind of knowledge by means different from those employed by the sighted, but more because it creates a different mode of being in the world. It is noteworthy that he terms the work of blindness as "a disruption of the fundamental nature of being in the world" (*On Sight* 181), a clear indication that for him as a person who became blind midway through life, perhaps sight will always remain richer and more fruitful than blindness. However, in "Blindness as a Way of Being in the World 4 January 1986" (*On Sight* 180–81), he does talk about the blind person becoming "familiarized to his or her new body and new world" (*On Sight* 181), and about the role of the white cane in such a person's mobility. In this offering of an alternative conception, it is clear that Hull is different from his earlier self, who used to give in to sadness.

5.2 Social Interaction and Self-Knowledge

Hull offers sustained reflection throughout his diaries on his interactions with sighted friends, family members, and even with those who are blind or have other disabilities. Furthermore, as indicated in the opening paragraph of this chapter, he considers self-knowledge to arise from interactions with other people (*On Sight* xiii). Let me, then, briefly examine the dynamics of this activity as he carries it out in the blind condition. Turning to sexuality, the diarist expresses deep anxiety about sexual arousal since, as a heterosexual man, he no longer has visual access to how women look. I wish to call the reader's attention here to Hull's conditioned reliance on a sighted colleague's description of "[the] beauty or [the] plainness" (*On Sight* 18) of "a new female acquaintance" to reach a conclusion in his own mind about her worth. Thus, at this point in the diaries, he still displays a sighted man's mode of sexual response. In the entry, "Face to Face 11 January 1984" (*On Sight* 47–8), discussing the significance of "the face-to-face position" (*On Sight* 47) in lovemaking among sighted people, he describes the change in the position taken in sexual intercourse by a couple in a film about primitive humans:

> One of the most dramatic scenes was when a couple making love abandoned the position, which the film shows as being universal, in which the male partner is behind the female, for the face-to-face position. This is portrayed as the development of mere sexual intercourse into an act of communion between two persons.
>
> (*On Sight* 47)

However, the face-to-face position loses its significance for the blind lover because he cannot turn his gaze upon his beloved while making love, and pay visual attention to her. Hull wonders whether this changed circumstance diminishes the sexual power of blind persons:

> How does blindness affect lovemaking? Must not blind lovers become more primitive? Must they not regress, as it were, to the situation described in the film as being pre-personal? On the other hand, is it not possible that the blind person, dependent so heavily upon touch, smell and taste, might develop new gentleness and sensitivity in that situation which is tactile all over?
>
> (*On Sight* 47–8)

We thus see, along with Hull, how utilising the power of "touch, smell and taste" can make the blind person a more gentle and sensitive lover.

To this potent realisation of the power that the blind man possesses to please the loved woman, we may oppose Hull's experiences of being infantilised. On one occasion, a stranger in the street hands him some sweets, and says that he was planning to give them to a child (*On Sight* 95). On another occasion, a good friend lies alert through the night, even in his sleep, to warn Hull about a bathroom overflow the moment he awoke, instead of waking him earlier to tell him about it. When asked, the friend tells the diarist that this experience is similar to looking after a child. A wheelchair-using friend tells Hull how people "tend to speak to him in a gentle, slow and compassionate sort of voice. It is a kindly, condescending voice, the way some people speak to children" (*On Sight* 96). These incidents show that non-disabled people view persons with disabilities as incomplete beings who really are ineffectual, and can never be as good as themselves. Related to this attitude is the practice of speaking about the disabled "in third person, to someone else" (*On Sight* 101) in their presence. Hull recognises, however, that people do such things because they are not certain how to deal with disability (*On Sight* 96).

Hull reports further that the blind tend to be perceived by the sighted world as supernatural symbols. One night, as he is walking home from the university, a man stops him because a car has climbed onto the footpath. His brother has been driving, and is hurt. But this man explains to Hull that he himself is not hurt because he shows care towards the disabled: "'This thing has never happened to me because I always look after people like you'" (*On Sight* 34). So the blind man who walks into sight "around the corner" (*On Sight* 35) tapping his white cane instantly gets converted by the shaken man's mind into "a sort of signal from heaven" which warns him to be kind towards the disabled.

Interactions between the blind and the sighted can result in misunderstandings as well. As the diarist records in the entry entitled "Misunderstandings 26 November 1983" (*On Sight* 38–9), these situations "arise from sighted people's difficulties in realizing the problems of blind mobility" (*On Sight* 38), and consequently from the image of the blind person that they conceive in their minds. In the two examples that Hull presents, the sighted persons do not realise that the blind man has to walk along a route that is defined by objects he can feel in order to find the required gates. The former, who work by using sight to access their environment, fail to recognise the difference in the method that the non-sighted latter must use in mobility. Due to this misunderstanding, Hull reflects, the sighted end up thinking that the blind are ineffectual and need help all the time. He also remarks that, if people would follow his instructions regarding his mobility, he would be "able to do this reasonably gracefully, with only a few swings of my cane" (*On Sight* 39). So the difficulties that the sighted have in understanding how blind persons move end up affecting Hull's own behaviour. To the question as to why the blind should even get affected by what sighted persons think of them, the answer is that the reactions of the former come spontaneously. Undergoing the experience of being watched and evaluated (negatively) is like being swept down a river by a sudden flood, in which case it is but natural to react. This is a fact of intersubjectivity in the human world. When a person interacts with others, how those others behave towards them influences how they react.

Hull also reports incidents where sighted people behave with overt negativity towards him due to his blindness, on one occasion with malice (*On Sight* 77–8). In the entry, "A Visit from a Faith Healer 5 March 1984" (*On Sight* 63–5), we meet a faith healer whom the diarist calls Mr Creswell. He attempts to heal Hull of his blindness through faith and purificatory actions (*On Sight* 63–4). Soon after this incident, a hypnotherapist urges Hull to undergo healing at his hands (*On Sight* 75). However, the latter declines the offer because he considers acquiescing to faith healing as a futile exercise that degrades and humiliates him (*On Sight* 76). Accordingly, the next time at church when Mr Creswell gives him an instruction in a particularly intrusive manner, Hull directly confronts the faith-healing man, and lets him know in no uncertain terms that he is "'not prepared to be put under emotional pressure to do all these strange things week by week'" (*On Sight* 77) in a bid to regain his eyesight. What is interesting about faith healers who claim that they can heal the blind is that they are obsessed with the 'normal' body (*On Sight* 82), and are not able to accept disability and illness in their religion. They consider persons who are ill or disabled to be afflicted. This attitude is in line with the medical model of disability, which views the disabled individual as defective. By the time Hull writes *In the Beginning There was Darkness*, he has come to realise that the compulsive desire to regain lost sight expresses merely a limited, normative outlook on life 'with blindness':

> To be delivered from the restrictions of blindness into the freedom of a sighted person's life is one of the most desirable transformations that a sighted person could imagine. Naturally, blind people get caught up in this point of view.
>
> (45)

Here he recognises the dynamics of the relationship between the sighted (non-disabled) and the blind, who are actually disabled by the social expectation of 'normal' sight. So, in 1997, when a proponent of faith healing for the ill and disabled (including blind persons) writes him a patronising, intolerant letter, Hull replies in a way that is accepting of his blindness. He acknowledges his disability, and says that he is blessed with "a wonderful wife and five beautiful children" (*In the Beginning* 47), and a good job with the University of Birmingham which enables him to provide for himself and his family very well. Further, he states in his letter, "I am a Christian like yourself. My Christian life has been deepened since I lost my sight"

(*In the Beginning* 48). So he interprets his blindness "as a strange, dark and mysterious gift from God" which has strengthened the primary way of being that he embraces. He arrives at this understanding by the date 21 April 1986, when he articulates the possibility of blindness being a gift (*On Sight* 188). He reflects on this realisation in four diary entries (*On Sight* 188–90). In this way, he rebukes proponents of faith healing who look down upon the blind, ill, and other disabled people as being not only inferior to the sighted, healthy, and non-disabled, but also as incomplete Christians.

Coming to the dynamics of Hull's interactions with other people, especially new colleagues or delegates at conferences, he says that he has to learn their names in order to know them. After he meets a person for the first time through their name, "[hears] the voice and [feels] the hand clasp which would, from now on, be associated with that name" (*On Sight* 89), he builds up "the story of that person" around "the verbal cue" of the name. So, he knows friends and acquaintances through their voices and touch, which aspects of their personalities get attached to their names. People are present to Hull, he explains further, in the form of "voices suspended upon stilts – a present emerging out of a past, in time rather than in space" (*On Sight* 90). This experience may be understood when we recognise that speaking with a person takes place in time, while they are visually available to a sighted person in space. The diarist is particularly concerned about his passivity as a blind person in the social activity of "getting to know people." Since he cannot look around a room in order to find people and greet them, he has to engage the help of whoever he happens to be talking with at the moment to introduce him to other people they know (*On Sight* 90–1). This initiative on his part enables Hull to make and keep "human friendships" (*On Sight* 90).

During the years Hull grapples with his blindness, he is deeply concerned about creating opportunities to help his children understand him as a blind person. For example, he trains his son, Thomas, from a very young age to show him things by putting them into his hand, or by placing his hand on them (*On Sight* 30–1). He explains to the little boy what blindness is when the two of them listen "to the story of Rapunzel on cassette" (*On Sight* 53, 68–9). Hull writes in "Feeling Beyond Feelings 3 February 1985" (*On Sight* 133–36) that when he and Thomas play with "a large construction set" (*On Sight* 133) which he is able to handle easily due to the size of its pieces, he has "a splendid time." This activity gives him great joy because of its "reciprocal" nature. But he undergoes deep suffering when he is not able to play with his children with the assurance of a sighted person. As he is unable to see what the children are doing and what their reactions are during playtime, he feels uncontrollable sleep come over him. He comprehends this phenomenon as "a protection against an unbearable situation" (*On Sight* 134), namely his lack of adequate knowledge. It is precipitated by at least three factors, viz. his understanding at the time that sight alone can provide him access to crucial information about his children's activities, the inability of sighted persons to include him in social situations, and inaccessible toys (*On Sight* 133–35).

However, as time goes by, Hull devises ways of interacting with his children more effectively. Although "Entering a Birthday World 1 September 1985" (*On Sight* 163–64) initially records the failure he encounters in playing with Thomas, the entry goes on to tell how the former takes the initiative and gets his son to describe "every toy or game" (*On Sight* 164) the latter has got as a present on his birthday. This way, Hull is able to participate in his son's enjoyment of the "birthday world." While the entry "Leading Daddy 6 September 1985" (*On Sight* 164–65) talks about how Hull's children enjoy leading him, the one entitled "Ludo 7 September 1985" (*On Sight* 165) describes how the diarist is now well able to play various games with his children since many of them are "designed for blind people, but just as good for the sighted" (*On Sight* 165). Even when Hull is unsure of which board game the children and he are playing, because it is not "adapted for blind people," he is content to simply follow the directions given him by his children, and talk with them enthusiastically. This success in both playing with the children and accepting his own limitation evidences a significant change in his consciousness and self-conception.

Having examined the multiple ways in which, for Hull, knowing the world and being with other people constitutes selfhood, we will now move on to the next chapter. In it, I write about blindness in Kuusisto's life, memory, and art.

6 The Poetical Subjectivity of Kuusisto

Stephen Kuusisto's writings embody a self-conscious art of blindness in two ways, which are not separate but contiguous: the art of living as a blind person, and the art produced in and through blindness. This position of Kuusisto with regard to blindness is different from the positions taken by Borges and Hull. While Borges deals with blindness in his art after the aesthetic turn to experience during the late 1950s (discussed earlier in this book [ch. 2, pp. 47–58; ch. 3, pp. 73–79]), his writings still display ambiguous feelings about his blindness, bordering on a largely melancholic stance. Hull grapples with the reality of living 'with blindness' in his two diaries, and in the two books on the Bible; at times gaining insights into his existence, and coming upon moments of aesthetic experience. However, an art of blindness may not be perceived in his writings. Kuusisto, on the other hand, explores the experience of blindness employing a narrative aesthetics that is deeply aware of the artistic potential of this way of being-in-the-world. His three autobiographical works, namely *Planet of the Blind: A Memoir* (1998), *Eavesdropping: A Life by Ear* (2006), and *Have Dog, Will Travel* (2018), embody an aesthetic shaped by sensory experience. The first book is a long narrative with "a dramatic scenario" (*Eavesdropping* xi), the second, a collection of twenty-nine essays called "auditory postcards or tone poems" (*Eavesdropping* xii), and the last, a narration of the story of Kuusisto's partnership with his guide dog.

The memoirs tell the story of how Kuusisto's difficult journey embodies a movement over several years from an outright rejection of blindness to embracing it. Early in the first book, the memoirist writes, "Raised to know I was blind but taught to disavow it, I grew bent over like the dry tinder grass" (*Planet of the Blind* 7). It is worth comparing the previous statement with the following one from the preface to the second book: "Happily I no longer crave recognition as a sighted person. At fifty I've learned how to be as much of myself as possible" (*Eavesdropping* ix). While the former clearly indicates that Kuusisto's long-term rejection of blindness is strongly influenced by his parents' and society's negative attitudes towards blindness, the latter leaves the reader with little doubt that the memoirist has grown into a complete blind person. Taken together, the two memoirs tell the story of his development from the state of disavowal to the total acceptance of blindness, together with its artistic potential and the world that it creates.

DOI: 10.4324/9781003399667-6

The works harness the metaphoric power of sensory deliverances to render the richness of Kuusisto's experience comprehensible to the reader. The narrating voices in the memoirs are those of the grown-up Kuusisto who has come to terms with his blindness. Hence, the books may be considered to be the fruition of the blind artist's labours. His narrative technique involves presenting the viewpoint of the experiencing self and analysing the writing self in a complementary fashion. This method may be elucidated by citing Penelope Scambly Schott's words defining the genre of memoirs: "Memoirs are about seeing—what you saw then, and how you see it now" (218). Although Kuusisto takes forward his story in a chronological order, he alternates between various times in his life to build the narrative. Describing a particular episode or occurrence, he narrates incidents from either the future or the past to illustrate a point relevant to that time of his life. He tells his multifaceted story in tight prose which combine narrative, poetry, and reflection. Another important feature of the narratives is that, in them, Kuusisto connects his experiences to those of other disabled persons and artists who lived in the past, or who are still living whenever relevant (*Planet of the Blind* 22, 30–1; *Eavesdropping* 3, 9, 14). In this way, he locates his experiences in the wider world, thereby indicating that they may not be isolated in an atomistic fashion.

6.1 Being Bound with the Minute Threads of Normalcy

Born "three months prematurely, in March 1955" (*Planet of the Blind* 5), Kuusisto is placed in an "overly oxygenated" (*Planet of the Blind* 6) incubator. As a result, he is left with the visual impairment called the retinopathy of prematurity (meaning his "retinas are scarred"), and he also has additional ophthalmic complications, viz. nystagmus and strabismus. This compounded impairment foregrounds his body in its difference from that of a 'normal' person. Although in childhood he has barely enough sight in his left eye (he cannot focus the other eye) to read "dark and large" (*Planet of the Blind* 6) print from very close, he is definitely a blind person "who possess[es] some marginal vision" (*Planet of the Blind* 6). For this reason, the memoirist says that blindness should not be regarded "as an either/or condition" (*Planet of the Blind* 5) in which the person "[either] sees or does not see" (*Planet of the Blind* 5). Instead, his blindness may be described as a "series of veils" (*Planet of the Blind* 5) constituted by "heliographic distortions of sunlight or dusk" (*Planet of the Blind* 5). He experiences what he calls, with humour, "a mad, holy vision, the repeated appearance and disappearance of the physical world" (*Planet of the Blind* 7). Thus, his sensorium is characterised by abstract shapes and colours that are unreliable, "disturbing" (*Planet of the Blind* 6), and blinding. Kuusisto repeatedly mentions the effects of his residual vision. When, for instance, he says, "Even today I live in the 'customs house' between the land of the blind and those who possess some minor capacity to see" (*Planet of the Blind* 11), it is clear to the reader that he is bringing the narrative (which, at this point, is dealing with his childhood) to the present to show how the thread of residual sight runs through his life. This point is also made clear when he explains, in the preface to *Eavesdropping* (ix–xiv), what his "own version of blindness" (xii) entails: "Blind people who have this condition [the retinopathy of prematurity] often see the world in fragments.... . This kind of seeing is both beautiful and worrisome" (xii). As this quotation suggests, residual vision shapes the particular form of his subjectivity.

Kuusisto characterises his boyhood as dominated by the twofold behaviour of denial of blindness and the need to 'pass,' that is, to appear as a sighted child. Simi Linton explains the idea of 'passing' as follows:

> Disabled people, if they are able to conceal their impairment or confine their activities to those that do not reveal their disability, have been known to pass ... passing may be a deliberate effort to avoid discrimination or ostracism, or it may be an almost unconscious, Herculean effort to deny to oneself the reality of one's ... bodily state. The attempt may be a deliberate act to protect oneself from the loathing of society or may be an unchecked impulse spurred by an internalized self-loathing.... . When disabled people are able to pass for nondisabled, and do, the emotional toll it takes is enormous.
>
> (166)

Kuusisto engages in 'passing' (that is to say, he conceals his disability) over many tormenting years, from childhood to the age of thirty-nine (*Planet of the Blind* 41, 171), for the reasons mentioned above. He confirms this assertion when he writes about how his mother, motivated by "a horror of blindness" (*Planet of the Blind* 14), enforces on him from a very tender age the attitude of rejecting his disability. In *Eavesdropping*, he offers a related reason for his persistent effort to 'pass' as a sighted boy: "Like many children with disabilities, I was eager to be a part of the world around me and capable of denial if denying my blindness allowed me to join in the activities of normal children" (ix). Besides the desire to protect himself from discrimination and loathing, the wish to participate in the activities of "normal" children encourages him to engage in this behaviour. Thus, he shuns life as a blind person in accordance with his mother's attitude towards the disability:

> I am going to be dimly sighted and normal. According to her, I will damn well ride a bike and go sledding, and do whatever the hell else ordinary children do. To her the prospect of the white cane denotes the world of the invalid. But I need that cane. I am about to begin an impossible contest with the sighted world, a display that today is known as "passing" or more correctly, "trying to pass."
>
> (*Planet of the Blind* 14–15)

This passage encapsulates the clash between the blind person and the over-whelming sighted world which dictates norms to the blind regarding the 'right' way to live. Kuusisto explains that in his strenuous attempts 'to pass' as a sighted boy, he is egged on by his mother's good intentions:

> I begin this eccentric waltz with my mother's own fears that blindness means a reduced life for her child. But behind every facsimile of accomplishment lies that word, like a corset with a thousand minute laces, each one a thread of normalcy.
>
> (*Planet of the Blind* 42)

Although his mother strongly desires that her son should lead a full life, and in this light considers blindness as a limiting condition, the memoirist suggests that her attitude of rejection towards his disability was conditioned by normative ideas about life and embodiment. The struggle that he goes through due to these societal and maternal demands for normalcy, his attempts to fulfil them, and his final embrace of blind selfhood form the major themes of *Planet of the Blind*.

This devaluation of the "blind self" (*Planet of the Blind* 7), which the memoirist calls "that blackened dolmen" with reference to his self-conception at the time, is enforced on the disabled individual from above, as is clear from this discussion, by society and their family. It is with this complex, normative "web of beliefs" (Hagberg 123) as the background that Kuusisto comments,

> I couldn't stand up proudly, nor could I retreat. I reflected my mother's complex bravery and denial and marched everywhere at dizzying speeds without a cane.... . The very words *blind* and *blindness* were scarcely to be spoken around me. I would see to this by my exemplary performance. My mother would avoid the word, relegating it to the province of cancer.
>
> (italics as in the source, *Planet of the Blind* 7)

Thus, from childhood onwards, he learns how not to be (and works hard not to appear as) a blind person in the eyes of the sighted world and for himself, living according to the scarring thought, "Who would choose to be blind?" (*Planet of the Blind* 8). He is very active, doing the things that sighted boys (and later, adolescents and men) do in order to 'be' a sighted person in a 'normal' world.

6.2 Boyhood and Adolescence

The memoirist writes that when he was given his "first pair of glasses at the age of three" (*Planet of the Blind* 7), he did not want to wear them. So, he continues, "I carried them in secret to the garden and buried them under the wide leaves of a rhubarb plant." This (almost strange) action suggests that the small boy had already come under the influence of normative beliefs concerning blindness and sight. The problem is highlighted by the encounter the boy and his father had with an "old crone" (*Planet of the Blind* 10) when the family lived in Helsinki, Finland. One day, when the three-year-old boy and his father were "climbing the stairs ... in [their] apartment building," the former became an "object of scrutiny" for "a severe old woman." This woman pointed out that the boy was blind (later in this chapter, I write more about becoming an exhibit [141–42]). This insensitive act angered the young target. Kuusisto writes,

> I was not quite sighted; I wished to never be blind. Didn't this old crone know that I'd buried my first pair of glasses under the rhubarb? This will be a nearly lifelong puzzle for me: Am I not a sighted boy? Am I not attempting bravely to see? What must I do?.
>
> (*Planet of the Blind* 10–11)

The incident shows that, even at the tender age of three, he knew the dilemma of a blind person: how to live in the sighted world in which one is sightless? Although he was blind, and his marginal vision did not aid him in any way, he refused to regard himself as a blind boy (person), and the memoirist indicates the child's desire: "I wished to never be blind." This is because, as he states in the preface to *Eavesdropping*, "I was ashamed of my disability throughout my childhood and this sadness was compounded by my mother's militant refusal to use the words 'blind' or 'blindness'" (xii). The three questions concluding the above quotation concerning the boy's helpless anger at the words of the "old crone" (*Planet of the Blind* 10–11) speak volumes about the normative, sighted world's hold on the minds of blind persons. It is this tyrannical requirement to "bravely" attempt to live like 'normal,' sighted people which impoverishes the lives of the blind.

When the Kuusistos return to the United States, the boy's mother has to struggle to enrol her blind son in an ordinary school. The memoirist writes, "... my mother decides to enrol me in public school instead of an institution for the blind and finds both consternation and disapproval from school and staff officials" (*Planet of the Blind* 12). Moreover, some parents of 'normal' children, due to their ignorance of disability, prevent the disabled boy from playing with their children. This is because they "think [he] might break during ordinary play." However, this concern appears to be only an excuse, because when the boy asks them, "'Why don't you tell them to play with me?'" (*Planet of the Blind* 13), they avoid giving any answer to the child. This is probably because they do not want their children to play with a disabled boy. Thus, we get glimpses of societal prejudice against the disabled, and of the pressure brought to bear upon the mother and child to govern themselves on account of the latter's disability.

An episode narrating a painful encounter between a blind social worker and Kuusisto's mother demonstrates the complex choices that the disabled and their families are faced with while trying to live life in a society not prepared to accept its disabled members. The social worker advises the mother to enrol her blind son in a school for the blind because, at such an institution, the child would learn the life skills necessary for the blind. That would include Braille, and how to use the white cane, both of which skills he would never be able to acquire in "the public schools of the day" (*Planet of the Blind* 14). The mother lives in denial of her son's blindness, and wants him to live as a 'normal' person with his residual sight. As suggested earlier, she is impelled by the desire for her son to have "the same kind of social experience" as other, non-disabled children. Contrasting the schooling system available for the blind in the 1960s with those functioning today, the memoirist writes that life for blind and visually impaired children in America of the 1960s and 1970s was extremely limiting. Out of necessity, they had to attend segregated institutions devoted to educating and giving them vocational training instead of enabling them to gain full exposure to social life. Kuusisto interprets his mother's decision as follows: "Hers is an urgent and primitive choice, one that today would be unnecessary as blind children regularly attend public schools and receive cane, travel, and Braille lessons at the same time." Be that as it may, his mother decides that her son should attend a public school, and her resistance to the white cane proves to be a terrible deprivation for the boy. As we will see, he grows up rejecting his blindness due to shame, thus shunning his disabled self for several years.

So, when the boy starts attending the public school, the memoirist writes, "I am without assistance" (*Planet of the Blind* 18). Due to the lack of "special education standards" to get schools to accommodate blind and visually impaired students and guide them in this task, his school does not provide him with educational facilities adapted to the needs of visually impaired children, such as Braille lessons and "large print materials." As a result, he cannot follow classes efficiently: "My fingers slide in all directions. I clasp and unclasp the lid of my pencil box, trace the scars on my desk." This narrative description captures the blind child's reaction to the inability to understand lessons without suitable help. The adult memoirist's retrospection brings out the bewilderment and boredom of years ago very well. In the following passage, he stresses the boy's isolation in class:

> While the class reads aloud, I watch the spirals of hypnotic light that ripple across my eyes when I move them from side to side. I do not belong here. My little body at this desk is something uncanny – a thing that belongs in the darkness and that has been brought to daylight.
>
> (*Planet of the Blind* 20)

These words indicate the blind boy's dilemma about sight – which the child cannot articulate – and feeling of not belonging to the sighted world of school. His form of blindness means that he is painfully exposed to the "hypnotic light" of "daylight" which renders him vulnerable. Under such circumstances, the boy cannot restrain himself from talking during class hours. The teacher, Mrs. Edinger, catching him whispering to a child sitting beside him, immediately inscribes his name on "a Photograph above the blackboard [of] two chubby infants swaddled in diapers" (*Planet of the Blind* 17–18). The ashamed boy, "swollen shut" (*Planet of the Blind* 18), has to endure his classmates' derisive laughter. Another method the teacher adopts to get the students to do their work efficiently results in Kuusisto's mistreatment by a classmate. The memoirist describes the pedagogic method in question here: "Students who finish their in-class assignments before the rest will henceforth be 'astronauts'—permitted to orbit the classroom and peer over the shoulders of others" (*Planet of the Blind* 19). A boy who finishes his work before the rest of the children takes advantage of the blind Kuusisto's inability to read print, and makes fun of him. Thus, the teacher fails to realise that such inducements to get the children to obey may cause unnecessary pain to those who are slow, and who require help and support.

Despite the difficulties the boy has to undergo, most crucially the agony of having to rely entirely on his damaged sight, he gains some knowledge in school, as the memoirist states: "[I follow] lessons without usable print or concrete numbers... . I follow the teacher's words and make a kind of caged progress, trapped as I am in my own neural nets" (*Planet of the Blind* 19). In the absence of facilities such as Braille, usable print, or concrete numbers, the boy listens to the teacher's words and makes limited progress. Listening and "repetition" allow blind children to acquire a surprising amount of information in the classroom and from their environment.[1] In *Eavesdropping*, Kuusisto stresses the importance of listening in the classroom:

> [I] listened to teachers when I was a small boy and developed an auditory version of what was happening around me. Unable to see the chalkboard or read a standard book, I learned by necessity how to hear both for content and splendour.
>
> (xi)

Kuusisto was, even as a child, keenly aware of the power of listening. Further, he receives unexpected encouragement and additional academic help from Mrs. Edinger, who we learn is a black woman. The memoirist recognises that the marginalised status shared by the teacher as an African American and himself as a blind boy helped in bringing them close to each other. Mrs. Edinger, as he writes, has "noticed my determination and has figured out that I have a photographic memory" (*Planet of the Blind* 20). This observation motivates her to give him additional lessons.

1 This observation holds true to my experience as well.

However, the heroic act of reading with one eye causes the boy great physical agony. Merleau-Ponty's discussion of what he calls "an example of morbid motility" (117) or, in other words, of difficulties faced by a person with a nervous disorder is important in the discussion of problems encountered by blind persons (due to their impairment) in doing their work. Kuusisto writes,

> I have to hold my book an inch from my eye and try hard to hold the hot, spasming muscle. The exhaustion of this is like the deep fatigue drivers feel after being too long on the road. The ordinary effort of reading is, for me, a whole-body experience. My neck, shoulders, and, finally, my lower back contract with pain. The legally blind know what it is to be old: even before the third grade I am hunched and shaking with effort, always on the verge of tears, seeing by approximation, craving a solid sentence.
>
> (*Planet of the Blind* 21)

This passage vividly represents the sheer corporeality of the boy's experience of reading with his damaged "left eye" (*Planet of the Blind* 6). As Merleau-Ponty points out, we find here that Kuusisto's visual impairment has "its repercussions on the main body of experience and open [s] the door to its disintegration" (157); that is to say, it affects "the whole of consciousness." Such a thing happens because "the life of consciousness ... is subtended by an 'intentional arc' ... which brings about the unity of the senses, of intelligence, of sensibility and motility." So, blindness results in a different mode of being which the boy is not able to accept and make his own. The blind boy's painful physical state of being "hunched and shaking with effort" (*Planet of the Blind* 21) while attempting to read may be contrasted with "the uprightness of the [blind] man" (*Planet of the Blind* 1, 171) portrayed in the prologue and towards the end of the memoir. This interpretative exercise paradoxically gives us a quasi-visual image of the movement in Kuusisto's self-conception from one who labours under the tyranny of norms dictated by the non-disabled world to one who is at home 'with his blindness' in the world (or planet) of the blind.

As Kuusisto is able to keep up with the class with help from Mrs. Edinger, he is treated better by his classmates. He is now able to maintain the appearance of not being blind. However, ironically, the next recorded experience belies the child's sense of achievement, and shows him that he is still only "blindo" (*Planet of the Blind* 21) – a weak boy to be made fun of – to his sighted peers: "... a boy I think of as a friend," writes the memoirist, harasses him at school by stealing his glasses. "More than thirty years" after "that moment," Kuusisto continues to be "disconcerted by what it felt like to belong so thoroughly to other people, to be, in effect, their possession." The panic and confusion he experiences in this situation literally make him an exhibit. (This feeling of having become a spectacle is familiar to most disabled persons.) Thus, the memoirist describes the corporeal experience of the boy in order to bring out the social dynamics of disability, which act of representation allows him to integrate that experience of humiliation into his subjectivity.

By depicting the classroom as a microcosm of society, for such is true in the case of children, Kuusisto shows how teachers and parents are responsible for the continuance of prevailing attitudes towards the disabled. The truth of this assertion becomes abundantly clear when, in accordance with normative preferences, the blind boy's doctor and parents make him wear "glasses fitted with telescopes" (*Planet of the Blind* 22). This imposition leads to his being harassed with labels such as "Martian" and "Magoo." The popular representation (in a magazine) of Mr. Magoo, who is a blind fool, belongs to "a long line of comic blind characters playing the role of the sighted man." The boy's harassment by his classmates may be interpreted as the enactment of the ideology of the 'normal' body which objectifies blind people. "When Mr. Magoo drives a car" (*Planet of the Blind* 23), explains the memoirist, "America's television audience experiences the same comic frisson as Hauy's villagers who laughed at the beggars wearing cardboard spectacles. But the blind are seldom depicted as being more than this. They are blind fools, or conversely, they're suddenly cosmic." Here, Kuusisto draws the reader's attention to the representational aesthetic that conceives of disabled characters either as freaks or as heroes. Thus, the lives of disabled persons come to be defined by their disabilities. These identity markers are perceived as being so important in such people's existence that other aspects of their personalities become obscured (as happens to the memoirist at school). When the ophthalmologist ignores him as a person and talks "about [him] in the third person" (*Planet of the Blind* 28), we see how the blind child is reduced to merely an object of study as a patient. In writing about these experiences, Kuusisto sketches the direct consequence of the medical model of understanding persons with disabilities according to which the impaired individual must be normalised by repairing their body.

In contrast to the painful experiences just described, Kuusisto next moves to activities which shape his self 'in blindness.' Following his mother's decision, he discovers typing at school. It quickly becomes a means of fostering creativity: "Soon I am left to writing stories... . Because I'd been reading Kipling on records, I fashion a primeval forest and fill it with conversational birds. Sometimes I write about submarines, sinking ships, people lost at sea" (*Planet of the Blind* 29). Now that he has a suitable instrument in the typewriter to develop the art of expression, he takes early steps in that direction. The memoirist relates an anecdote about Borges to suggest the crucial importance of practising literature: As "the blind poet who lived in Buenos Aires" and a "woman friend" walked together in the city, the former

would narrate ... funny, involuted, decorous stories about the world that he could invent as a means of navigating the hours. The stories were an amusement, the intellectual equivalent of card playing, a pictorial solitaire that could be shared, a demarcation of art and of mental health.

(*Planet of the Blind* 30)

Clearly, these stories which arise from the isolation of blindness enable both the boy and the poet not only to amuse themselves and their friends, but also to fashion new worlds. Thus, Kuusisto draws a strong connection between his own storytelling activity as an eager boy on the typewriter and Borges's stories, and casts art as a means of preserving sanity and the self. The world of literature, the sound of voices on the radio, and music are Kuusisto's companions as an isolated child with no boyhood to speak of in the blind condition. We read about Mary Day, a blind woman in 19th-century America, through whose story Kuusisto emphasises the power of art to shape the self. Referring to the "music lessons" (*Planet of the Blind* 30) she gladly took in the "blind asylum" where she was living, he says that "they gave her the means to shape her blindness, her days could become a tapestry of sounds." This brief sketch exemplifies a significant feature of the narrative method employed in the memoir, namely the technique of compressing memories and stories about other blind people into vivid vignettes.

The memoirist describes in minute tactual detail the discoveries he makes as a boy in his grandmother's house. It is "a long-in-the-tooth yellow Victorian" (*Planet of the Blind* 31) which reminds him of a "four-story museum." The house is located in New England, and is a place where the boy finds playmates in his cousin Jim and his sister Carol. For one who is denied the pleasures of playing with other children, it is no coincidence that he discovers a few joys of blindness in the solitary attic of his grandmother's house while enjoying a game of hide-and-seek with the two children:

> There are doors in the attic that open into the deepest closets, places of rich concealment, rooms without lights, rooms that have never had lights. In here I am not at a disadvantage: my body is like a falling silk scarf in the blackness... My hands are actually breathing. This is pleasure: to be blind in the museum dark, unwrapping and holding.
>
> (*Planet of the Blind* 32–3)

Moving stealthily in the darkness of the attic, exploring the innumerable strange objects he discovers in there, the boy comes to realise the pleasures that the non-visual world offers. Away from this exciting world that is friendly to him as a blind boy, the "daylight world" (*Planet of the Blind* 33), in sharp contrast, reduces him to a tormented loiterer "on the sidelines" of school life.

With the passing of time – now he is in "the fourth grade," and his schoolmates use the f-word to abuse him – he has grown despondent due to exclusion and loneliness. He eats uncontrollably to comfort himself: "With no exercise plan, I've ballooned. By the fourth grade, I am buried in my girth, fat with anguish and defeat" (*Planet of the Blind* 33). The memoirist writes that as this lonely, excluded boy, he would spend his nights feeling ugly and inferior (*Planet of the Blind* 34). He has internalised the social rejection resulting from people's negative attitudes towards the blind, and towards those who are fat. After a particularly stinging, humiliating experience in class, the narrator describes the helpless vulnerability of the blind boy:

> More laughter. I stumble into the hallway like a child who has wet his pants. For refuge I have the nurse's office, where I lie in the dark like Tutankhamen. My mask is a cold cloth. There are headaches that spread from my skull to my stomach. My entire body is uninhabitable. I have backaches from leaning and straining to see. The heat inside my body is oppressive: I'm parched, clogged. Never have I been so thirsty.
>
> (*Planet of the Blind* 43)

Under the hammering impact of societal pressure (or power), it is difficult to explain the psychological reason(s) for someone who is disabled to give in to the desire 'to pass' even if it leaves them exhausted and broken. It may be said that such behaviour is impelled by the person's nature of being a social animal. This gives other non-disabled people the power (and ability) to reduce that person to a palpitating wreck. Thus, Kuusisto moves into his teens, still hungering to see.

Using a nimble method of telling his story, with the help of which he weaves ideas and memories born of association, Kuusisto narrates how, as a child, he read (or listened to recorded) books voraciously: "I stayed alone in rooms, listening as a daily ritual, hardening my memory, making my tongue sharp" (*Planet of the Blind* 40). However, his immersion in language increases his desire to see: "My appetite for seeing is fed by lingo as vanilla." His parents encourage him in his denial of blindness. Derisive peers force him to reject who he is. And so, the words "the addiction to pass" (*Planet of the Blind* 41) are significant. The narrator asks,

> Why can't I tell him [his father] how little I'm seeing? What's wrong with a life of color and light, inferences pouring through my skin like dream-water?
>
> How do you personalize darkness, make it yours, if you're living in denial?.
>
> (*Planet of the Blind* 41)

Here Kuusisto wonders why as a boy he was unable to figure out the value of his kind of blindness, which exposes him painfully to "colour and light," and forces him to infer, as in dreams, the nature of the world around him. He recognises the suffering of the child, his inability to accept blindness, which state of self, as he realises later, would enable him to flourish.

This reflection brings us to the question of sexuality. Kuusisto describes his sexual awakening by offering an early scene of masturbation. It is important to point out here that this activity requires visual excitement:

Blind Portnoy!
This is what girls look like! Look at this! Its perfection! Curve of
breasts, hair cascading!
My God!
I'm Quasimodo.
Who would ever accept my passionate approach?
How will I ever get close enough to see a girl's face?
                                                    (*Planet of the Blind* 45)

Here the memoirist indicates that the blind adolescent's sexual expectations
are shaped by sighted male values of ideal female sexual bodies, and the
improbable depictions of pornographic perfection. He suggests the boy's
excited and despairing thoughts through the exclamatory throes of language. So, in the midst of his sexual thrill, he is discouraged by the thought
of his own disabled body's yearning. The fix he finds himself in concerning
girls and sex is well articulated in the following quotation: "... desire is
conveyed by a fixed eye. The steady eye makes one available, places us in
the centre of a room. But my eyes would not hold still" (*Planet of the Blind*
51). Since he is caught in the sexual paradigm of the sighted world, we find
here the dilemma faced by a blind person who is expected (forced) to behave
according to social norms that favour the sighted. The blind boy is thus
disabled by society, which does not accommodate his needs by providing
accepted means of socialising with potential sexual partners.

As a teenager, Kuusisto encounters "a dozen blind men [who] sit at a table
in a coffee warehouse" (*Planet of the Blind* 48) depicted in an 1885 photograph. Then the memoirist offers a history of the blind encompassing the
civilisations of the world, which reveals various stereotypes used over time to
characterise them:

> Their one talent was their compensatory payment from God—all
> human feats of memory or articulation became the proof of a divine
> intervention. As a result, the blind have appeared throughout history as
> bearers of divine judgment... . The coffee drinkers are descended from
> a vast and powerful clan.
>
>   (*Planet of the Blind* 49)

The narrator says that the fifteen-year-old boy sat in an octagonal room
(which had been built in the nineteenth century for the purpose of conducting
séances) in the Kuusistos' residence at Geneva, New York, and dreamt about
the long line of blind people down the millennia (*Planet of the Blind* 48–50).
This may suggest a recognition of the self as an inheritor of all that blindness
entails personally and socially "throughout history" (*Planet of the Blind* 49).
Thus, Kuusisto recognises historical continuity in the types of relationships
existing between various societies and the blind.

Then Kuusisto's social life begins to change along with his self, which shrinks from his blindness due to shame:

> ... in all the fractions of denial, I'm growing thinner. I conjure tutelary angels, seraphs who will spin me faster, burning my incompleteness into blackened sugar.... .
>
> I tell my parents I have a stomach ache, and I do. I'm overflowing with blind shame, embarrassments of the flesh, humiliation of the demiurge: I cannot look you in the eye.... .
>
> Weight is vanishing, and no one looks at my face. My identity is being solicitously honed.
>
> (*Planet of the Blind* 52–3)

Here, the memoirist fuses the personal and the social aspects of identity through his corporeality. He talks about his "incompleteness," "blind shame," and the erosion of his self-worth because no one looks at his face, that is, no girl shows any interest in him.

Later, he grows dangerously thin: "Upstairs I'm free to be urgently thin, inverted around my disappearance. My shrinking is an abstraction, just as I am. Together we are a species" (*Planet of the Blind* 56). He starves himself in a sign of surrender to his shame of the disabled self. So, in the case of Kuusisto (as with Borges and Hull), we find a doubling of the self in the form of two abstractions, viz. "my shrinking" and the blind "I" (*Planet of the Blind* 58). Interestingly, this phenomenon of psychological doubling accompanies the experience of being, or the desire to become, invisible in Borges (Ubelaker Andrade 59; Hull, *On Sight* 51–52; Kuusisto, *Planet of the Blind* 56). The memoirist indicates that both his obesity and anorexia are expressions of his shame as an 'incomplete' person. He experiences a diminished self-worth on account of lacking a sex life (*Planet of the Blind* 58). Sexual hunger, and the blind teenager's despair that he can attract no girl due to his disability, clash to produce a conflicted selfhood.

Later, just before he receives his first kiss from a girl, says Kuusisto of his friends and himself:

> We are each seeking some kind of transparent nourishment. Moira wants to act. Teddy needs a town where he can play the horn. I'm under the roof of disability, an iron-coloured room. I belong to fruitfulness but have no idea that blindness does too.
>
> (*Planet of the Blind* 59)

Here Kuusisto talks about "fruitfulness" in blindness, which refers to his future as a poet and writer. The image of his being trapped in a confining space, i.e., a restrictive conception of disability, suggests that the narrating voice is that of the Kuusisto who is writing his memoir. Unlike the boy, the writer clearly regards his blindness as "a rich way of living" (*Planet of the Blind* 59), that is, it is a creative force "rich as an oak tree or strong grapes." That the memoirist writes of his future creativity along with the narration of his first kiss with a girl suggests a link between fruitfulness and sexual fulfilment.

One day, Kuusisto is touched by the suggestion by his eleventh-grade English teacher, Mr Morton, that his class "pray for [him]" (*Planet of the Blind* 60). After ascertaining that the teacher and class were not being derisive of him, the teenager responds in his mind to Mr Morton's kind thought:

> I wouldn't be telling the truth if I said that at that moment I regretted taking the acid. But I make a resolution that I should go to school. The teacher said the truth. I haven't been there in over a month. I've spent days roaming around like a sleeping wanderer. Blind Huck... .
>
> I'm trying to imagine the power of prayer—other people's prayers. I don't quite get it, the connection between faith and reward in my life seems so far apart. But lately, I have been eating without appearing to have made a conscious choice. I don't know what changed me, but to this day, the Eucharist can start me weeping.
>
> (*Planet of the Blind* 61–2)

He has been shunning school because, for too long, teachers and his peers have regarded him only as an inferior creature due to his blindness. Shame about his blind self also plays a major role in his behaviour. Kuusisto indicates that, touched by the teacher's gesture, he has emerged from his eating disorder a changed person.

In 1973, Kuusisto enters college, but he still denies his blindness. He refuses to use the white cane for mobility and soldiers on using his damaged eye to read the nearly inaccessible print. This behaviour and barriers erected in his path such as "unreadable print in books, the dark dormitory room, the inaccessible library books" (*Planet of the Blind* 64) make up the familiar forces that disable him. However, he finds that reading books and poetry "are wholly necessary" (*Planet of the Blind* 65). He has a way with language, and he experiments with words to fashion something fruitful:

> I often go home from the library with the few words I've been able to see and absorb still vivid in my imagination. Alone, I take the words apart and rearrange them like Marcel Duchamp playing chess with his own private rules ... exploring what words can do when placed side by side, I'm starting to build the instrument that will turn my blindness into a manner of seeing.
>
> (*Planet of the Blind* 66)

The idea that poetry is "the instrument that will turn [his] blindness into a manner of seeing" suggests that artistic expression allows the young man to "see" in a different way, that is to say, it is somehow visionary. This conception of poetry means that it enables the solitary, anguished disabled student to be with himself, and also find fruitfulness later in his life as a poet.

Kuusisto writes that his experience of being read to by a young woman called Ramona has a liberating effect on his social life. As he listens to her inspiring reading of poetry, lying flat on his back in a quiet room of the college library, his sexual nature is awakened: "Oddly enough, eros, syllables, and alchemy are facts, particularly in the lives of young people ... my habitual shyness around women begins to fall away. Outside the library, I find myself conversing with my female classmates with ease" (*Planet of the Blind* 69). Thus, from the splendour of spoken poetry, we move with the blind man to matters of romance and sex. He finds love with an "altogether irreverent young woman" (*Planet of the Blind* 70) whom he calls Bettina:

> I begin to cry. I who cannot see a woman's face, who can't look someone in the eye, I, I, who, what, never thought this could happen. I'm crying in earnest, copious sparkles... .
>
> Bettina refastens her dress, retrieves a tortoiseshell hair clasp, arranges it, sings very softly some lines from Yeats... .
>
> I'm unimaginably blessed. The crystallography of sharpened syntax, image, her voice behind it, wash of water on stones.
>
> (*Planet of the Blind* 71)

This poetic passage shows that the blind young man discovers peace in himself for the first time in his sexual relationship with Bettina. However, even in his relationship with his first girlfriend, he needs to show that he can see: "Even while I know she knows I can't see, I still need to appear sighted. Manage my steps. Look forceful. Race-walk in the white foam" (*Planet of the Blind* 78). Travelling with Bettina and other college mates in Greece, the young man experiences agonies due to his denial of blindness:

> There is oil on the paving stones. I'm beneath a wave of light, my arms and legs so tense, I must look like a child wearing clean clothes. Hypersensitive, holding my breath, I try to navigate the narrow walks impossible for footing.
>
> (*Planet of the Blind* 79)

He finds it terribly difficult to walk in the streets of Athens because he does not carry even a white cane. The above quotation acquires its semantic force when we recognise that the memoirist is writing from the perspective of a blind man who knows how to use the white cane, and who has mastered mobility with the help of his guide dog. Due to his difficulties in walking and inability to see, he starts hating his blind self again (*Planet of the Blind* 84–6). He longs to accept his blindness and be at peace with himself by asking Bettina to take his hand and guide him through the ruins and wherever else they might travel together. However, he cannot open his lips to utter the words about his disability (*Planet of the Blind* 86–7).[2] Then he and Bettina part ways because she chooses to take her own path in life. Kuusisto remarks that in the 1970s, both young women and young men in the United States have the liberty to choose their fields, though the latter do not like this (*Planet of the Blind* 90).

On graduating "from college with highest honours in English and a cum laude diploma" (*Planet of the Blind* 91), Kuusisto must confront the uncertainty of what to do as a blind person. Wishing to study further, he has applied to graduate schools but is not certain about the results. He hates the thought of living in dependence on somebody else. So he decides as follows: "Roaming in needy tandem with the others who can see is no substitute for a room of one's own—this I understand. I need to live somehow, I don't know" (*Planet of the Blind* 93). Here the intertextual allusion to Woolf's essay with the crucial expression "a room of one's own" spells out the one principle important to the selfhood of the blind man. Then he joins the graduate programme of the Writers' Workshop at the University of Iowa (*Planet of the Blind* 95).

6.3 Struggles with Normativity: The Adult Years

Enrolled as a graduate student at the University of Iowa, although Kuusisto experiences considerable difficulty finding readers (peers who would read to him his course material), he is eligible to receive "social security assistance" (*Planet of the Blind* 96), which translates into a stipend. Also, for the first time, he finds an organisation – the Commission for the Blind – that exists for the sole purpose of supporting blind people living in Iowa State. Thinking about the academic difficulties he experiences in the 1970s, the memoirist contrasts the situation then with the technological facilities for the blind and a powerful legal tool to enforce rights of the disabled in the form of the Americans with Disabilities Act in the 1990s (*Planet of the Blind* 103). Barry, a "very secure, compact, cool" (*Planet of the Blind* 97) blind man who is comfortable using the white cane, works for the commission. Kuusisto accords him great respect: "He's the second angel in my life after Mrs. Edinger, who thought I could read with a little extra effort." Barry understands the blind student's disability like no one before in his life. Kuusisto writes, "Here's a stranger who understands me: this is as beautiful and unforeseeable as the guest who appears in poems by Kabir, the guest who is really a god, but a god who has known you all along" (*Planet of the Blind* 98). Thus, we see a mystical strain in the memoirist. Barry, whom he calls "my first ever blind adviser" (*Planet of the Blind* 97), tries to nudge him out of his long-ingrained denial of his own blind self by encouraging him to carry

2 Here, I wish to call the reader's attention to an episode narrated later on in *Planet of the Blind*. As a Fulbright scholar in Helsinki, Kuusisto finds love with a young woman named Karina, who is a student in the city. He experiences the same difficulty due to his rejection of the blind self.

the white cane (*Planet of the Blind* 99–100). However, despite this help, Kuusisto persists in not carrying a cane, and rejects his being-in-blindness. As a child, he faced prejudice due to his disability, and was sidelined at school and outside. Therefore, he finds it agonisingly difficult now as a young man to come out of the trap of sightedness forced upon him. Kuusisto describes his younger self as being "in my self-constructed village of St. Ovide, a blind man in a charade" (*Planet of the Blind* 103) because he still dances to the visual-normative tune played by the sighted world.

In Helsinki on a Fulbright scholarship for literature, Kuusisto continues to 'pass' as a sighted person. However, he feels the desperate need to articulate his problem of rejecting the blind self without feeling ashamed about it: "I desperately need words, ones that will point my sharp prow toward the great green water of my blindness" (*Planet of the Blind* 121). His loneliness in the secret of his disability makes him ripe for poetry: "And there is an ache in me like wind through an open door, a complete, unadulterated fervor for poems" (*Planet of the Blind* 119). He fools his companions about his useless sight, and puts on a show for himself, making believe that he is not blind. As a result of this policy, he must "act more sighted, seem jaunty and independent" (*Planet of the Blind* 122). Ironically, this admission is predicated upon a well-founded assumption that sight gives most people greater independence to move unhindered through the world. Blind persons need assistance, a dependence that is construed as diminishing their worth as human individuals.

Back in the United States after his Fulbright tenure, Kuusisto meets with an accident to his reading eye while opening a book (*Planet of the Blind* 129). Stopped short in his foolish rejection of blindness, the young man undergoes a change. He starts considering the situation which he is faced with as a blind person who can no longer 'pass' as a sighted member of the 'normal' world. Then he becomes a teacher of creative writing at his undergraduate alma mater, Hobart and William Smith College, and works there for "seven good years" (*Planet of the Blind* 136). After losing his job "owing to campus cutbacks" (*Planet of the Blind* 136), he experiences the sharp anxiety of being unemployed. He discovers that it is very difficult for a blind poet and creative writing teacher to land a job, and starts receiving social security disability payments (*Planet of the Blind* 138). Walking home one day, he barely escapes being run over by a car. At home, and badly shaken, he admits to himself, "I can't get from one point to another. Can't sleep. Can't pray. Can't find intelligence because I am without humility. I can barely bathe" (*Planet of the Blind* 142). He feels that he has no purpose in life. He recognises the need to acknowledge his own blind self and seek help. The memoirist wonders why he could not accept himself:

> Why should it take so long for me to like the blind self? I resist it, admit it, then resist again, as though blindness were a fetish, a perverse weakness, a thing I could overcome with the force of will power.
>
> (*Planet of the Blind* 142)

The younger self of the memoirist regards his blindness as a weakness that mars his dignity and manhood. Shaken by the close shave with death, however, he calls the New York State Commission for the Blind to seek help with walking (*Planet of the Blind* 143), which means that he wishes to be trained how to use the white cane.

When Kuusisto starts carrying the white cane, walking becomes much easier for him, and he develops a more engaged style of self. The memoirist's words, when he describes his younger self's acceptance of the white cane, reveal a change in his self-conception, thus signifying the recognition of blindness and the welcoming of the blind way of life:

> He [Mike Dillon, an orientation and mobility expert] hands it to me, and I take it. Finally.
> Nothing terrible happens.
> He shows me how to use it, sweeping it from side to side like an electronic metal detector.
> The paradox is that my cane produces only casual regard.
> Cars slow for me. An old man on a porch calls out cheerfully.
> I'm wrapped in the silence of discovery.
> I'm an acrobat walking on the wings of a biplane. I'm both light-headed and somber, bending to a delicate task.
> Nothing terrible happens. I can be disabled. On this ordinary street.
> I need to touch my hair. I want to feel my own face.
> (*Planet of the Blind* 145)

The acceptance of his blind self is clearly evident in this passage. Moreover, his desire to touch his hair and feel his "own face" also suggests a blind person's behaviour, since these are gestures used to know oneself (*Selected Poems* 357; *On Sight* 48). However, his acceptance of his self brings with it the necessity of dealing with both societal prejudice towards the disabled and friendliness.

Kuusisto's poetic musing about a planet of the blind in outer space (*Planet of the Blind* 147–48) strikingly communicates his desire not only for societal acceptance of the blind, but also for the peaceful coexistence of sightless and sighted people. This imagined planet is shaped by the blind, and its inhabitants experience blindness and the world in all its physical, aesthetic, and spiritual richness. With this conception, we realise that the blind man has reached a new phase in his selfhood. The cane is, for him, only a temporary instrument. He wants to walk and travel everywhere, and decides to be partnered with a guide dog. This realisation comes after a reckless driver almost mows down the narrator and his friend, Mike:

> There's danger out here. I need something more powerful than the cane. I need eyes. Now that I'm out of the closet, and blind for everyone to see, the cane has done all that it can do. I'm thinking: dog.
> (*Planet of the Blind* 150)

He has accepted his blind self, and it is important to note that he articulates this acceptance with the phrase "out of the closet," which is used by homosexual persons to indicate that they are openly gay. Now Kuusisto wishes to unleash the traveller in himself by getting a guide dog. Therefore, he applies to a school called Guiding Eyes for the Blind in order to achieve his goal of learning how to work with a guide dog, and attends the training programme. This is how he comes to find his canine companion, Corky.

We may, then, conclude this chapter, wherein I have traced a trajectory in Kuusisto's life from a rejection of blindness and the consequent struggle manifested in the social and personal spheres of his existence to an acceptance of the blind self. This exposition, which drew on critical concepts from disability studies and phenomenology, has prepared the ground for an elucidation of Kuusisto's narrative aesthetics in the next chapter.

7 The Narrative Dialectic of Silences and Articulations in the Memoirs of Kuusisto

As we have just read, in the previous chapter, I analysed Kuusisto's first memoir, *Planet of the Blind*, and showed how he came, over many years, to acquire a political and philosophical understanding of himself. The present chapter will first treat the aesthetic of listening he fashions in his second memoir, which is a collection of essays entitled *Eavesdropping*, and will subsequently elaborate an aesthetic dialectic that may be discerned in the two memoirs; the third memoir will be touched on to meet potential objections to the argument presented here.

7.1 Questions and Answers Regarding Blindness

Eavesdropping is a book which grows out of a conversation about the lack of eyesight and the worth of travelling as a blind person which takes place at a talk Kuusisto delivers to blind people in Boston. The essayist writes,

> Suddenly a woman called out from the back of the room. Her voice was fierce. "Why travel anywhere if you can't see?" she asked. Her words seemed to linger in the air... . This woman was in her mid-fifties; she'd gone blind from diabetes; her husband had recently passed away—her question was complex and it had a good deal to do with faith. What would the future hold? What is the use of going forward? Without eyesight aren't we selfless in the worst sense? How can one live in a world without independence or the daily therapy of sight-seeing?
>
> (x)

Rephrasing this dilemma slightly differently, what relationship can the newly blind person develop with his or her surroundings, and, more fundamentally, what relationship does blindness make possible and necessary between self and world? The newly blind woman's self-conception is almost identical to the one held by Hull when he "began to sink into the deep ocean" (*On Sight* 9) and started facing the reality of being blind. This fact becomes clear from the woman's linking of sight with her selfhood. The desperate question asked by her is similar to the ones dealt with by Hull in his books on blindness. The

DOI: 10.4324/9781003399667-7

validity of my (metaphysical) rephrasing of the newly blind woman's question to Kuusisto is proved by the subtitle of the memoir: *A Life by Ear*. The question which troubles her – and once she has asked it, even Kuusisto – has philosophical implications for the way the blind person lives and moves in the world. *Eavesdropping* is constituted by Kuusisto as a book of essays which indirectly offers answers to his interlocutor at the meeting, and to other readers about "living or travelling by ear" as a veteran blind person (x).

7.2 The Aesthetic of Listening

In an essay entitled "Tchaikovsky" (*Eavesdropping* 27–30), Kuusisto narrates the camaraderie that he and his Finnish father share during the former's childhood. One day, the latter takes the seven-year-old boy to a circus. The memoirist's auditory description of walking with his father "through the circus tent" (*Eavesdropping* 28) skilfully brings out the child's association of similar memories by weaving them together. He remembers how adults never failed to comment on his physical appearance after his recent eye surgery: "... all [those who saw him] had ways of suggesting that [he] was terribly unfortunate." He recalls the "fat and bored" (*Eavesdropping* 29) grunts of lions, the feel of his father's hand as the two "walked arm in arm," a question concerning the boy that a Russian clown asks the older Kuusisto in a "baritone voice," and innumerable other sounds. In this essay, Kuusisto presents a striking (even jarring) contrast between two realms, namely the blind boy's personal experiences and social perceptions of him as a disabled person. This point is brought out by the boy's love for the music of the Russian composer, Pyotr Ilych Tchaikovsky. In fact, this contrast differentiates the two volumes of memoirs, the earlier *Planet of the Blind* and the later *Eavesdropping*. as recorded in both works, on the one hand, the personal experiences of Kuusisto, his understanding of them at the time of having them, and at the time of writing them display a remarkable artistic subjectivity. On the other hand, the social attitudes that he encounters as a blind boy and as a man attest to the lack of awareness of blindness and other disabilities among the members of twentieth-century American society.

Whereas in *Planet of the Blind* Kuusisto talks about the dilemma he faces (as a small boy, teenager, and man) of a blind person in a sighted world, and deals only secondarily with the joys of listening, he writes with great lyrical beauty about his listening life in *Eavesdropping*. He understands that "Knowing and savoring the world by ear is really an impressionistic subject" (*Eavesdropping* xi). The preface to the latter book indicates a number of times the aesthetic of listening which the author develops in the auditory essays contained in the collection. He first offers a description of how he experiences delight in travel: visiting "hundreds of cities" (*Eavesdropping* x) with his guide dog, Corky, the man does "all the listening" as his canine companion "watche[s] the traffic," thereby helping him to be safe. The memoirist provides a sketch of how the (fortunate) blind eavesdrop:

Veteran blind people know that it's possible to sightsee by ear, for we do it all the time. Alone in unfamiliar hotel lobbies, we survey our surroundings and hear in the ambient curves of architecture a hundred oddities. We hear the movements of strangers; hear their laughter; hear pennies dropped in the Hilton's fountain; the bristles of a shoeshine brush; the wings of a pigeon that has made its way indoors. The blind hear all this while they're locating the chiming bells of the elevators.

(*Eavesdropping* x–xi)

The essayist describes the fruit of his hard labour over many years to develop his method of "living or travelling by ear" (*Eavesdropping* xi) in the passage. The rhythmic prose writing, with its emphasis on hearing, itself constitutes part of this achievement.

He elaborates further on the effort required to become a practiced listener: "This is how I navigate the world. I enter unfamiliar environments and I listen with everything I have, finding inchoate music in what happens around me" (*Eavesdropping* xii). His rich artistic and philosophical awareness comes through clearly in the recognition that auditory events have meaning, which idea is expressed when he combines two elements: "treasures of sound and sense" (*Eavesdropping* xiv). So he says,

Blindness often leads to compensatory listening [or "creative listening"] (if one has the fortune of a hearing life).... Blind people are not casual eavesdroppers. We have method. As things happen around us we reinvent what we hear like courtroom artists who sketch as fast as they can.... In reality I cannot see the world by ear, I can only reinvent it for my own purposes. But admitting this may make me lucky. I am free to daydream for survival or amusement.

(*Eavesdropping* xi)

This passage reveals a poetic aesthetics which, in Kuusisto's words in *Planet of the Blind*, has the power of water to sustain life (30). The essay "Dog-Man: The Action Figure" (*Eavesdropping* 63–8), appearing in Part Two of the collection, demonstrates the truth of Kuusisto's friend and guide-dog trainer, Dave See's words (as the essayist expresses them) that "letting the dog navigate would free up my ability to listen" (*Eavesdropping* 67). Kuusisto narrates the absorbing activity of listening in the streets as he walks with his dog. The writing pays close, phenomenological attention to the sounds which carry meaning for the narrator and paint a vivid auditory picture in his mind. This character of his auditory journey becomes the foundation for his creative work.

"The Invention of the Cell Phone" (*Eavesdropping* 69–79) is an essay that possesses a complex structure like a musical composition. It begins with the narrator listening to non-digital, classical music, moves on to ugly sounds heard in airports and streets, also occasional beautiful sounds, and ends with him resolving "to live as much as possible like a man waking up" (*Eavesdropping* 79) in accordance with a new aesthetic of listening that he develops in the course of the essay. He dwells on the lonely art of listening, describing the ever-present quality of sound in mystical terms: "Birds scurry on my roof. *The ears, I think, are a dream we will never be rid of.* Forget serendipity—all the luck of chance music, sound, even the most ineffable sound is permanent—a continuous wave throughout creation" (italics as in the source, *Eavesdropping* 70). He displays an attunement to sounds in his environment which isolates him from the sighted world. He traces the accumulative experience of listening to "chance sounds" (*Eavesdropping* 71) in a stream-of-auditory-conscious technique. He writes,

> Whitman could reconstruct a whole day from sounds remembered in sequence. This was my ambition, at least for the moment; an idea as ephemeral as a New Year's resolution... .
> I sensed that one could listen to sounds in a sequence just like Whitman did. But how could I learn Whitman's patience and live the whole day with open ears? The days turn ugly... . *Let the ugly be ugly... .*
> *... And let the ugly be part of the daylong Whitman method.*
> (italics as in the source, *Eavesdropping* 71–72)

The narrator quotes the words of the Estonian poet Jaan Kaplinski, who was a Buddhist, and we find in his own attitude to the world and in his poetic method, as is expressed in the above passage, a Buddhist acceptance of the beautiful and the ugly with equanimity. He describes the method used by the composer John Cage, who creates music from sounds heard in city environments humming with machines. Kuusisto compares the composer's art to Whitman's poetic method: "The modernist composer wants the ugliness of both the notes and the intervals to have meaning" (*Eavesdropping* 75). The memoirist makes this method his own and pays attention to "the quick transformations in a soundscape, especially the ugly ones" in order to mark the development of a situation, the change in human relationships, and important shifts in the modes of communication (*Eavesdropping* 73–4). His musical practice structures this essay. He bases it on an aesthetic principle that he has come to through long and careful reflection: "If you really want to hear with penetration and find its associated pleasures," the author emphasises, "you must imagine you are waking up over and over again—waking on your feet, becoming aware in medias res" (*Eavesdropping* 75). Thus, the essay and his other auditory postcards develop an understanding of listening that links the blind person's chance hearing of everyday sounds with the careful comprehension of (classical and other kinds of) music.

The two essays, "Albatross" (*Eavesdropping* 121–28) and "Letter from Venice" (*Eavesdropping* 129–42), explore two kinds of difficulties that Kuusisto faces in his project of developing an aesthetic of listening: the former dwells on its abstractness, and the latter is concerned with the puzzle of appreciating a world of visual forms as an 'eavesdropping' blind tourist[1] in a city famous for its architecture. In the play about a Finnish man called Heiskanen and his friends, which Kuusisto listens to in "Albatross," the Finn finds himself living in a trailer park in Sweden, not liking his new home but confused and not appearing to consider returning to his beloved Finland (*Eavesdropping* 121). The albatross, the famous symbol from S. T. Coleridge's long poem "The Rime of the Ancient Mariner," here connotes the burden of a limiting culture. The narrator calls this way of life 'provincialism' and employs the trailer park as a symbol for this unsatisfactory culture of self (*Eavesdropping* 122). The reason for the narrator's dissatisfaction with himself stems from his inability to figure out a way to listen to the sounds of the world intelligently (*Eavesdropping* 123). It is in this situation that his statements about his being "an exile from visual culture" (*Eavesdropping* 122), and the desire to be "an advanced ear man" assume importance. Although (as described in *Planet of the Blind*) the memoirist has embraced the blind self and its mode of being, he is seeking a way (with difficulty) to develop the art of listening which would enrich his life. Thus, he says,

> I had the feeling that I was both solitary and simple. The sensation had been building for months. I walked around without knowing exactly where I was going and gave myself over to chance soundscapes. Hardly anyone does this, and though you can find writing about soundscapes and the music of what happens, well it's all rather abstract. Sitting in that theatre listening to Heiskanen and his friends, I recognized my true situation. I was declaring myself to be a rube.
>
> (*Eavesdropping* 124)

Kuusisto's reflection upon the self, which is prompted by the aesthetic appreciation of the burlesque performance, illustrates Danto's understanding of literature as a mirror that shows the reader an aspect of themselves (63–4). The blind man's concern relates to a sense that he has no method as yet of practising the art of listening to "chance soundscapes" and comprehending "the music of what happens." However, he thinks of Walt Whitman's lines on listening (*Eavesdropping* 124), and finds in poetry solace and encouragement for this art, as in the earlier essay entitled "The Invention of the Cell Phone."

In "Letter from Venice," Kuusisto writes that he comes "to Venice precisely because [he] was blind" (*Eavesdropping* 129) since, as he explains it, the city of canals "has endless distractions for the listener." He wants to "prove it" as he is interested in sightseeing by ear. However, he recognises the difficulty involved. Citing "the Florentine translator of Plato," Marsilio

---

1 Here, I enclose the adjective 'eavesdropping' within single quotation marks in order to avoid confusion. What I want to suggest by this phrase is expertise in listening.

Ficino's claim that "sound equals form," he wonders if this is strictly correct: "... could I, for instance, listen to the accidental music of a place like Venice while my wife explored the architecture? Could I find corresponding pleasure in merely listening?" While Ficino might mean by "form" Plato's conception of ideal forms, the word that appears ("shapes") in his description of the world as being "'just shapes and sounds'" suggests that he intends it to signify visual forms. Kuusisto wonders if it is possible to equate auditory occurrences such as "the accidental music of a place [sound]" with "the architecture [of that place, that is, forms or shapes]." In the latter's understanding, "form" clearly means a configuration or arrangement.

Kuusisto recognises the care required in developing "the art of hearing" (*Eavesdropping* 139) when he says that "hearing has only its acquired nobility, sequenced and slow" (*Eavesdropping* 130–31). This statement means that it takes time and patience to (learn to) hear intelligently. So he must, as he puts it enthusiastically, "wander in a delirium of sound in a vast city with no cars. I had to get lost there" (*Eavesdropping* 131). While walking around the city with his dog, Corky, he stands on a bridge and wonders about the possible answer to the newly blind woman's question (see this chapter, p. 153) introduced in the preface to *Eavesdropping* ...

> *Guesswork and understanding create a knowing man*, I thought. *The subjectivity of Kant. . . Why go anywhere when you can't see? Is it because the spirit of man and the world of form are identical? Because even with eyes shut my spirit and the narrow alleys of Venice were one and the same?*
>
> (italics as in the source, *Eavesdropping* 135)

Thus, his speculation yields a poetic/philosophical answer: it is the character of man's being to be one with the world, and from that integrated state comes the desire to travel. However, he acknowledges the limits of sightseeing by ear: "There were limits to how much listening I could do without the consoling balance of visual description" (*Eavesdropping* 138). So Kuusisto accompanies his wife, Connie, to see Venice. She describes in detail the various buildings and architecture of the city. He concludes that "the sounds of a place" (*Eavesdropping* 139) cannot reveal physical form: they constitute different and equal realms, and the blind person must therefore rely not merely on sighted help, but on "a nobility of descriptive engagement" to appreciate architectural beauty. He states, "Walking in Venice in long, slow circles, I realized that sound is to shape as thirst is to hunger. Ficino understood the nature of the meal" (*Eavesdropping* 140). So, Kuusisto comes to understand the way in which sound can be equal to form through his walking exploration of Venice with help from Connie. The two types of phenomena are separate, and need to be understood by means of different sensory modalities. This requirement fosters partnership between the blind and the sighted – here, between the memoirist and his wife. Instead of relying solely on the self *"all our days"* (italics as in the source, *Eavesdropping* 141) in most matters including that of art and becoming absorbed *"in the geometry of self,"* he feels that it is *"all right"* to appreciate the world through the eyes of another and asks, "Why not *get lost in someone else's wonder?"*

In "Letter from Venice," as we have just seen, Kuusisto comes to the conclusion that since "[his] own hearing had become careful and algebraic" (*Eavesdropping* 130), he can appreciate the city partially by listening to the sounds in its streets and buildings. However, in the end he does need sighted help to see the beautiful architecture. But in "The Twa Corbies" (*Eavesdropping* 147–54), he narrates his experience of going alone into the woods and enjoying the music ever-present in the natural world without any help. The essay starts off by presenting, through the figure of "a ten-year-old [boy] who plays too much Nintendo, but [who's] now ... delirious because he's got the birds talking" (*Eavesdropping* 147), a contrast between the technological world of mankind and the world of talking and singing birds. But Kuusisto immediately bridges this gap by offering a harmonious incident involving the boy: "I picture Yamaguchi Goro playing the shakuhachi flute in the woods of Nara. Music, even a child's primal music, pays homage to the soundscape." This quotation suggests that man, woman, and child can all participate in the soundscape of what we know as the natural world. The singing human voice and musical sounds produced by playing instruments enrich the narrator's life.

The memoirist narrates memories of listening to music as a four-year-old boy – he was born in March 1955 (*Planet of the Blind* 5): "I spent the better part of the summer of 1959 listening to records or walking the woods, where I thought I might find the singing soldiers of the Red Army. Instead, I found the crows" (*Eavesdropping* 148). This combining of singing men heard on records from the Soviet Union, the woods of childhood in New Hampshire, and calling crows residing there becomes a memory path on which Kuusisto treads the way to narrating his "first job of the new summer," that is, listening "to the crows all day." He goes on to describe (in minute detail) how he sits under a tree for hours without moving, and listens to the music that first two crows, and soon many crows, produce – initially in friendship, and then in a mighty fight. The narrative moves between his childhood and present as a "blind man [in] the forest [listening] to the unmusical corvidae—the ugly crows" (*Eavesdropping* 150). Here he makes an important statement that connects his experience of listening to birds in childhood and as an adult:

I've wriggled into a nest of childhood [in "a grove of spruce trees"].

As a visually impaired kid who played no baseball, I spent a thousand hours in places like this. I learned how to spin a story in a sheltered place. Writers are all orphans of a kind... . I learned my listening early. Knew the cicadas from the katydids. Knew starlings from grackles.

(*Eavesdropping* 150)

Thus, for Kuusisto, the art of listening and the creativity of a storyteller are closely connected. Two similar auditory events related in the early essay on childhood, "Victrola" (*Eavesdropping* 15–17), and in the late essay on listening in adulthood, "The Twa Corbies," respectively, strengthen the connection between them: "a noise like thrown buttons" (*Eavesdropping* 16) to describe hornets hitting a window, and "a sound like buttons thrown against glass" (*Eavesdropping* 151) to indicate the rhythmic sounds made by "crows' beaks." This solitary listening in the forest that the latter essay narrates not only contrasts with sightseeing in Venice, but also represents the method that Kuusisto has fashioned in his practice of the art of hearing, which was a problem he faced earlier (*Eavesdropping* 124). Thus, "The Twa Corbies" expresses the joy of being alive and blind in the woods, listening to the music of the crows (*Eavesdropping* 154).

"Skull Flowers" (*Eavesdropping* 155–56) is a brief, exquisitely written essay that treats the physical activity of listening. The narrator describes how he listens to birds going about their business, and provides a detailed commentary on the sensory process of hearing, which is jointly performed by the ears and the brain. He takes the two themes forward in a harmonic form, as in a musical composition, weaving them into four movements (in two paragraphs): an introductory paragraph, a brief outline of how the perception of sound takes place, then a longer description in which the listener plays an active role in channelling "molecular vibrations" (*Eavesdropping* 156) through the ears to the brain, and a very brief concluding section summarising the experience.

If "The Twa Corbies" explores the practice of the patient aesthetic of eavesdropping that Kuusisto has developed through the collection of essays, "Skull Flowers" revels in its rich potential. In the process, it outlines the corporeal self's active involvement in its environment in performing the activity of listening. The narrator begins,

> I sit all afternoon in a low-slung canvas chair and keep still because I can hear the blue heron tracking mice through pond grass. It is good just sitting here. My ears know the sky, the opaque and impossible air is filled with purple feathers martins catch mosquitoes even in a light rain.
>
> (*Eavesdropping* 155)

Kuusisto listens with all his attention to the sounds of nature, and reinvents the world through this experience. This passage brings out what is remarkable about his art: it is his "ears [which] know the sky," and not his eyes, although he can catch sight of the opaque air filled with the purple feathers of the insect-hunting martins. His objective is to know as much of the world as is possible through his ears and brain (thereby not giving room for regret at the lack of sight). Thus, he describes the process whereby auditory experience is produced:

Human ears stand like dried flowers. The pinna, the twin flowers of cartilage, dry, without much blood, they hang out there, transparent crescent moons. The purple martin drops from the barn's roof quick as a flying mongoose, dropping fast as gravel in a well. And air, obedient, moves with him, and molecules are pressured, and the vibrations rush into my dried flowers. The cartilage shakes, hot sounds reach the brain-stem faster than the purple martin can swallow the errant hornet.

(Eavesdropping 155)

This scene, although it includes a couple of images drawn from sight, possesses a rare power that literary language usually derives from the strength of visual observation. Here, however, auditory metaphors simultaneously, and fittingly, build a picture of the experience through the sound of a fast-diving ("dropping fast as gravel in a well") bird's activity, and of audition itself in descriptions such as "the vibrations rush into my dried flowers." This discussion of Kuusisto's art of listening and writing, developed with sustained effort and richly represented in the essays, brings us to the aesthetic dialectic mentioned in the introduction to this chapter. It turns on a crucial difference in the author's artistic approaches in the two memoirs, *Planet of the Blind* and *Eavesdropping*.

7.3 The Narrative Dialectic in Kuusisto's Memoirs

Planet of the Blind and *Eavesdropping* present two startlingly different pictures of Kuusisto's life as a child and adolescent (which constitute only a part of the works' narrative content). The former narrates his denial of blindness, and the painful lengths to which he goes to 'pass' as a sighted boy in a world obsessed with the 'normal' body. The latter contains essays called "auditory postcards." This descriptor is appropriate because the compositions describe in careful detail – initially the boy's and subsequently the man's – life listening to the varying sounds of the natural and human worlds,[2] as well as to the popular songs of the 1950s and 1960s. Kuusisto explains the reason for the difference between his first two prose works as follows: "*Eavesdropping* differs from *Planet of the Blind* because its hopes are different" (Purpura and Kuusisto 674): he sets out to write the latter in such a way that its narrative would unfold "the histories and mythologies of blindness as culturally received" while he explores his "own childhood, adolescence, and adulthood" – in other words, his development as a disabled person who has to grapple with the ableist notions prevalent in his society. However, as he explains, "With *Eavesdropping* I was driven by something far more elemental." As discussed in section 7.1 above, he writes the book in answer to a fierce question asked by a newly blind woman in Boston who was around sixty years old: "'Why travel anywhere if you can't see?'" (*Eavesdropping* x;

---

2 For the memoirist, these auditory events carry a rich suggestion of musical experience.

cf. Purpura and Kuusisto 674). This collection of lyric essays is, in Kuusisto's words, a travelogue "that allowed me to throw myself into different situations to see what I could hear" (Purpura and Kuusisto 675). In it, he tries to take "the best of all the different forms – the image of the poem, the metricality and musicality of language, the abstract propositions of prose written without a plot, sometimes the framing of a plot" (Purpura and Kuusisto 677) in order to clarify "the relationship between the body – our own individual, subjectivized bodies – and the imagination" (Purpura and Kuusisto 676). Thus, *Eavesdropping* offers a poetics of listening in the blind condition by going far beyond the socio-cultural dimensions of the memoirist's life to touch the visceral parts of his remembered experience. The dialectic that concerns us here turns on this point. This section of the chapter shows why delving into the difference between the memoirs of Kuusisto is warranted.

Interestingly, in *Planet of the Blind*, Kuusisto fails to narrate a number of experiences which he includes in *Eavesdropping*. Of particular importance to the argument in this chapter are remembrances which are narrated in three early essays of the latter book: these memories are, first, of listening as a young boy to birdsong and other remarkable sounds in the environment; second, of being acknowledged in his boyhood by a lawyer as a remarkable listener; and, third, of the teenager's public declaration of his blindness by playing in his class an audio book of Milton's *Paradise Lost*. I argue that the author remembers these details after embracing blindness and welcoming his own self into his life. He is able to utilise the creative power that is released when he has wandered "the galleries of self, pausing to read the hard words about failure, incompleteness, and self-forgiveness" (*Planet of the Blind* 123). This difference between the artistic approaches manifested in the two memoirs indicates the author's differing narrative plans for them. Thus, the two works enact a significant dialectical movement in his life and art which is motivated by the related questions of selfhood and aesthetics.

Although Kuusisto writes in the preface to *Eavesdropping* that in *Planet of the Blind* he describes how as a child he listened to teachers and developed "an auditory version of what was happening around [him]" (xi), and also learned "by necessity how to hear both for content and splendour," certain crucial auditory experiences are not mentioned in that memoir; or if they are, they do not receive much attention. Kuusisto writes,

> I remember Helsinki's open-air fish market, where I ran through the crowds of winter shoppers. The green and gold of vegetables and fruits, and the icy chill of the butchers' stalls where the walls were blood-red— all of it drew me on and on. I could run in abandon bouncing off strangers, wild to elude my mother and absorb the colors. The market became my customs house between the ocean of blindness and the land of seeing.
>
> (*Planet of the Blind* 12)

Curiously, Kuusisto (like Hull) uses the ocean as a symbol of blindness, and the land as that of sight. Living in the "customs house" between the two worlds of blindness and sight, excluded from the one for his severely imperfect vision, and not wanting to be in the other due to shame, the small boy is "inordinately active" (*Planet of the Blind* 11). He eludes his mother, and runs "in abandon" because he thirsts to "absorb the colours." Thus, at the time of writing *Planet of the Blind*, the memoirist remembers the inexpressible yearning of the child to be a part of the sighted world. However, he recalls neither the experience of listening to the sad, dark singing of the old, carpet-beating women "on the shore of the frozen [Baltic] sea" (*Eavesdropping* 3) in Helsinki, nor "the polyphony of hungry birds" (*Eavesdropping* 4) near the south harbour of the Finnish capital, nor even "the chance music of the city" (*Eavesdropping* 5), all of which he narrates in an essay entitled "Harbor Songs" (3–6) in *Eavesdropping*.

In *Planet of the Blind*, he recalls an experience he has around the age of five in the hospital:

> After the surgery I have bandages on my eyes for several months, and that is when I learn to hear. I spend whole afternoons listening. I can hear the wooden gears of the railroad clock that hangs on the far wall.
>
> (17)

Two aspects in this remembrance are worthy of attention. First, he states that he learns to hear when he is required to "have bandages on [his] eyes for several months," but we learn from the essayist's words in *Eavesdropping* that "By the age of four [he'd] found the intricacies of listening were inexhaustible" (6). Secondly, the sentence ending the above quotation from *Planet of the Blind* (17) suggests that the boy "can hear the wooden gears of the railroad clock" when he is recovering from the operation (perhaps at his home). While this may well be true, he fails to mention his adventure with the grandfather clock (*Eavesdropping* 23) which he has in his grandmother's old Victorian house. He narrates this adventure, which takes place before the operation, in the essay entitled "House Music" (*Eavesdropping* 18–26). In the second work, he writes about the connection between his eye surgery and hearing the clock as follows: "It seemed like one minute I was listening to the gears of a clock and then I was in a hospital bed" (*Eavesdropping* 27). These words, appearing in the essay called "Tchaikovsky," suggest a subtle difference in the ways that the memory is recalled and narrated in both books. This shift in the mode and content of remembrance concerning the same collection of experiences in two books, which are separated by a few years,[3] may be explained by citing Hull:

> Many adults, when trying to remember their childhood, search for visual images of the sort that they would now be able to collect if they

---

3 This gap of eight years or so may be inferred from the date "*July 2005*" (italics as in the source, xiv) inscribed at the close of the preface to *Eavesdropping*.

were in those places ... The point is, however, that to the young child things did not look like that, and thus could not be stored in a form which the adult can recollect or can recognize as being similar to more recently stored images. Now and again, back and beyond the occasional visual inspiration, lies something deeper which can be called body memory. This is not so much memory of what things looked like, but recollection of how things felt.

(*On Sight* 123)

Since this "body memory" can be described as "recollection of how things felt," Kuusisto may, on embracing his blind self and growing to think and feel as a complete blind person, be said to begin to recall memories of childhood occurrences in accordance with body memory.

In *Planet of the Blind*, the memoirist describes his loneliness as a small boy in this way: "I stay at the piano for hours.... . Later, alone in the woods, wet elbowed and wet kneed, I catch my trousers on a sunken rock, lean into the ground, press my chin into the moss" (15–16). This picture vividly shows that the boy is forced to spend much time in solitude. This is because neither his parents nor other children give him any company (*Eavesdropping* 10, 15). Writing about his first memoir in the preface to *Eavesdropping*, he summarises it by saying, "In that book I described growing up with a visual impairment in the late fifties and sixties" (ix). This quotation points to the main topic of the memoir, which is (as we have seen in the previous chapter), his life of struggle with the social and personal rejection of blindness as a child and youngster. While the narrative in this memoir gives a poignant sense of the boy's solitude, *Eavesdropping* contains at least six essays in Part One which deal at length with his loneliness and the power of listening he develops in that condition. Again he writes in the preface, "I realize now that I had the good fortune to live my early years in provincial places" (*Eavesdropping* xiii). This might seem to be an innocuous statement, but the fact proves to be of the greatest significance to Kuusisto. He explains,

My father was a professor at the University of New Hampshire, and we lived in the woods. We also lived in Helsinki, Finland, when that rare and beautiful city was largely an unknown destination for tourists. I heard reindeer bells and ancient folk songs long before I heard a transistor radio.

(*Eavesdropping* xiii)

While living in these isolating locales (*Eavesdropping* ix) increases the child's loneliness, it simultaneously helps him to grow into "a hearing life" (*Eavesdropping* xi).

This change becomes clear when we recognise the important gap perceivable between the subjectivities presented in the two memoirs. Kuusisto writes in the first book about his discovery as a college student of an interest in bird-watching (which is aroused after listening to "a recorded bird-watching disk" [*Planet of the Blind* 72]). Curiously, he does not say in this memoir that he used to listen avidly to various birds as a small boy of seven. He describes this passion in detail in the essay "Birds" in *Eavesdropping* (10–12):

> I knew the birds from a radio program. I'd wake early on Sundays and listen to a solemn old man guiding listeners through the calls of New Hampshire's birds. The purple finch sounded more contented than any creature I knew of. He sounded like the world's fastest wind chimes. The old man and the purple finch gave me my first lesson in timbre.
>
> "Sounds," he said, "even bird sounds, have character... ." ...
>
> ... Alone in the woods, I could spend a whole hour listening to a single bird. I had a bed of moss where I'd lie for the concert... .
>
> My early childhood occurred in the last moments of unmediated listening.
>
> (*Eavesdropping* 10–11)

This quotation demonstrates that the boy is well-versed in listening and tracking birds by means of their calls. It is the openness of this careful listening to ambient sounds in nature, and the absence of electronic technology in audition that the essayist calls "unmediated listening." Further, in a later essay, he writes about how as a teenager he "could identify the call of a purple finch without confusing him with a thrush" (*Eavesdropping* 58). Despite his long association with birdsong, he writes in *Planet of the Blind* that he has been a stranger to birds till the discovery of the disk in the college library:

> I'm completely jazzed: all my life I've been a stranger in this neighbourhood. I've never seen a bird. Now, hearing them has made a place in my imagination... .
>
> I've been missing out on something huge. But where are they?
>
> (72)

The silence about his childhood interest in birdsong in the context of a re-discovery of "bird-watching" is noteworthy. In the interim between the publication of *Planet of the Blind* in 1998, and that of the essay on birds in *Eavesdropping* in 2006 Kuusisto recalls his jaunts in the New Hampshire woods in pursuit of the varied song of birds while searching for "the flower known as the lady's slipper—a violet-going-to-rose-colored orchid" (*Eavesdropping* 10). Almost certainly, during these years, he explored his early childhood experiences from a new standpoint as a consciously blind writer.

As I have explained above in detail, after embracing his blind self, Kuusisto sets out to become "an advanced ear man" (*Eavesdropping* 122) and fashion an aesthetic of listening. Moreover, it is clear from my discussion thus far that travelling by ear forms the major theme of *Eavesdropping*. In a creative frame of mind that makes life 'with blindness' yield rich analogies, he composes some exquisite essays that resurrect important memories from his childhood. They may be read in the first section of the collection, which is entitled "Sweet Longings" (*Eavesdropping* 3–60). The auditory memoiristic compositions recreate the world of the blind child as he listens and feels his way through a vivid world in solitude. What stands out in "Harbor Songs" is the total sense of being at home in the world of blindness and sounds that he shows as a boy of three or four years: "But what a thrill it was to be a sightless child in a city of sounds" (*Eavesdropping* 6), Kuusisto states emphatically, narrating his family's two-year sojourn in Helsinki. In the manner of the blind man in Borges's "The Maker," he draws up a tender memory from early in his life:

> A little girl whose name I can no longer recall taught me to waltz. I'm sure that her parents must have told her I was blind. She must have been around eight years old. She swayed me back and forth in the light of the birches. The old man played slowly and I felt something of the Zenbody: wherever I was I was there.
>
> (*Eavesdropping* 6)

While the passage shows the boy's total presence in the activity of listening and waltzing, the essay "Ice" (*Eavesdropping* 13–14) describes how Kuusisto creates music by making use of unusual things available in his environment. He produces "instantaneous" music with ice that forms "between the trees behind my house" (*Eavesdropping* 13) by plucking "a wire fence in the woods" (*Eavesdropping* 14), by shaking the ice-covered birch trees, and by "tapping" on "large metal drums" placed by his mother in the basement of their house. The memoirist reflects that when a child is lonely, "One simply pushes his or her homemade music and gets through the dark that way." Again, it is this same loneliness in his grandmother's large house that leads to his discovery of the music of rain against windows (*Eavesdropping* 15), of flying creatures, and of Enrico Caruso's singing voice in an old victrola (*Eavesdropping* 16). Thus, the author, on delving into his memory, realises that he as a blind boy did engage in creative play.

In the second essay of *Eavesdropping*, "Horse" (7–9), Kuusisto relates an adventure he has as a five-year-old boy in a lyrical style. He wanders through the woods, enchanted by "the beams of light or depths of shade that fell between trees" (*Eavesdropping* 7), and meets a horse in a barn full of the smells given forth by "hay and leather and turds." The boy wants to touch the fascinating horse. Kuusisto writes, "And so I reached out and there was the great wet fruit of his nose, the velvet bone of his enormous face. And we stood there together for a little while, all alive and all alone" (*Eavesdropping* 8). When the boy touches the horse's face, the latter accepts the contact. The togetherness of this moment stands in sharp contrast to the solitariness of the "very small boy." At a deeper level, then, the child makes an aesthetic journey, discovering unexpected things of beauty. The memoirist composes the essay with these sensuous moments – the misleading visual, auditory, tactile, and olfactory – as the basic material.

"The Voice of the Dark" (*Eavesdropping* 41–5) dwells on misery and death. In it, we read about the blind boy being bullied at school, and his way of "reclaim[ing] the world after these moments by entering a self-made audible environment" (*Eavesdropping* 42). The memoirist foregrounds the theme of death in the music that the boy listens to, namely Hector Berlioz's "treatment of the death of Ophelia," and what he simultaneously listens to on a talking book, that is, an excerpt from *The Adventures of Huckleberry Finn* by Mark Twain, which describes "the drawings of a death-obsessed girl, Emmeline Grangerford, who in fact dies early from a fever." These artistic works represent the darkness in the boy's mind which is generated by his experience of being bullied and of solitude, both on account of his blindness. Kuusisto makes this link explicit a few pages later when he underscores the absence of either of his parents when he needs comforting: "I was alone in my suburban bedroom, chewing black licorice, listening to Twain and Berlioz. I could still smell Jerry's sweat on my torn sleeve: it was an odour like apples and methane" (*Eavesdropping* 44). He finds it difficult to forget the bullying and broods since he is unable to find an outlet for his misery.

"The Sound of My Mother's Body" (*Eavesdropping* 46–9) demonstrates what the recognition of one's talent by another, especially that of a sensitive boy by an adult, can do for the confidence of the former. The essay narrates an important episode in the blind boy's life. He is required to be the chief witness in a case filed by his mother against a supermarket where she had suffered a severe injury to her elbow due to a faulty door slamming into her. It so happened that, as she entered the shop and the accident came to pass, recalls the memoirist, "I was just a few steps ahead of her" (*Eavesdropping* 47), and goes on to relate,

> I heard the sequenced sounds of the door and elbow and then her torso hitting the plate glass. I was fascinated by radio sound effects and knew that the noise of her body hitting the window sounded exactly like a dropped bag of apples. Then there was a gasp—her gasp, different from any cry I'd ever heard.
>
> (*Eavesdropping* 47)

He proves his ability to stand as a witness in the court by talking to his mother's lawyer about his skill in listening:

> And then I was in the cold, clear sky of facts, my favorite place. The lawyer was asking me about listening. I told him what I'd heard in the supermarket and what the store manager had said about the door being broken again. Then the lawyer asked me if I was sure about what I'd heard. I told him how I treated every day like a requiem.
>
> "… You can think of a whole day as a kind of musical pattern… ." …

... I said that with your eyes closed you could confuse one noise with another unless you really knew the character of a sound... . I was flat out happy, talking about the wilderness of noises and the hours in a day.

(*Eavesdropping* 48–9)

The two quoted passages bring out the boy's precise attention to detail in his awareness of the sequence of noises, including the words spoken by the store manager, and the unique artistic inclination in his treatment of every day as a musical composition – a requiem – that is made up of melodic patterns. The mother knows that her son is well-versed in the art of listening, and at the end of the blind boy's words about his art practised all day, on a daily basis, the lawyer says, "'You are the finest listener I've ever met. I have learned something here'" (*Eavesdropping* 49). When a stranger appreciates his remarkable skill in picking out auditory details, distinguishing among a variety of complex sounds, and building a precise world from sounds heard in his environment, the boy feels good about his blind self more or less for the first time. "I was a designated listener," writes the essayist. We should note here that this experience does not find a place in the narrative of *Planet of the Blind*. However, Kuusisto finds enough material to compose an essay in *Eavesdropping*. In the course of the short composition, he reveals how the lawyer's earnest recognition of the boy's powers as a listener amounted, at least in the mind of the latter, to "the status ... of a recognizable athletic skill." This birth, in him, of the consciousness that he can develop a mode of being which is different from mainstream sighted culture marks the origins of Kuusisto's poetic art.

"Paradise Lost" (*Eavesdropping* 50–60) narrates how Kuusisto's understanding of listening deepens when, as a fourteen-year-old adolescent, he discovers Milton's great epic bearing the same title. He first listens to *Paradise Lost* when Mr Mercer, "[a] substitute music teacher" (*Eavesdropping* 51) who is a Miltonist, recites it in class because he loves the poem. Kuusisto describes it as "the sound of iniquity" (*Eavesdropping* 50) for its concentration on Satan's story. Sitting alone in his room, he would listen to the audio book of the epic for hours together. Reflecting on that experience, the memoirist writes, "I'd discovered the gift of Milton: the soul's path is in the ear— not in the mirror." As a gift from Milton, he conceives of the self as being an entity which is susceptible to understanding through "the ear," that is, through listening and not through the sight of the self "in the mirror." This discovery also has important implications for intersubjectivity. When the boy realises that his parents' relationship is breaking down because they do not understand how to listen to each other (*Eavesdropping* 57), his newly gained wisdom from Milton sheds light on the true meaning of listening: "... the difference between speaking and being," the boy understands, is "what listening is, true listening, the lonely but open mind" (*Eavesdropping* 50). From the context of the narrative, true listening may be comprehended as pausing the unceasing expression of one's own point of view, and keeping the mind open to receive the other's views. Then the teenager declares his inheritance from Milton:

> "There's Braille on the label because this record is for blind people," I said. "Can you imagine how solitary John Milton must have been in the days when there was no Braille and no blind person could read a book without help? He had to listen to voices. He had to figure out who was telling the truth without seeing their faces."
>
> There was a long silence. I was in the midst of people whose ways were not my own. I was alone with the spirits of Milton and the vanished Mercer.
>
> (*Eavesdropping* 59)

These poignant words to his classmates about blindness, isolation, and literature constitute self-identification in the blind condition. Like Borges in his essay "Blindness" and the poem "A Blind Man," Kuusisto recognises literary kinship with the blind poet of 17th-century England. It may be added that Hull too derives self-constitutive strength from *Paradise Lost*. He memorises Milton and recites the poem to himself as he waits for sighted people and while walking to work (*On Sight* 160).

The reader might wonder whether the narrative divergences identified in the first two memoirs, and the aesthetic dialectic marked by those differences are not similar to Kuusisto's re-assessment and fleshing out of certain memories in *Have Dog, Will Travel*. I will answer this proleptic question by briefly commenting on relevant narrative sections in the three prose works. Writing in *Planet of the Blind* about his effort to learn how to use the white cane, the author says that he contacted Mike Dillon, "a senior orientation and mobility specialist for the State of New York" (144), soon after he was nearly run over by a speeding car (142). In *Have Dog, Will Travel*, he clarifies that he "called Mike Dillon, a well-regarded orientation and mobility teacher for the State of New York" (22) after first contacting "Guiding Eyes for the Blind, a guide-dog school" (19), following his close brush with death on the road (18). The reader understands that the memoirist is telling in greater detail an experience that he has already narrated in a previous memoir. Again, while in *Planet of the Blind* (36) and *Eavesdropping* (39) Kuusisto hints that his mother was an alcoholic, he devotes a full chapter to her addiction in *Have Dog, Will Travel* (31–9). We know that this is an extended narration of a memory which was only touched upon in earlier books. Although the teenager's depression and the resultant anorexia, and his emergence from it through the strange power of prayer and the Eucharist, are narrated with slight differences in *Planet of the Blind* (56–62) and *Have Dog, Will Travel* (192–95), they represent a continuity in memory. However, the silences and articulations that define the dialectic of blind self-knowledge in the first two memoirs are significantly different from mere narrative elaborations.

As we have seen in the current chapter, *Planet of the Blind* and *Eavesdropping* demonstrate the artistic development of Kuusisto as he fashions an aesthetic of listening, and achieves poetic and narrative fulfilment. The two memoirs complement each other, because the second work re-examines the author's experiences from a standpoint vastly different from that adopted in the first work. Significantly, the essay "The Sound of My Mother's Body" in Part One of *Eavesdropping* prefigures Kuusisto's aesthetic by relating an event in his boyhood, which attests to his remarkable skill in listening, and the essay "The Twa Corbies" in Part Two of the collection weaves, thematically and formally, the threads of his childhood memories and his practice of the listening art as a blind adult. Thus, the aesthetic dialectic discussed herein is twofold in character. In the next chapter, I will sum up the arguments presented in the monograph by exploring some salient narratological issues thrown up by the preceding multilayered discussion.

8 Artistic Subjectivity, Narrative Choices, and the Author

Their Relation as a Function of Bodily Being

In this chapter, I present some concluding reflections on the narrative modes used by Borges, Hull, and Kuusisto to tell their various stories. Doing so will help me tie together arguments presented in the preceding chapters in such a way that the authors' individual artistic subjectivities stand forth. Literature may be considered as an effective form of art for self-examination and self-care. As Shusterman states,

> … there is a need to objectify the self in some way in order to examine it. The examining subjectivity (or "I") must be directed at some representation of the self (or "me"). Verbal descriptions and expressions of that self provide such representations. Without gainsaying the important presence of nameless feelings and non-verbal images that stream through consciousness, it is clear that our most precise, articulate, and examinable representations of the self are expressed in language, and thus formulated in terms of words and meanings that are public and shared.
>
> (11)

Thinking about verbal "representation of the self" for self-examination, Merleau-Ponty's discussion of "abstract movement" (139) proves to be especially relevant in interpreting Borges's short stories that deal broadly with the experience of disability, and Hull's diaries as well as Kuusisto's memoirs which directly treat varying experiences of blindness. The phenomenologist explains the above-mentioned concept as a power that "is not triggered off by any existing object," but as that which outlines "in space a gratuitous intention which has reference to one's own body, making an object of it instead of going through it to link up with things by means of it." This phenomenological concept may be glossed as the symbolic power that enables the subject to achieve "'projection'." It facilitates acts that give meaning to sense-data and centre "a plurality of experiences round one intelligible core." This power enables the subject not only to give meaning to their perceptual

DOI: 10.4324/9781003399667-8

experiences, but also "to objectify the self" (Shusterman 11). With the projective power of consciousness in focus, Merleau-Ponty describes it as follows: "The essence of consciousness is to provide itself with one or several worlds, to bring into being its own thoughts before itself, as if they were things" (150). Drawing on Shusterman's thought as expressed in the previous long quotation (11), if imaginative – or artistic – projections in language are considered as belonging to this category of representative acts, the portrayal of blind and other disabled characters, and the exploration of related themes in fictional and non-fictional worlds may be conceived as attempts to personalise them and give "a form to the stuff of experience" (Merleau-Ponty 139). This literary projection also "has reference to one's own body," which means that the author engages in self-examination and self-dramatisation in this form. If abstract movement in its symbolic and representative capacity is considered to be consciousness itself, as Merleau-Ponty does, then we may conclude that subjectivity and the artistic potential of consciousness are closely allied to one another.

Pursuing this line of thought further, the question of subjectivity in literary composition may be illuminated by stepping back from twentieth- and twenty-first-century intellectual achievements and turning to the writings of Kierkegaard, which were first published in mid-nineteenth-century Denmark. His authorship covers the period from 1843 to 1855, and is divided into two parts, namely the aesthetic and the religious (Pattison 76). He developed his views on Christianity, faith, subjectivity, representation, and so on as an *Aufhebung* of Hegel's impersonal system (Westphal 101, 114; cf. Plunkett ch. 1). As already discussed in Chapter 1 (13–14), the Danish thinker wrote the works both under his own name and a number of pseudonyms. His reason for developing the technique of writing, known in Kierkegaard scholarship as "indirect communication," is explained by Howard V. Hong and Edna H. Hong as follows: "Kierkegaard expressly employed indirect communication in works such as *Fear and Trembling* and *Repetition* in order to take himself as author out of the picture and to leave the reader alone with the ideas" (x; Poole 59). Pseudonyms indicate diverse individualities, and Kierkegaard accomplishes his *Aufhebung* of Hegel's system through a number of works in differing voices. In "A First and Last Explanation" as found in *Kierkegaard's Writings, XII. Volume I*, he states,

> My pseudonymity or polyonymity has not had an accidental basis in my *person* ... but an *essential* basis in the *production* itself, which, for the sake of the lines, of the psychologically varied differences of the individualities, poetically required an indiscriminateness with regard to good and evil, brokenheartedness and gaiety, despair and overconfidence, suffering and elation, etc., which is ideally limited only by psychological

consistency, which no factually actual person dares to allow himself or can want to allow himself in the moral limitations of actuality.[1]

(625)

By extrapolating from Kierkegaard's explanation of his pseudonymous authorship, we can elucidate the divergent literary practices of Borges, Hull, and Kuusisto across different temporalities. As has become evident in the course of seven chapters, these authors engage in personalising the blind condition by objectifying their experiences through the literary art. These linguistic acts acquire a special significance when we recognise that the said authors dramatise experiences of differing disabilities in fictional and nonfictional stories on their own terms, and scrutinise societal definitions of disabled lives. The dialectical arc thus constituted involves a narrative transformation from the empirical author to the 'implied' author.

8.1 Subjectivity through the Alter Ego, Voice, and Perspective in Borges

Kierkegaard's intention "to take himself as author out of the picture and to leave the reader alone with the ideas" throws light, analogically, on Borges's auctorial technique of creating alter egos. It is appropriate at this point to recall what Laraway says about the Argentine's stance on literature:

> If nothing else, we should have learned from the canonical Borges that the particulars of an author's life are not sufficient to explain the meaning of the texts that bear his name. Empirical causes and literary effects may in fact be correlated, but the nature of their relationship is anything but clear.
> ("The Blind Spot in the Mirror" 308)

Thus, reducing Borges's works into mere autobiographical pieces which directly reflect their author's life would be naïve. Similarly, Ronald M. Green states, "The ordinary cautions against using the facts of an author's life to interpret his writings have special relevance to a writer like Kierkegaard" (274). As the Hongs explain this matter, "No writer has so painstakingly tried to preclude his readers' collapsing writer and works together and thereby transmogrifying the works into autobiography or memoir" (xi). It should be noticed that both Kierkegaard and Borges consider it necessary to deal with this issue consciously. While the former creates pseudonymous authors in order to distance himself from his readers, his pseudonymity may be compared and contrasted with Borges's alter egos. As Kierkegaard clarifies

---

1 This method of philosophising evidences the rich and varied aesthetics of the novel, a literary genre devoted to the representation of consciousness (Fludernik 19–20). Besides analysing literary works while examining philosophical problems, Kierkegaard has also written a few pseudonymous novelistic works (Westphal 123; cf. Plunkett). He discusses ancient Greek drama, modern theatre, and the novelistic art to explain the human condition broadly, and the existence of the subject in particular, in the modern age.

in the long quotation (625) above, the pseudonymous authors present "psychologically varied ... individualities" in their works. In light of this representational technique, Borges may be understood as creating alter egos in the form of first-person narrators with the objective of carrying out intricate forms of self-examination in diverse fictional worlds. This way of articulating fictional subjectivities through partial distancing from the self provides the key to dealing with plurality and change in selfhood and world.

Authorial voice may be inflected, then, through the creation of alter egos or authorial doubles, and not solely through the employment of a point of view. Laraway comments on "the impressive array of voices found in Borges's mature verse" ("The Blind Spot in the Mirror" 319) in order to show the "plasticity" of "the first-person voice" there. The multiple voices point to the proliferation of identities that are assumed in Borges's poetry. Concerned as we are with his short stories, it may in turn be said that he creates a number of alter egos and doubles with the purpose of exploring his blindness and subjectivity. Here we should not underestimate the importance of the role played by the narrator in the short stories that feature Borges's alter egos. As Gregory Currie reminds us, it is the narrating agent who provides the reader with all the "information about the story, the one whose choice of words and their order sets the emotional and evaluative tone of the work and the episodes it contains" (339). Thus, the narrator's technique, the tropes and language he uses, and the thoughts he foregrounds not only build the story, but also constitute an exploration of subjectivity. In this regard, it should be noticed that many of Borges's narrators bear his name.

The quest motif appears in short stories such as "Tlön," "The Library of Babel," "The Secret Miracle," and "The Immortal." These short works present meandering narratives where the characters search for various things. Instead of moving directly to the referent, such narratives self-consciously wend their ways through books and time. For example, in the first-mentioned short story, Borges the narrator and his friend, Bioy Casares, look for a country that exists only in an encyclopaedia and not in the world of the story. The second short story deals with the search for meaning in books. The quests in both stories should be understood as a metaphor for language's search for meanings or referents. Further, narration in these short stories is in actuality more about the narrator than it is about what is narrated, viz. the ideal realms "of Uqbar and Tlön and Orbis Tertius" (71) in the former narrative, or the library in the latter. The encyclopaedic article on Uqbar in "Tlön" treats a country that exists in a book (or in the mind) rather than in the geographic world. At the opening of the story, the narrator discusses with his friend the compositional aspects of "a first-person novel" (68) whose narrator is unreliable. He presents a "horrifying or banal truth" in a veiled manner. The foregoing turns out to be a self-conscious description of "Tlön" because the narrative, in taking the reader through a maze of ideas, hides the truth (until the postscript) about the power of simplistic, idealist creeds to devastate the world. As discussed in Chapter 2 (43–5), the librarian narrator in "The

Library of Babel" realises that meaning exists in the readers' selves rather than in texts. All this goes to show that a connection exists between narrative meandering and self-reflexivity. These esoteric features act as metaphors for the difficulty (or lack) of reference. Such a narrative is, then, about itself rather than about its referent. This point speaks to the psychological response of a person who loses his or her sight late in life, namely of withdrawing from the external world. This reaction is indirectly impelled by the problem of reference. The provisional character of knowledge also acts as a link in the self-reflexive narrative. These reflections on what constitutes a narrative not only highlight the basic difference between mirror epistemology and aesthetic self-reflexivity, but also form an aesthetic of blindness.

Remarking on the "unclear distinction" (135) existing between the author and the protagonist in much of Borges's writing, Hagberg observes that the Argentinian "has repeatedly called attention to the autobiographical content of his writing..." We must, in this respect, consider the short story "The Maker." In it, Borges presents a dramatisation of himself as the poet who gradually became blind, and in the process, discovered creativity. Significantly, this poet's name is never mentioned but only suggested as being that of the archetypal blind singer of Greek epics, Homer. Borges draws experiences from his own life in the telling of his tale. Here is an example of an experience that a person becoming blind might undergo. Describing the disposition of the character who lived in the ancient Mediterranean world, the author says that one of the impressions the man took in was "the sky-vault filled with stars that were also gods" (292). Thus, the celestial bodies visible in the sky were, for him, living gods. As he started losing his sight, we read that "the night lost its peopling stars, the earth became uncertain under his feet." These words represent the sensitive, widely-travelled man's style of thinking. The next example relates to the representation in the story of a particular occurrence in the author's life. As Williamson elucidates, a crucial episode in the narrative is fashioned from Borges's personal experience. The biographer writes that Borges describes a "transcendent episode when he first sensed the magic power of his father's dagger and his subsequent failure to realize that power in his writing" (Williamson 343). As mentioned in Chapter 2, Borges wrote the short story when he was in despair (Williamson 338). Thus, the poet's despair in the story mirrors the state of mind the real author, Borges, found himself in. Further, as the former went on to realise his poetic power in the course of the narrative, the author's "failure to realize that power in his writing" gets reversed. It should necessarily be noticed, however, that while Borges shows an intimate awareness of the difficult feelings that the protagonist grappled with while losing his vision, the former cannot report what the latter felt "as he descended into his last darkness" (293). This admission means that while the author can imagine the experience of the character in his fiction, he lacks omniscience. He cannot penetrate all the way into Homer's consciousness, and must acknowledge the residual opaqueness of his personhood.

Sexuality is a vital facet of corporeality, but it does not receive much attention in Borges's work. Appearing in the short stories and poetry in an obscured manner, it forms the main theme of only four narratives, viz. "Emma Zunz" (1948), "The Cult of the Phoenix" (1952), "The Interloper" (1970), and "Ulrikke" (1975). E. D. Carter Jr. cites the first and last short stories listed above as containing rounded portrayals of women characters. Apart from the ones in the list above, stories such as "The Circular Ruins" (1940) and "The Garden of Forking Paths" (1941) have sexual dimensions. Daniel Balderston writes about homophobia in Borges's writings (2004). While this indeed is the case, it is clear that Borges avoids treating any sexual relationship in a complete manner.

Coming to the question of narration in the short stories analysed in Chapter 3, it may be dealt with by examining the issues of narrative mediation and narrative agency. This matter assumes significance when we deal with the articulation of disabled characters' subjectivities in the short stories. In "The End," the impersonal narrator attempts to articulate the thoughts and feelings of the characters. This type of narrator, common in traditional narratives, cannot, as explained in Chapter 2 (53–4), be distinguished from the author (Walsh 510–11). Phrases and sentences like the following indicate the narrator's intent: "… the ordinary things that now would always be just these ordinary things" (168), "He looked down without pity at his great useless body," and "… there was neither destination nor destiny on earth for him, and he had killed a man" (170). While these quotations evidence the narrator's desire to represent the inner lives of characters in the story, the narrative statements come across as being ambiguous. The narrator may thus try very hard to express the inner being of another person, but it is not possible to achieve this goal due to epistemological limitations and language barriers. The narrative desire to express, and the impossibility of its fulfilment give rise to narrative tensions which become apparent in ellipses, ambiguities, and gaps in the short story. In "The Maker," the narrator tries very earnestly to understand the "soul" of the maker. Words and expressions like "impressions," "vivid," "sensitive," "keen, curious," "gazed," "sensed," "sought," "understood," indicate his intention. At the end of the narrative, however, he confesses, "These things we know, but not those that he felt as he descended into his last darkness" (293). This statement is an explicit recognition of the fact that it is not possible for an impersonal narrator – or the author – to grasp fully the self of another. Thus it is that the narrator of "The End" compares Recabarren to animals (168), not comprehending the man's attitude of acceptance towards his paralysis. Similarly, the phrase "the thick bars at his window" seems to imply that the paralysed man is in a prison. However, as I have argued in Chapter 3 (63–6), Recabarren knows his self and has accepted life with disability.

In "Funes, His Memory," we have a narrator-character who tells the story of Funes, a young man who is paralysed and who has a remarkable memory, in his own words half a century after the encounter between the two. The narrator declares that his "dialogue [with Funes] half a century ago" (134) is the only justification for the short story-as-biographical account to exist. Despite the central importance of that dialogue to the narrative, he does not "attempt to reproduce the words of it, which," according to him, "are now forever irrecoverable" presumably due to the lapse of such a long period of time, as a result of which he has forgotten them. As he states below, this narrative choice to employ "indirect discourse [which] is distant and weak" sacrifices "the effectiveness of my tale." This decision of the narrator to "summarize, faithfully, the many things Ireneo told [him]" is significant because, as a result of it, Funes cannot narrate his version of the story and his understanding of paralysis. This narrative tension can be sensed in the following passage: "It was shortly afterward that he learned he was crippled; of that fact he hardly took notice. He reasoned (or felt) that immobility was a small price to pay. Now his perception and his memory were perfect" (135). The expression "he reasoned (or felt)" shows that the narrator is not sure of Funes's state of mind regarding his paralysis. The narrator's failure to grasp Funes's individuality may be seen in his assertion that "Funes either could not or would not understand me" (136).

In the short story "Hakim, the Masked Dyer of Merv," the author cites a number of sources of information throughout his narrative about Hakim, the Veiled Prophet of Khorasan (40). By employing this narrative strategy, he makes explicit the process of research, gathering of information, and writing. Some of the sources he cites are genuine while others are imaginary. This approach shows that he blends fact and fiction and thus fictionalises a person who once existed. The narrative also makes explicit the inherent mediation involved in the telling of the story of Hakim, the dyer of Merv, because of the fact that we have access to innumerable sources about his life, but no access whatever to the person himself. He is thus reduced to a sign (42–4).

We can discern a shift in the paradigm of narration in "The Other" and "August 25, 1983." Here the characters who are blind, "auctorial doubles" as mentioned in Chapter 3, themselves narrate their stories. Thus, in the former, the narrator-character is able to access the depths of his being and talk about the state of his mind. Pertinent here is his reference to his sanity, and his statement: "I know that it was almost horrific while it lasted—and it grew worse yet through the sleepless nights that followed" (411). Similarly in the latter, the narrator-character says, "I experienced, as I had at other times in the past, the resignation and relief we are made to feel by those places most familiar to us" (489). In the former, the narrator is blind, and the two selves part from each other (417). However, in the latter, the narrator is sighted, and the two selves merge into one (493). But the two short stories are, it must be noted, dream narratives referring to Jorge Luis Borges (412, 489). Thus, when the older selves tell their younger selves in the respective short stories what it is like to be blind (417, 491), we may understand their statements as the articulation of a desire to tell what life with a disability is, and as the fulfilment of the need to tell their stories on their own terms. This narrative freedom enjoyed by the narrator-characters enables the reader to sympathise with them.

8.2 Reflecting on Experience: Narrative Form in Diary and Memoir

Drawing on Fludernik's narratological model based on the concept of experientiality, the entries constituting Hull's diaries may be described as "conversational storytelling." Fludernik writes as follows on the significance of this conception: "The narrativity which can be observed to emerge from spontaneous conversational storytelling is a holistic or organic as well as dialectically constituted phenomenon" (11). Since Hull records his experiences and dreams as diary entries, these incorporate spontaneity and, therefore, may be understood to be "holistic or organic" in composition. Further, we have seen that he wishes to explain his life in the blind condition to his sighted friends so that it might become possible for them to understand him (*On Sight* xi). This aspect demonstrates that the diaries are "dialectically constituted" phenomena.

The relatively small temporal gap existing between the narrating self and the experiencing self in the two diaries is important because it is the former that analyses the experiences that the latter has had in the recent past. The narrating and reflecting self records the narrative-reflective sections sometimes on the same day, but mostly a day after, or a few days after, and rarely even months or a few years after the experiences. This narrative feature leads to a uniquely short-term retrospective character being written into the entries. As mentioned in Chapter 7 (161–63), the narrating self in Kuusisto's first memoir, *Planet of the Blind*, and in Part One of *Eavesdropping*, "Sweet Longings" (3–60), are two selves (separated more or less by eight years) of the older artist. They describe and analyse experiences undergone by Kuusisto as a child, and later as a young man who is a student and then teacher. The difference between Hull's and Kuusisto's works lies in the narrative aspect. While the former gives an ongoing commentary on the evolution in his selfhood, the latter looks back at his younger selves – some in his remote past (childhood and adolescence), and some in the recent past – as the memoirist who writes. This is to say that the gap between the writing, or reflecting, self and the experiencing self, or selves, is wider in Kuusisto than it is in Hull. This observation implies that while the latter's diaries present largely immediate, fragmentary narratives, the former's memoirs, although they evidence an aesthetic dialectic, are able to present more unified narratives.

Writing on biographical narratives "about psychological problems like addiction" (140), Gosselin says,

> Telling a story is necessarily selective, as an author must decide which elements to include and which to exclude. Nevertheless, a causal explanation should suggest the complex interaction of multiple relevant factors rather than over-simplistically suggesting that one factor is more relevant than others.
>
> (140)

The significant point here is that the memoir acquires a circumscribed focus due to the selective way in which the author must pick out "elements" or events and other details relevant to the focus of the story he is telling. However, the narrative "should suggest the complex interaction of multiple relevant factors" in presenting the designated themes of the story. Explaining how he came to write *Eavesdropping*, the collection of essays on the role of listening – or eavesdropping – in his life, Kuusisto clarifies that it was in response to a troubling question posed by a newly blind woman about blindness and travelling, as discussed in Chapter 7 (153, 158, 161). However, the essays themselves do more than just providing answers to that question. They elaborate its implications, which the memoirist formulates as further questions. In the connected narrative essays, Kuusisto describes his experiences from childhood onwards, dwelling on events involving his insubstantial sight of things and fleshing out the world through sounds, music, touch, and art – not least the art of writing. While he struggles with his disability over a long period of time due to his denial of blindness and societal rejection, he leads a life of solitude. This fact encourages the development of an artistically inclined mind in him.

We have seen that the texts under study belong to different genres of literature: short stories, diaries, and memoirs. Further, it is clear that these narratives require varying interpretative approaches which are sensitive to their differing aesthetics. I have interpreted the short fiction of Borges on the basis of "cognitive parameters gleaned from real-world experience" (Fludernik 26) of gradually becoming blind. I have also explained that the diary entries recorded by Hull express his being-in-the-world. This is because, in them, he narrates his recent experiences and reflects on them in such a way that his immediate concerns relating to blindness come to the fore. In the long narrative memoir, *Planet of the Blind*, and in the essays forming *Eavesdropping*, Kuusisto selectively narrates memories and experiences with a view to emphasising certain themes. This narrative technique distinguishes the memoir from other forms of life writing. In interpreting the diaries and memoirs, I have adopted a phenomenological method that pays attention to sensory life and experientiality.

I will conclude the chapter by briefly presenting the reader with the findings of the research project. I set out to study the influence which blindness exercises on literary composition and the resulting artistic subjectivities of three blind authors, viz. Borges, Hull, and Kuusisto. Two philosophico-narratological questions and concepts flowing out of them have shaped my method in the monograph. It has uncovered interesting patterns in the evolution of selves 'in blindness.' Borges's 'fictions' show a strong awareness of blind experience, and a dialectical movement between the ideal and the experiential. This is emblematic of his shifting attitudes towards his disability over a long period of time. Hull's diaries record a transition in his self-conception from one oriented towards sight to that which is comfortable in the blind condition. Kuusisto makes a comparable but long journey from rejecting blindness to embracing his blind self, and beyond to developing a rich aesthetic of listening. In this way, the book demonstrates the importance of variable corporeality in writing. This also means, however, that the study is limited in scope. It is restricted to narrative prose works by three blind male authors. Embodied experience is defined not only by disability, but also by gender and sexuality. This point raises further questions for inquiry in feminist and queer literary theories of disability, and in criticism of poetry by Borges and Kuusisto.

Afterword

One day on a car drive, my brother-in-law and I were chatting about the Indian author, Ruskin Bond, and his remarkable way with words. I said to my companion, who was driving, that writing quotidian happenings into stories does something indefinable to the former. To elaborate, the literary art enriches our engagement with the human and non-human world by giving both writer and reader the means of recognising, through words, the significance of that interaction. It not only throws a new light on what is experienced, but also allows us to examine ourselves as observers.

But even so, this linguistic art has a downside to it, an unexpected effect I have grappled with since at least February 2016 (so a verse I keyed in tells me), as somebody who is marginalised by society due to his blindness. (Similarly, other people facing social exclusion may perhaps attest to such an experience while reading literature.) This essential feature consists in the illusion of materiality spun by literary texts.

Let me explain. In *Planet of the Blind*, Kuusisto relates an anecdote about Borges. During his years of blindness, the Argentine poet walked every day with a woman friend and "told funny, involuted, decorous stories about the world that he could invent as a means of navigating the hours" (*Planet of the Blind* 29–30). In turn, Borges states, "I have always come to things after coming to books" ("Autobiographical Notes" 9). Concerning his own reaction to language as a small boy, Kuusisto says, "My appetite for seeing is fed by lingo as vanilla" (*Planet of the Blind* 40, 91; cf. *On Sight* 14, 21, 144). These quotations highlight the ways in which language acts as a screen between blind persons and the world, precluding a spontaneous contact with people and things. Might this awareness of language's distancing nature help explain why linguistic pyrotechnics in novels fail to interest me?

As a result of inaccessible surroundings, because roads, footpaths, and public transport in India are regularly built and run without taking into account the needs of disabled people, my social life is severely limited. When I read literature in which people get to experience human relationships without having to struggle even to come into contact with one another, or travel,

DOI: 10.4324/9781003399667-9

or have adventures, my sense of isolation and inadequacy gets intensified. It is but cold comfort to realise that most literary works depict only non-disabled people as enjoying the benefits of society and mobility.[1] Because, you see, I regard myself as a regular man needing the human contact and excitement that make one whole; it is non-disabled people who perceive me as lacking something essential.

But I am forced to flip the coin and consider its obverse. The first epigraph to the article "Writing, Identity, and the Other: Dare we do Disability Studies?" (2001), "I can't ignore my disability, why would you?" (107), may be complemented with a forceful question I once expressed to my friend, Max: "Blindness impacts everything in my life, but why should I allow my identity to be defined by it?" This belief ties the sensory-corporeal facet of personhood with the cultural dimension of human existence, viz. how societal practices and thought comprehend and deal with disability.

That rhetorical query put to Dr Ubelaker Andrade around seven years ago has led to a gradual realisation. My fifteen-year engagement with literature composed by blind and visually impaired persons, disability studies, and philosophy has given me the critical power to write on reading, writing, and the experience of blindness. I am aware that these creative and academic efforts, borrowing from Borges's text "The Yellow Rose" (1960), can only "allude to" (310) situations and things in the world, not "truly express" them. However, the value of these essays (meaning "attempts" here) lies in projecting a fresh perspective on matters of import to more than just one person.

So, love, family, and friends make life worth living.

I awaken fairly early in the morning and go about my business just as you do.

I freshen up, eat breakfast, go to my department in an auto-rikshaw, prepare for classes on my computer which has a screen-reading software installed on it, teach my students, read for my research, come home for lunch, go back to my college, take a walk with my parents in the evening, rest a while at home, do a workout, eat a light supper, read some more, and go to bed.

To stand in the cool dark with my father and hear a cricket punctuate the quiet.

To drink strong, aromatic coffee early in the morning from my wooden cup.

To smell wood smoke in the half light of mornings and evenings.

To think on ideas and ponder about my writing.

To inhale the fragrance of the Parijata flowers at night.

To listen to the white-cheeked barbet which my mother caught sight just once, recently.

---

1 I think that referring to individuals portrayed in literature as "characters" is simply an empty, pedantic gesture whose use is necessitated by the prevalent standards of academic writing. It is more honest to call them what they are meant to be understood as: persons living in the imaginations of writers and readers.

What a strikingly loud call the little green bird has!: "kukroo, kukroo, kukroo."

I believe in the power of advocacy and education to raise awareness about the value of disabled lives and create change for the better in society.

Works Cited

Asbury, Herbert. *The Gangs of New York: An Informal History of the Underworld.* Garden City Publishing Company, 1927.

Balderston, Daniel. "The 'Fecal Dialectic': Homosexual Panic and the Origin of Writing in Borges." *Studies on Line, J. L. Borges Center for Studies & Documentation,* 2004, www.borges.pitt.edu/bsol/bgay.php. Accessed 23 Sept. 2022.

Beiser, Frederick. "The Enlightenment and Idealism." *The Cambridge Companion to German Idealism,* edited by Karl Ameriks, Cambridge University Press, 2000, pp. 18–36.

Bergson, Henri. *Introduction to Metaphysics.* Translated by Mabelle L. Andison, Philosophical Library, 1961.

———. *Matter and Memory.* Translated by N. M. Paul and W. S. Palmer, Allen and Unwin, 1911.

Berkeley, George. *A Treatise Concerning the Principles of Human Knowledge* (Part I). 1710, Project GUTENBERG, www.gutenberg.org/files/4723/4723-h/4723-h. Accessed 28 July 2022.

Bhat, Aravinda. "Being on the Brink of a Blind Abyss: Stepping Back from a Religion Defined by the Opposing Archetypes of Light and Darkness." *De Natura Fidei: Rethinking Religion across Disciplinary Boundaries,* vol. 3, edited by Jibu Mathew George, Authorspress, 2021, pp. 259–94.

———. "Borges's Aesthetic of Blindness: The Dialectic of the Ideal and the Experiential." Blind Creations: An International Colloquium on Blindness and the Arts, 29 June 2015, Royal Holloway, University of London, Egham, Surrey. Conference Presentation.

———. "Faith Healing and Blindness across Cultures: Disability, Religion, and the Scientific Milieu." *Finding Blindness: International Constructions and Deconstructions,* edited by David Bolt, Routledge, 2023, pp. 83–92.

———. "Narrative Lacunae and Variable Articulation in Stephen Kuusisto's Memoirs: Uncovering an Aesthetic Dialectic." *EFL Journal,* vol. 13, no. 2, 2022, pp. 1–11.

Booth, Wayne C. *The Rhetoric of Fiction,* 2nd ed., University of Chicago Press, 1983.

Borges, Jorge Luis. "A Blind Man." *Selected Poems,* edited and translated by Alexander Coleman, Viking, 1999, p. 357.

———. "After Images." *Selected Non-Fictions,* edited and translated by Eliot Weinberger, Penguin, 2000a, pp. 10–11.

———. "Autobiographical Notes." *The New Yorker,* 11 Sept. 1970, www.newyorker.com/magazine/1970/09/19/jorge-luis-borges-profile-autobiographical-notes. Accessed 31 Oct. 2022.

———. "Blindness." *Selected Non-Fictions*, edited and translated by Eliot Weinberger, Penguin, 2000b, pp. 473–83.

———. *Collected Fictions*. Edited and translated by Andrew Herley, Penguin, 1998.

———. *Poems of the Night*. Edited by Efrain Kristal and S. J. Levine, Penguin, 2010.

———. *Seven Nights*. Translated by Eliot Weinberger, New Directions, 1984.

Carter, E. D. "Women in the Short Stories of Jorge Luis Borges." *Pacific Coast Philology*, vol. 14, 1979, pp. 13–19. JSTOR, www.jstor.org/stable/1316433. Accessed 23 May 2023.

Cixous, Hélène, et al. "The Laugh of the Medusa." *Signs*, vol. 1, no. 4, 1976, pp. 875–93. JSTOR, www.jstor.org/stable/3173239. Accessed 28 July 2022.

Currie, Gregory. "Narration, Imitation, and Point of View." *A Companion to the Philosophy of Literature*, edited by Garry L. Hagberg and Walter Jost, Wiley, 2010, pp. 331–49.

Danto, Arthur C. "Philosophy and/as/of Literature." *A Companion to the Philosophy of Literature*, edited by Garry L. Hagberg and Walter Jost, Wiley, 2010, pp. 52–67.

Davis, Lennard J. "Bodies of Difference: Politics, Disability, and Representation." *Disability Studies: Enabling the Humanities*, edited by Sharon L. Snyder, Brenda J. Brueggemann and Rosemarie Garland-Thomson, MLA, 2002, pp. 100–106.

Davis, Lennard J., editor. *The Disability Studies Reader*. 2nd ed., Routledge, 2006.

Descartes, René. *Meditations on First Philosophy: With Selections from the Objections and Replies*. Edited and translated by John Cottingham, Cambridge University Press, 1996.

Fishburn, Evelyn, and Psiche Hughes. *Dictionary of Jorge Luis Borges*. Duckworth, 1990.

Fludernik, Monika. *Towards a 'Natural' Narratology*. Routledge, 2005.

Foucault, Michel. "The Subject and Power." *Critical Inquiry*, vol. 8, no. 4, 1982, pp. 777–95. JSTOR, www.jstor.org/stable/1343197. Accessed 4 Aug. 2022.

Gatzia, Dimitria Electra, and Berit Brogaard, editors. *The Epistemology of Non-Visual Perception*. Oxford University Press, 2020.

Genette, Gerard. *Narrative Discourse: An Essay in Method*. Translated by Jane E. Lewin, Cornell University Press, 1980.

George, Jibu Mathew. Interview. By Aravinda Bhat, 1 Oct. 2015.

Gosselin, Abigail. "Memoirs as Mirrors: Counterstories in Contemporary Memoir." *Narrative*, vol. 19, no. 1, 2011, pp. 133–48. JSTOR, www.jstor.org/stable/41289290. Accessed 3 Jan. 2021.

Grayling, A. C. "Berkeley's Argument for Immaterialism." *The Cambridge Companion to Berkeley*, edited by Kenneth P. Winkler, Cambridge University Press, 2005, pp. 166–89.

——— *The Refutation of Scepticism*. Open Court, 1985.

Green, Ronald M. "'Developing' *Fear and Trembling*." *The Cambridge Companion to Kierkegaard*, edited by Alastair Hannay and Gordon D. Marino, Cambridge University Press, 1998, pp. 257–81.

Guyer, Paul. "Absolute Idealism and the Rejection of Kantian Dualism." *The Cambridge Companion to German Idealism*, edited by Karl Ameriks, Cambridge University Press, 2000, pp. 37–56.

Hagberg, Garry L. "Self-Defining Reading: Literature and the Constitution of Personhood." *A Companion to the Philosophy of Literature*, edited by Garry L. Hagberg and Walter Jost, Wiley, 2010, pp. 120–58.

Hannay, Alastair, and Gordon D. Marino. Introduction. *The Cambridge Companion to Kierkegaard*, edited by Alastair Hannay and Gordon D. Marino, Cambridge University Press, 1998, pp. 1–15.

Harris, John. "Is There a Coherent Social Conception of Disability?" *Journal of Medical Ethics*, vol. 26, no. 2, 2000, pp. 95–100. JSTOR, www.jstor.org/stable/27718461. Accessed 3 Jan. 2021.

Heaney, Seamus, et al. "Borges and the World of Fiction: An Interview with Jorge Luis Borges." *The Crane Bag*, vol. 6, no. 2, 1982, pp. 71–8. JSTOR, www.jstor.org/stable/30023907. Accessed 26 Nov. 2020.

Helbeck, Jochen. "The Diary between Literature and History: A Historian's Critical Response." *Russian Review*, vol. 63, no. 4, 2004, pp. 621–29. JSTOR, www.jstor.org/stable/3663983. Accessed 3 Jan. 2021.

Hong, Howard V., and Edna H. Hong. Historical Introduction. *Fear and Trembling; Repetition*. By Soren Aabye Kierkegaard, edited and translated by Howard V. Hong and Edna H. Hong, Princeton University Press, 1983, pp. ix–xxxix. Questia, www.questia.com/library/99509227/kierkegaard-s-writings. Accessed 22 July 2016.

Hull, John M. *In the Beginning There was Darkness: A Blind Person's Conversations with the Bible*. Trinity Press International, 2001.

———. *On Sight and Insight: A Journey into the World of Blindness*. Oneworld Publications, 1997.

———. *The Tactile Heart: Blindness and Faith*. SCM Press, 2013.

———. *Touching the Rock: An Experience of Blindness*. Pantheon Books, 1990.

Kant, Immanuel. *Critique of Pure Reason*. 1781 and 1787. Edited and translated by Paul Guyer and Allen W. Wood, Cambridge University Press, 1998.

Kierkegaard, Soren Aabye. "A First and Last Explanation." *Kierkegaard's Writings, XII. 1*, edited and translated by Howard V. Hong and Edna H. Hong, Princeton University Press, 1992, pp. 625–30.

Kitcher, Patricia. "Kant's Epistemological Problem and Its Coherent Solution." *Philosophical Perspectives*, vol. 13, 1999, pp. 415–41. JSTOR, www.jstor.org/stable/2676111. Accessed 27 Jan. 2021.

Kottman, Paul A. Translator's Introduction. *Relating Narratives: Storytelling and Selfhood*. By Adriana Cavarero, Routledge, 2000, pp. vii–xxxii.

Krentz, Christopher. "Borges in the Mind's Eye." *Journal of Literary and Cultural Disability Studies*, vol. 10, no. 1, 2016, pp. 37–51. Project Muse, www.muse.jhu.edu/article/611311/pdf. Accessed 13 Mar. 2023.

Kumar, Shiv K. *Bergson and the Stream of Consciousness Novel*. Mackie & Son, 1962.

Kuusisto, Stephen. *Eavesdropping: A Life by Ear*. W. W. Norton, 2006.

———. *Have Dog, Will Travel*. Simon & Schuster, 2018.

———. *Planet of the Blind: A Memoir*. Faber, 1998.

Lacey, A. R. *Bergson*. 1989. Routledge, 1999.

Laraway, David. "Dis-semblances: Physiognomy and Fiction in Borges's 'historia universal de la infamia'." *Confluencia*, vol. 17, no. 1, 2001, pp. 52–62. JSTOR, www.jstor.org/stable/27922823. Accessed 23 May 2021.

———. "The Blind Spot in the Mirror: Self-Recognition and Personal Identity in Borges's Late Poetry." *Revista Canadiense de Estudios Hispánicos*, vol. 29, no. 2, 2005, pp. 307–25. JSTOR, www.jstor.org/stable/27763987. Accessed 23 May 2023.

Linton, Simi. "Reassigning Meaning." *The Disability Studies Reader*, 2nd ed., edited by Lennard J. Davis, Routledge, 2006, pp. 161–72.

Manguel, Alberto. *With Borges*. Telegram, 2006.

Melancon, Michael L. "'A River that No One Can See': Body, Text, and Environment in the Poetry of Stephen Kuusisto." *Journal of Literary & Cultural Disability Studies*, vol. 3, no. 2, 2009, pp. 183–94. Project Muse, www.muse.jhu.edu/journals/jlc/summary/v003/3.2.melancon.html. Accessed 27 Jan. 2021.

Merleau-Ponty, Maurice. *Phenomenology of Perception*. Translated by Colin Smith, Routledge, 2005, www.eBookstore.tandf.co.uk. Accessed 27 Jan. 2021.

Merry, Bruce. "The Literary Diary as a Genre." *The Maynooth Review*, vol. 5, no. 1, 1979, pp. 3–19. JSTOR, www.jstor.org/stable/20556925. Accessed 27 Jan. 2021.

Mills, Selina. Interview. By Aravinda Bhat, 28 June 2015.

Mitchell, David T. Foreword. *A History of Disability*. By Henri-Jacque Stiker, translated by William Sayers, University of Michigan Press, 1997, pp. vii–xiv.

Nun, Katalin, and Jon Stewart, editors. *Kierkegaard's Pseudonyms*. Routledge, 2015.

Núñez-Faraco, Humberto. "In Search of the Aleph: Memory, Truth, and Falsehood in Borges's Poetics." *The Modern Language Review*, vol. 92, no. 3, 1997, pp. 613–29. JSTOR, www.jstor.org/stable/3733389. Accessed 27 Jan. 2021.

Oliver, Mike, and Colin Barnes. "Disability Studies, Disabled People and the Struggle for Inclusion." *British Journal of Sociology of Education*, vol. 31, no. 5, 2010, pp. 547–60. JSTOR, www.jstor.org/stable/25758480. Accessed 15 June 2022.

Pattison, George. "Art in an Age of Reflection." *The Cambridge Companion to Kierkegaard*, edited by Alastair Hannay and Gordon D. Marino, Cambridge University Press, 1998, pp. 76–100.

Pfeiffer, David. "The Disability Paradigm." *Journal of Disability Policy Studies*, vol. 11, no. 2, 2000, pp. 98–9. Sage Journals, dps.sagepub.com/content/11/2/98.extract. Accessed 27 Jan. 2021.

Piper, Paul S. "For Jorge Luis Borges, Paradise Was Not a Garden but a Library." *American Libraries*, vol. 32, no. 7, 2001, pp. 56–8. JSTOR, www.jstor.org/stable/25645997. Accessed 27 Jan. 2021.

Plunkett, Erin. *A Philosophy of the Essay: Scepticism, Experience and Style*. Bloomsbury Academic, 2019.

Poole, Roger. "The Unknown Kierkegaard: Twentieth-Century Receptions." *The Cambridge Companion to Kierkegaard*, edited by Alastair Hannay and Gordon D. Marino, Cambridge University Press, 1998, pp. 48–75.

Popkin, Richard H. "So, Hume Did Read Berkeley." *The Journal of Philosophy*, vol. 61, no. 24, 1964, pp. 773–78. JSTOR, www.jstor.org/stable/2023392. Accessed 27 Jan. 2021.

Purpura, Lia, and Stephen Kuusisto. "Attendant Surprise: An Interview with Stephen Kuusisto." *The Georgia Review*, vol. 62, no. 4, 2008, pp. 673–86. JSTOR, www.jstor.org/stable/41403043. Accessed 1 Aug. 2020.

Quian Quiroga, Rodrigo. *Borges and Memory: Encounters with the Human Brain*. Translated by Juan Pablo Fernández, The MIT Press, 2012.

Rao, D. Venkat. Interview. By Aravinda Bhat, 5 Oct. 2015.

Reid, Alastair. Introduction. *Seven Nights*. By Jorge Luis Borges, New Directions, 1984, pp. 5–8.

Rimmon-Kenan, Shlomith. *Narrative Fiction: Contemporary Poetics*. 2nd ed., Taylor & Francis e-Library, 2005.

Ryan, Marie-Laure. "Meaning, Intent, and the Implied Author." *Style*, vol. 45, no. 1, 2011, pp. 29–47. JSTOR, www.jstor.org/stable/10.5325/style.45.1.29. Accessed 27 Jan. 2021.

Sachs, Joe. Introduction. *Poetics*. By Aristotle, The Focus Philosophical Library, 2006, pp. 1–17.

Saverese, Ralph James. "Lyric Anger and the Victrola in the Attic: An Interview with Stephen Kuusisto." *Journal of Literary and Cultural Disability Studies*, vol. 3, no. 2, 2009, pp. 195–207. Project Muse, www.muse.jhu.edu/journals/jlc/summary/v003/3.2.savarese.html. Accessed 27 Jan. 2021.

Schor, Naomi. "Blindness as Metaphor." *Differences*, vol. 11, no. 2, 1999, pp. 76–105. Project Muse, www.muse.jhu.edu/article/9603/summary. Accessed 27 Jan. 2021.

Schott, Penelope Scambly. "Planet of the Blind: A Memoir, and Under a Wing: A Memoir." *Fourth Genre: Explorations in Nonfiction*, vol. 1, no. 2, 1999, pp. 218–19. Project Muse, www.muse.jhu.edu/article/388893/pdf. Accessed 27 Jan. 2021.

Shusterman, Richard. "Philosophy as Literature and More than Literature." *A Companion to the Philosophy of Literature*, edited by Garry L. Hagberg and Walter Jost, Wiley, 2010, pp. 7–21.

Siebers, Tobin. "Disability in Theory: From Social Constructionism to the New Realism of the Body." *The Disability Studies Reader*, 2nd ed., edited by Lennard J. Davis, Routledge, 2006, pp. 173–83.

Stiker, Henri-Jacque. *A History of Disability*. Translated by William Sayers, University of Michigan Press, 1997.

Stoffregen, Thomas A., and John B. Pittenger. "Human Echolocation as a Basic Form of Perception and Action." *Ecological Psychology*, vol. 7, no. 3, 1995, pp. 181–216. TANDFONLINE, www.tandfonline.com/doi/pdf/10.1207/s15326969eco0703_2. Accessed 23 May 2023.

Swan, Jim. "Disabilities, Bodies, Voices." *Disability Studies: Enabling the Humanities*, edited by Sharon L. Snyder, Brenda J. Brueggemann and Rosemarie Garland-Thomson, MLA, 2002, pp. 283–95.

Tink, Amanda. "The Nuances of Memory." *Sydney Review of Books*, 4 Mar. 2016, www.sydneyreviewofbooks.com/the-nuances-of-memory/. Accessed 24 May 2023.

Tomlinson, Tim. "Fiction." *The Portable MFA in Creative Writing: Improve Your Craft with the Core Essentials Taught to MFA students*, 1st ed., edited by Michelle Ehrhard, Writer's Digest Books, 2006.

Toombs, S. Kay. "The Lived Experience of Disability." *Human Studies*, vol. 18, no. 1, 1995, pp. 9–23. JSTOR, www.jstor.org/stable/20011069. Accessed 27 Jan. 2021.

Tremain, Shelley, editor. *Foucault and the Government of Disability*. University of Michigan Press, 2005.

Tremain, Shelley. "On the Government of Disability: Foucault, Power, and the Subject of Impairment." *The Disability Studies Reader*, 2nd ed., edited by Lennard J. Davis, Routledge, 2006, pp. 185–96.

Ubelaker Andrade, Max. "Against Seeing: Jorge Luis Borges' Literary Imagination." Blind Creations: An International Colloquium on Blindness and the Arts, 29 June 2015, Royal Holloway, University of London, Egham, Surrey. Conference Presentation.

———. "Blind Narrations and Artistic Subjectivities-Foreword." Email Interview. Received by Aravinda Bhat, 19 Aug. 2022.

———. *Borges Beyond the Visible*. Pennsylvania State University Press, 2019.

———. Interview. By Aravinda Bhat, 13 Sept. 2014.

Walsh, Richard. "Who is the Narrator?" *Poetics Today*, vol. 18, no. 4, 1997, pp. 495–513. JSTOR, www.jstor.org/stable/1773184. Accessed 1 Aug. 2022.

Ware, Linda. "Writing, Identity, and the Other: Dare We Do Disability Studies?" *Journal of Teacher Education*, vol. 52, no. 2, 2001, pp. 107–23. www.doi.org/10.1 177/0022487101052002003. Accessed 23 May 2023.

Weinberger, Eliot. A Note on This Edition. *Selected Non-Fictions*. By Jorge Luis Borges, Penguin Books, 1999, pp. xi–xvi.

Westphal, Merold. "Kierkegaard and Hegel." *The Cambridge Companion to Kierkegaard*, edited by Alastair Hannay and Gordon D. Marino, Cambridge University Press, 1998, pp. 101–24.

Williamson, Edwin. *Borges: A Life*. Penguin, 2004.

Wilson, Jason. *Jorge Luis Borges*. Reaction Books, 2006.

Wilson, Kirk Dallas. "Kant on Intuition." *Philosophical Quarterly*, vol. 25, no. 100, 1975, pp. 247–65. JSTOR, www.jstor.org/stable/2217756. Accessed 19 June 2014.

Woolf, Virginia. "On Being Ill." *Collected Essays*, Vol. 4, edited by Leonard Woolf, Chatto, 1969, pp. 193–203.

Yudin, Florence L. *Nightglow: Borges' Poetics of Blindness*. Universidad Pontificia de Salamanca, 1997.

Index

For Product Safety Concerns and Information please contact our EU
representative GPSR@taylorandfrancis.com
Taylor & Francis Verlag GmbH, Kaufingerstraße 24, 80331 München, Germany

www.ingramcontent.com/pod-product-compliance
Lightning Source LLC
Chambersburg PA
CBHW071110100726
47908CB00008B/2328